Jim Crow North

T0355478

Jim Crow North

The Struggle for Equal Rights in Antebellum New England

RICHARD ARCHER

OXFORD
UNIVERSITY PRESS

OXFORD
UNIVERSITY PRESS

Oxford University Press is a department of the University of Oxford. It furthers the University's objective of excellence in research, scholarship, and education by publishing worldwide. Oxford is a registered trade mark of Oxford University Press in the UK and certain other countries.

Published in the United States of America by Oxford University Press
198 Madison Avenue, New York, NY 10016, United States of America.

First issued as an Oxford University Press paperback, 2020

Library of Congress Cataloging-in-Publication Data
Names: Archer, Richard, 1941– author.
Title: Jim Crow north: the struggle for equal rights in antebellum
New England / Richard Archer.
Description: New York, NY: Oxford University Press, 2017. |
Includes bibliographical references and index.
Identifiers: LCCN 2017033018| ISBN 9780190676643 (hardcover: alk. paper) |
ISBN 9780190676667 (epub) | ISBN 9780197532881 (paperback: alk. paper)
Subjects: LCSH: African Americans—New England—History—19th century. |
African Americans—New England—Social conditions—19th century. |
New England—Race relations—History—19th century. | Civil rights
movements—New England—History—19th century. |
Racism—New England—History–19th century.
Classification: LCC E185.917 .A73 2017 | DDC 305.896/07307409034–dc23
LC record available at https://lccn.loc.gov/2017033018

For Derek, Jason, Patricia, and Rose

Contents

PART IV—*Mixed Marriages*

PART V—*Hitting the Wall*

PART VI—*Epilogue*

Illustrations

Jim Crow North

PART I

Jim Crow in New England

I

The World of Hosea Easton
and David Walker

HOSEA EASTON MAY have seemed an odd choice to deliver the Thanksgiving address before the "colored population" of Providence, Rhode Island, in 1828. Only thirty years old and a resident of the small town of North Bridgewater, Massachusetts (now Brockton), he might have seemed too inexperienced for such a noteworthy gathering. Even his mixed heritage of Wampanoag, Narragansett, African, and European forebears may have made him suspect to a crowd partially composed of former slaves. But there was much more to Easton than his age and ethnicity. He came from an elite family of abolitionists with broad New England connections. He was a promising minister who recently had chaired an important meeting in Boston supporting the nation's only African American newspaper, and judging by the Thanksgiving oration he was a stirring speaker.[1]

Easton began conventionally enough by acknowledging the political leaders who had declared a day of Thanksgiving and praising the prosperity that providence had brought the nation. A white audience might have contently drowsed in this sea of pleasantries, but a black audience would have been alert to the storm approaching. Easton, for one, had referred to the leaders as "Rulers," not as democratic representatives, and providence's blessings clearly were for the nation as a whole, not necessarily for all of the individuals within it. Less subtly he attributed prosperity to "our forefathers . . . superior knowledge in the use of fire arms above that of the natives: by which means the latter were drove out before them, being slain by thousands, thus, leaving them in peaceable possession of the soil." Prosperity in turn promoted agriculture, skilled trades, scientific advancement, and the building of churches. God, Easton further intoned, blessed the nation with a constitutional commitment to liberty and equality. Here was cause for celebration and thanksgiving.[2]

By then Easton had established the contrast between the world of the forefathers and the world he and his audience experienced. They knew there was not prosperity, liberty, and equality for all. Brutal slavery in the land wrenched families apart, lashed bodies, and barred religious worship. Easton reminded them of the obvious. Former slaves and the descendants of slaves, though deemed free and better off than bondsmen, formed a caste unequal and unfree. With a call and response flourish, he asked: "Are we eligible to an office? No.—Are we considered subjects of the government? No." And on he went. Schools often were not available, well-paying employment was non-existent, transportation was segregated or refused, church attendees were separated so that even visiting African American ministers had to sit in distant black pews or balconies, travelers had to eat in kitchens rather than dining rooms and sleep in garrets rather than bedrooms. All that was abundant was humiliation and disdain. Compounding these troubles, the Colonization Society was attempting to send free American blacks to Africa. As Easton saw it, Africans had been stolen from their native lands, had worked as slaves, and now that the drudgery was completed were to be transported back.[3]

Despite these obstacles, Easton remained optimistic. His solution was "moral improvement." The community needed to unite and work together. In particular, oppressed people should demand that their children be virtuous. They should avoid the dance hall, the gambling den, and all "unnecessary diversion" and become "pious, industrious, and intelligent men and women." Then whites would respect them and equality would follow.[4]

Easton's views were not unusual in African American communities throughout New England. Two years earlier the Massachusetts General Colored Association had formed in opposition to slavery and for the promotion of equal rights, and black churches continued to serve as centers of discontent and reformist organization as well as religious institutions.[5] The most famous and effective protest of the plight of people of African descent in America written at this time, David Walker's *Appeal to the Coloured Citizens of the World*, appeared a year after Easton's Thanksgiving address.

Son of an enslaved father and a white mother, Walker was nearly forty years old when he moved to Boston in late 1824. He had lived most of his life in Wilmington, North Carolina, and in his mid- and late thirties had traveled widely in the South and mid-Atlantic, living for a few years in Charlestown, South Carolina. To him, slavery was not an abstraction; although he had not been a slave, he had seen its ugly face firsthand. The Boston used clothes dealer made an imposing figure physically and intellectually. Six feet tall, slender, with a dark complexion, Walker quickly rose to prominence in Boston's black community, joining the African Masonic Lodge, the African Methodist Episcopal Church, and the Massachusetts General Colored Association, and he acted as an agent for the African American newspaper, *Freedom's Journal*.[6]

Walker's *Appeal* was a slashing condemnation of American slavery and the blight of racism across the country and a plea for people of African descent to unite for radical reform. He asserted that African Americans in the United States were "the most degraded, wretched, and abject" people who had ever lived. Ignorance, clergymen who preached docility, and the threat of forced colonization in Africa contributed to their condition, but American slavery was the prime cause. Never in human history had there been a form of slavery so cruel. Slaveholders withheld education, broke up families, and beat and murdered their slaves. Elsewhere and in other times slaves could hold positions of authority, but in the United States neither slaves nor free blacks could hold elective office, practice law, or serve on a jury. Laws forbade free people of African descent from marrying whites, employment was limited to the most menial jobs, and education—where available—was inadequate. Worst of all, whites denied blacks their humanity. Their belief that people of color were inferior to themselves underlay slavery and racism.[7]

"You have to prove to the Americans and the world, that we are MEN, and not *brutes*," he exhorted his fellow blacks. They had to stop assisting "tyrants," as did drivers in the fields and informants. They had to curtail their servile ways. They had to improve themselves. They had to resist subjection and assert their humanity. If whites would change their ways, repent their past, and support African Americans' equality, all could live together peaceably and prosperously. But if not, and here is where he departs from Easton, violence might ensue. No matter how reluctant black people may be to harm others, Walker reasoned, it is better to kill than to be killed or have family members slain. Perhaps with a sly eye at whites who might read his *Appeal*, he commented that once blacks started killing they could be ferocious. Slavery and racism were bound to end one way or the other.[8]

Walker may have included such provocations primarily to encourage blacks to assert their rights and whites to mend their ways, but no matter

what his intentions, he sent shock waves through the South. State govern-
ments quickly passed laws banning the *Appeal* and other pamphlets like
it, and reputedly a bounty was offered for Walker's death or capture. When
he died at home the following year, rumors floated that he had been murdered; but it is far more likely that tuberculosis—a disease that had killed
his daughter three days earlier—was the culprit.[9]

New England was more receptive to its black population than were other
sections of the United States. African Americans could join congregations, own property, attend schools, and enter into contracts; and after the
American Revolution, all six New England states extended voting rights
to black males who met the qualifications demanded of all citizens. As
their populations of free people of African descent dramatically increased,
however, Connecticut and Rhode Island reversed themselves. In 1814,
the Connecticut legislature passed a law restricting the vote to qualified
"free white males," and four years later the state incorporated the law
into its constitution. In 1822, Rhode Island disenfranchised its African
Americans.[10]

    This was the contradiction for which both Easton and Walker bitterly
condemned white America. The United States, New England in particular, rejoiced in its revolutionary past, proclaiming its independence from
British "slavery" and its commitment to equal rights as espoused in the
Declaration of Independence. These were not empty platitudes. Each of
the New England states, some more gradually than others, had found a
way to terminate the institution of slavery. People truly believed in the principles of equal rights. But by 1776 and certainly by 1828, America—very
much including New England—already had a long tradition of racism. As
the number of free African Americans grew as a result of emancipation
and migration, the conflict of values became clear. The white belief in the
inferiority of people of color and the principles of the Declaration could
not consistently coexist. One or the other had to be modified, if not fully
eliminated.

    At the time of Easton's "Address" and Walker's *Appeal*, racism and the
construction of a society where people of African descent had a defined
and inferior place (in short, a caste system) were winning in New England.
African Americans could not serve on juries or in militias and only rarely
held public office. The eighteenth-century minister and historian Jeremy
Belknap vaguely remembered a mixed-heritage man who was a town
clerk in a "country town." On those occasions when they gained entry into

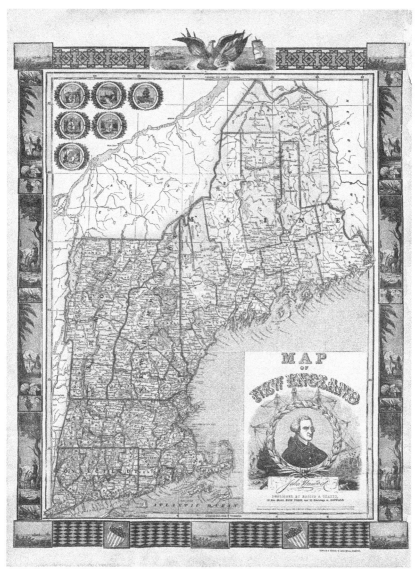

FIGURE I.I *Map of New England*, 1847. (Map image courtesy of the Norman B. Leventhal Map Center at the Boston Public Library).

theaters, hotels, and hospitals, African Americans still endured segregation. Company policies for stagecoaches and steamships as a rule separated blacks from whites, often requiring exposure to inclement weather above the coach compartment and on the deck of ships, or excluded them altogether. John Hooker recalled as a small boy in Farmington, Connecticut, witnessing a Captain Goodrich, "one of New Haven's aristocracy," ordering a black man out of a stagecoach and compelling the driver to enforce his demeaning command. "We boys looked on," Hooker related, "and could not help feeling a sympathy for the black man, but somehow it did not strike us that it was anything more than an unreasonable thing on Capt. Goodrich's part; that the rights of a man were assailed we hardly thought."[11]

Employment opportunities were grim. In the larger towns and cities where most African Americans lived, skilled jobs and entrepreneurial possibilities were seldom available. Women typically worked as servants, seamstresses, cooks, and laundresses. Most men toiled as unskilled laborers or sailors, including whalers from Nantucket, New London, and New Bedford. They lifted and moved cargo on wharfs, cleaned windows, swept chimneys, sawed wood, waited on tables, and took on odd jobs. Anyone who aspired to more skilled work had difficulty receiving the training. William J. Brown in later years reflected back on the rejections he had received in Providence. He applied for an apprenticeship to a carpenter, a shoemaker, a grocer, and several other businessmen. In each case he was rebuffed. "I could readily see that the people were determined not to instruct colored people in any art," he concluded. Even those already with the requisite skills, as Frederick Douglass discovered in New Bedford, would be denied employment. As a slave he had been a caulker along the Baltimore waterfront, but no such positions were open to him as a free man. Instead he had to take any menial job that came along. Ironically, some slaves in the South had a broader range of skilled opportunities than did most free blacks in New England. Their owners could place them in any kind of work they chose and didn't have to combat the antagonism of free workers. Still, a very few black New Englanders found skilled work. In Boston in 1830 there was a housewright, a soap maker, a cordwainer, a confectioner, three tailors, and thirty-four barbers. Cutting hair was the one trade African Americans monopolized. Others like David Walker sold used clothes, nine people ran boarding houses, and one person kept a bar. The professions included only three clergymen.[12]

Housing was not formally segregated, but in the larger towns some neighborhoods effectively excluded people of African descent. Because of white restrictions, limited employment opportunities, poverty, and the desire to live close to an African American church and business establishments that catered to black people, clusters of African Americans formed. Although in 1830 African Americans lived in all of Boston's twelve wards, the majority resided near the waterfront in ward 2 or on the north slope of Beacon Hill in the sixth ward or the adjacent fifth and seventh wards. Cheap rents drew poor whites to these areas as well, but the base of Beacon Hill still was designated as "Nigger Hill." Such racist names for black enclaves and satellite settlements could be found throughout New England—Nigger Hill in Middletown, Connecticut; New Liberia and New Guinea for two districts in New Haven, Connecticut; New Guinea near Nantucket, Massachusetts; Parting Ways or New Guinea near Plymouth, Massachusetts; Roast Meat Hill or Knockers Hole in Salem, Massachusetts; Nigger-town Crossing near Macchias, Maine; and Hardscrabble in Providence, Rhode Island. Rural communities with small black populations usually did not have residential segregation but rather experienced a scattering of African American farms and farmworkers.[13]

New Englanders had a long history of discriminatory church seating. In the seventeenth century, reformed Protestant churches seated their congregants according to each person's status. The higher the person's standing, the closer he or she sat by the pulpit. Men and women sat on separate sides of the meetinghouse, allowing for the possibility that a husband might sit forward from his wife or vice versa. Their children sat farther back, and servants and slaves were the most distant removed. In the eighteenth century these meetinghouses installed pews where entire families could sit together, although status and cash determined the placement of each family. African Americans remained in the farthest reaches of the church.[14]

After the Revolution when slavery rapidly ended except in Connecticut and Rhode Island, some New Englanders of color tested how far their freedom and equality went. Hosea Easton's father James Easton, a veteran of the Revolution and a successful manufacturer of iron products in Bridgewater, Massachusetts, objected to the construction of a separate balcony for black people in his Congregational church but to no avail. Leaving that church he joined a Baptist congregation and purchased a pew. After some white church members unsuccessfully attempted to block the deal, they tarred the pew. Easton and his family—Hosea then only a boy—brought chairs for the service. By the following Sunday congregants had torn down the pew. The conflict continued a while longer, but eventually the Easton family left the church in disgust. In 1830, Frederick Brinsley suffered a similar affront. Brinsley acquired a pew in Boston's Park Street Church, when its owner had no other way to pay a legal claim. He furnished it and offered it for sale. No purchasers came forward; so Brinsley decided to occupy the pew himself. Before the next Sunday a church committee warned him to go to the upper level or he would "hazard the consequences," and at the service it placed a constable at the door of the pew to ensure compliance.[15]

Many churches in New England retained segregated seating through-out the antebellum period. There were differences, of course, from place to place. In Brattleboro, Vermont, the town's first black landowner, Benjamin Wheaton, purchased a pew in 1803, and there is no evidence of reprisals or negative reactions. Rural areas with small African American popula-tions often were more inclusive than were cities, as was northern New England in comparison to Connecticut and Rhode Island. Shubael Clark of Hinesburgh, Vermont, for example, not only was a landowner and a member of the Baptist church of that town but also a leader of the congre-gation. He frequently was on investigative committees that evaluated the behavior of church members, overwhelmingly white.[16] But where most blacks lived—Boston, Hartford, New Bedford, New Haven, Providence, and other substantial cities—they clearly were a caste separate from peo-ple of European descent.

In response to such discrimination as well as a desire for more expres-sive religious services and for centers of black community life, African Americans in cities throughout New England created their own, separate churches. Here congregants could worship and socialize without fear of hostile treatment. Here potential leaders could gain experience that would serve them well in the struggle for equal rights. Here illiterate children and adults might learn to read, the poor receive aid, and a positive black identity be nourished. Not all people of African descent supported segre-gated institutions. The doubters questioned how black people could call for equal treatment and equal rights while at the same time maintaining their own separate churches, and they sometimes played it down the middle by keeping membership in a black church and in a white-led church. Others remained in their original churches or didn't participate in any organized religion. The disagreement between "segregationists" and "integration-ists" continued through the antebellum period, sometimes flaring up in destructive ways. All ultimately wanted equal rights and the dignity and recognition of their humanity, but they clashed on how to get there and on what was needed in the interim.[17]

Schools in New England had a similar history and outcome. The region deserves its reputation as the nation's leader in public education from the colonial period well into the nineteenth century. From the first, New Englanders agreed that all individuals needed to be able to read the Bible, and after the Revolution, an agreement developed that the well-being of the republic was dependent on the education of its citizenry and that free schooling should be provided. The sticking point was the question, who composed the citizenry? There also was the practical issue of funding, particularly since in most states it would be at the local level. Cities had tax bases that allowed them to create schools. Villages and hamlets often had to join together or do without. The result was a patchwork of systems, and African American education varied from quilt to quilt.[18]

As early as the first half of the eighteenth century in New England, there were some schools for black children; and as public schools emerged, they ordinarily admitted all boys and eventually girls, regardless of the heritage of the child. By the early nineteenth century, separate schools for African Americans began to appear in cities with substantial black populations. That left out Vermont, New Hampshire, and Maine, where only Portland had segregated schools. The situation in Connecticut, Massachusetts, and Rhode Island, however, was quite different. Until the nineteenth century, Connecticut was at the outmost extreme with a law prohibiting the teaching of reading to African American children. Then three women (the daughter of a signer of the Declaration, the daughter of a seated US senator, and the daughter of a framer of the Constitution) created a school in New Haven that offered instruction in reading and sewing to young children of African descent—and unavoidably challenged the law. New Haven officials confronted the women with the possibility of prosecution, but they would not yield. Faced with the choice of ignoring the school or enforcing the law and arresting the daughters of three prominent citizens, the authorities capitulated.[19]

By 1830, New Haven, Hartford, Newport, Providence, Boston, Lowell, Nantucket, New Bedford, and Salem provided only separate schools for their children. There were no laws requiring educational segregation, but once established it was difficult to curtail. In some cities, such as Salem in 1807, African Americans were forced to leave integrated schools, but in others, such as Boston, people of African descent initiated segregation. Integrated schools often were miserable centers of learning for black youth. Teachers disciplined students, black and white, by sending them to the "nigger seat," and the taunting, bullying, and general harassment led many a child to stay home. African American parents had little voice in determining educational policy and no control over the schools where they sent their children. There was little encouragement or opportunity for black children to advance beyond primary education. Like the dilemma over whether to create black churches, the decision to establish black schools offered parents a choice between accepting demeaning treatment of their offspring in the classroom but keeping the demand for equality front and center or becoming "segregationists" and possibly improving their children's education.[20]

In 1787, Boston black leaders petitioned for segregated schools. School authorities denied the request. Eleven years later in response to a second petition, the Boston School Committee turned them down again but allowed for the possibility of a private school with funding raised by the black community. Finally, by 1806, the School Committee tentatively approved funding for a separate school to be located in the basement of the African Baptist Church, and in 1812 it committed to annual support of segregated schools with the proviso that it would control all schools in its system. Parents had gained funding for their children's education but at the cost of their determining who taught and administered it.[21]

While Hosea Easton was delivering his "Address" and David Walker was writing his *Appeal*, African Americans in the large cities throughout New England began to have second thoughts. Black schools received less funding than white schools, their teachers were paid less, their buildings (some only basements) were less well maintained; black children typically attended school for fewer and shorter days, and, as in Boston, they had no opportunity to advance beyond primary school.[22] Without good education, African Americans would remain an inferior caste. There had to be change.

Few of these discriminatory practices came from the law. Laws prohibiting marriage between people of African descent and people of European descent were one important exception. Massachusetts was the only New England colony with such a law. In 1705, its General Court established that "none of her majesty's English or Scottish subjects, nor of any other Christian nation within this province, shall contract matrimony with any negro or molatto." The official or clergyman who conducted the ceremony paid the highest price, a fine of £50. Following statehood in 1786, Massachusetts reenacted the law but also included Indians as people beyond the pale and specified that mixed marriages would be null and void. Rhode Island passed an almost identical law in 1798, as did Maine when it split from Massachusetts and achieved statehood in 1820.[23] None of the remaining New England states ever had such a law.

The marriage prohibitions may have prevented some weddings, postponed others, or at least given a couple pause, but it appears the laws were rarely enforced. The officiator might have to pay a hefty fine in those atypical cases, but the marriage partners faced no punishment. And it was easy to outwit the law by wedding in an adjacent state and returning to the home state. Law enforcement officials, moreover, faced huge obstacles. How do you know, for example, where people fit on the broad continuum of color? Who is black, mulatto,[24] or white? Do you ask? Do you guess? Do you bother? For the most part, the bans on mixed marriages stamped in blood the idea that there were castes, and perhaps that was the prime intent.

There were some practical consequences, however. If the husband of a mixed marriage died intestate, neither his widow nor his children were legal heirs. If an offspring of such a union entered into a mixed marriage herself and was a pauper, it might be unclear which town—the town of her residence or the town of her father—was responsible for her maintenance. That was the context in 1810 for the important Massachusetts court decision of *Inhabitants of Medway v. Inhabitants of Natick*. Roba Vickons of Natick, Massachusetts, was the daughter of Ishmael Coffee of Medway, Massachusetts (whose parents were mixed) and of a white woman. Her husband was white. She was impoverished, a pauper. The question was, who was responsible for her welfare, Natick or Medway? If her marriage were valid, Natick would offer support. If not, her father's residence of Medway would be accountable. The court reached a unanimous decision that "a mulatto is a person begotten between a white and a black. . . . The pauper's father . . . was a mulatto, and her mother was a white woman. The pauper is then not a mulatto." By this decision the Massachusetts court declared Roba white and her marriage valid. Natick had to provide her support. The impact, of course, was much greater than the dispute between Natick and Medway. It defined white people in Massachusetts. Any person who had a mixed parent and a white parent was white. The definition was racial, if not racist, and it opened up "whiteness" well beyond the one-drop rule of the twentieth century. When Maine became a state, it incorporated the definition into its constitution.[25] There is no record of the standards the other New England states used to determine these vague and fluid categories.

It is impossible to know precisely how many mixed marriages there were, particularly before the federal census improved in 1850. During the colonial period there probably were few mixed marriages in any of the New England states, but after 1830 the number that is possible to know increased significantly.

Discriminatory laws and practices, frequent insults and occasional assaults, all these were bad enough; but African Americans in Boston, New Bedford, and Providence also became targets of race riots in the 1820s. Although miles apart and at different times, these violent attacks on people of color and their property had much in common. Each site was a substantial and growing urban center with a relatively large, poor black population. In 1830, Boston had 1,876 African American residents (3.1% of the city's total population), New Bedford had 383 (5.0%), and Providence had 1,205 (7.3%). By comparison, all of New England had 21,224 black residents (1.1% of the total population). Census workers acquired these numbers, and they underreported. Actual numbers almost certainly were larger, although small in comparison to the white population. It was easy to overlook people who were poor and black—the near invisible; and fugitive slaves in particular and people of African descent in general were wary of giving any personal information to inquiring government employees. Seaport centers, such as Boston, New Bedford, and Providence, moreover, had substantial groups of black whalers and sailors who could have been at sea when the census taker arrived.[26]

Each of these cities had poor sections where rents were cheap and small property affordable, at least for the fortunate few. Although not exclusively black enclaves, these areas were places where blacks located churches, schools, and benevolent societies. They were home for hardworking families. Unfortunately, they also were the site for brothels, dance halls, gambling houses, and drinking establishments—magnets for sailors, transients, and ne'er-do-wells. Respectable citizens, white and black, were uncomfortable with these businesses, and each race riot was initiated by a white attack on these seamy enterprises. Had the mobs limited themselves to the disreputable establishments, there might have been a tinge of racism evident but that would have been a minor part of the motivation. In all three cities, however, the mob's rage spilled over to the demolition of black homes, which leaves little doubt that the intent was both "moral" and racist.

Mayor Josiah Quincy led the charge in Boston. In 1823, he began a campaign to eradicate illegal and disreputable businesses. He went so far as to lead raids on the neighborhood on the north slope of Beacon Hill, the section of largest concentration of black residents in Boston. It was not the only area where such enterprises existed, but it was the only one he targeted. Two years later a white mob made a similar incursion, this time in the North End, an area heavily populated by black sailors and maritime

workers. These raids were prelude to the riot that occurred on July 14, 1826, when a mob invaded "Nigger Hill" and pulled down several houses. According to a historian of race riots, there was another assault in the same area on August 26 that first attacked brothels and then demolished a few houses. New Bedford witnessed similar riots in both 1826 and 1829, when white mobs attacked the Ark, a brothel in a predominantly black neighborhood of the city.[27]

The Hardscrabble riot in Providence was the most devastating of all. Hardscrabble, more formally known as Addison Hollow, was on the outskirts of Providence, on its northwest side. With both inexpensive houses and rooms, it attracted poor blacks as well as brothels and the like. White patrons of the disreputable establishments frequently taunted and harassed local residents, and Providence's white population in general grew alarmed as increasing numbers of African Americans from southern Rhode Island migrated to "their" city. Not long before the October 18, 1824, riot, the *Providence Gazette* published an editorial promoting the colonization of blacks to Haiti. The spark was lit on October 17 when a group of black men refused to leave the sidewalk as a group of white men approached. There was a scuffle but nothing else that night. The following evening a large mob returned. Forty or so of its members approached Henry T. Wheeler's residence whose ground floor was a dance hall. With clubs and axes they shortly demolished his house. Other black residents tried to protect their property, their dignity, and their rights; but when the sun rose the next morning, it revealed roughly twenty destroyed homes. One of the homeowners, Christopher Hill, a widower with three or four children, formed a roof over his remaining cellar and, refusing offers of help, lived through the winter there. As shameful as the episode itself, some city officials were among the spectators yet did nothing to halt the destruction.[28]

There should be no surprise that Hosea Easton lamented the condition of people of African descent or any shock at David Walker's appeal for blacks to stand up for themselves, violently if necessary. New England African Americans lived in a racist world, full of discrimination, insults, caste, and hostile assaults. Without slavery, the story would have been quite different.

2
——————

New England's Peculiar Institution

BY THE TIME Easton and Walker were condemning the racism of New England whites, nearly two centuries had passed since the first, few, enslaved Africans had arrived on New England shores. Seventeenth-century New England with a few small exceptions was never fertile ground for large-scale, commercial slavery. Its glacier-scraped, thin soil and short growing season limited what could be grown profitably, and markets for agricultural produce were almost always local rather than international. Trade, fish, shipbuilding, and maritime supplies were where the money was. In the 1630s, with the Great Migration of 20,000 people, there was a large demand for labor. This year's migrants in great need of supplies and house building skills became the next year's sellers and workers. People, even Puritans, were optimistic. Temporarily there was a huge bubble of prices and wages, and the well-off might buy an indentured servant's contract in payment for travel across the Atlantic. But in 1642, the bubble burst with the English Civil War. Migration declined to a mere trickle, demand for goods and services decreased, and prices and wages plummeted as the region sank into a depression. Most New Englanders on their small farms settled into a barter economy. By the time the economy improved there already was an alternative to an outside labor force—large families. Throughout the seventeenth century the population regularly doubled through natural increase with each new generation. An abundance of children put pressure on families to acquire sufficient land, but they provided much needed, inexpensive labor.[1]

Enslaved Africans were a luxury that few could afford or wanted, and there were alternatives. When family members were not sufficient, a person could exchange labor with a neighbor or hire a part-time worker or take on an apprentice or lease land to a tenant.[2] In all these cases, the New

Englander operated within a familiar cultural framework. The outsiders spoke his language, worshipped his god, ate similar food, and held more or less his same values. There was neither a purchase price to pay nor the responsibility to maintain sick or elderly slaves.

Despite all these obstacles and disincentives, slavery came to New England. The first slaves for whom there are reliable records were captive Native American women and children who had survived the bloody war that Massachusetts Bay and the Narragansett waged on the Pequots in 1637. Authorities sent the Pequot boys to Bermuda but kept the women and girls for themselves and others. Prominent New Englanders inundated Massachusetts Bay governor John Winthrop with requests for the bounty, and a minor feeding frenzy took place. Many magistrates and ministers were quite comfortable owning slaves, particularly if the bondsmen weren't Christian. Even the principled Roger Williams was among the applicants, although his motivation appears to have been to protect three Indian women from the mistreatment many slaves were receiving, on the condition "they would stay at my house and not run away."[3]

Africans arrived as slaves less than a year later. When Captain William Peirce anchored his ship *Desire* in Boston harbor in February 1638 after seven months in the West Indies, he brought a diverse cargo of cotton, tobacco, salt, and "negroes." How many slaves he held and whether he sold them in Massachusetts is unknown, but in 1639, the voyager John Josselyn reported three slaves owned by Samuel Maverick. Maverick had been in New England since 1624 and, at the time of Josselyn's visit, lived on an island in Boston Bay. One morning Josselyn was startled by an African woman's "very loud and shril" singing outside his bedroom window. When he ventured outside to find what was troubling her, she spoke only in her native tongue but conveyed her grief through gestures and facial expressions. Discussing the matter with his host, Josselyn learned that she once had been a queen and that Maverick, wishing to breed slaves, had attempted to force "a Negro young man" upon her.[4]

Governor John Winthrop's brother-in-law, Emmanuel Downing, also was an entrepreneur who enthusiastically advocated enlarging the African slave population in Massachusetts Bay. He envisioned a solution to the labor shortage caused by the slowed migration, profits, good works, and prosperity for the fledgling colony. He suggested to Winthrop that Massachusetts Bay should wage war with their former ally, the Narragansett. Combining a religious gloss and prospects for the colony's well-being in such a way that would appeal to his relative, he argued that an English victory would curtail devil worship and that the Indian captives could be exchanged for "Moores." Slavery, in Downing's estimation, was the only way the colony would thrive and "see this great Continent filled with people." Besides, he concluded, "you know verie well how wee shall maynteyne 20 Moores cheaper then one Englishe servant."[5]

Downing's argument for slavery was fifty years ahead of his time, and his pleas were ignored during the depression of the 1640s. Massachusetts Bay, nonetheless, had paved the way for the legitimacy and growth of slavery in its 1641 *Body of Libertyes*, the first code of law in British America. Its chief purpose was to protect its citizens from arbitrary magisterial decisions. The code was a comprehensive compendium of English and biblical law and practice, and attention to slavery constituted only a minor part. Article ninety-one stated: "There shall never be any bond slaverie, villinage or captivitie amongst us unles it be lawfull captives taken in just warres, and such strangers as willingly selle themselves or are sold to us. And these shall have all the liberties and Christian usages which the law of God established in Israell concerning such persons doeth morally require. This exempts none from servitude who shall be Judged thereto by Authoritie." Slavery, therefore, was lawful only when a person was captured in a just war and when outsiders sold themselves or were sold. The law as written could apply to people of European descent as well as to those of African or Native American descent. In practice, it applied solely to Indians and Africans. In 1670, the legislature expanded the definition of who could be enslaved by removing the word "stranger" from the law, thus determining that the children of slaves would follow the status of their parents. The second part of the article was equally important and suggests why New England slavery was distinctive. Slaves were persons entitled to all the rights and protections provided by Mosaic Law.[6]

The first test of Article ninety-one occurred in 1646 when authorities arrested James Smith and Thomas Keyser for "man stealing." Smith and Keyser brought across the Atlantic two Africans who had been captured in a raid on their village—not in a just war—and then sold them in Massachusetts Bay. The crime of the raid and capture was compounded, in the magistrates' eyes, by having taken place on the Lord's Day, a Sunday. They decided in the Africans' favor, freed them, and returned them to Africa.[7] The decision, in part, may have been an anomaly, for there is no evidence that authorities during the colonial period checked the background of other Africans who reached New England shores to be sold. The Smith/Keyser verdict, however, did reinforce the legal protections of the enslaved as required in Article ninety-one. Among other rights, slaves could sue for their freedom.

Massachusetts Bay, Connecticut, and New Plymouth incorporated Article ninety-one into their "Articles of the New England Confederation," thereby jointly accepting the conditions for lawful slavery and the protections for slaves. Rhode Island, as usual, went its own way. Its government in 1652, with only the two northern towns of Providence and Warwick represented, passed a law ostensibly outlawing perpetual slavery. No one, white or black, could be held in bondage for more than ten years or to the age of twenty-four, if a person first was enslaved younger than fourteen. But there was a loophole. Although the penalty for violations was £40, there was no requirement that the slave then must be freed.[8] Forty pounds was a substantial sum, but people who were willing to pay the fine could hold their slaves indefinitely. Whether there were people who paid the penalty or whether the law was not enforced, slavery, though on a small scale in the seventeenth century, continued in Rhode Island.

Historians have differentiated between "slave societies" where slavery was central to the economy and the culture and "societies with slaves" where slavery was consequential but peripheral to the core institutions. New England in the seventeenth century nearly requires its own category: a society in which if you searched diligently you might find a few slaves. In 1676, Edward Randolph reported to the Lords of Trade that there were "not above 200 slaves" in all of New England. Massachusetts Bay governor, Simon Bradstreet, reinforced the estimate in May 1680 when he wrote that there were between 100 and 120 blacks (he used the word as a synonym for slaves) in his colony. He claimed that in the fifty-year history of Massachusetts Bay there had been only two large ship loads of slaves brought to port. More typically, two or three slaves periodically trickled in on ships from the Caribbean, apparently remnants from the slave trade there. Bostonians had engaged in the commerce of selling humans since at least 1645 and occasionally at the end of a voyage brought a few Africans to their homeport to be sold for around £20 per person. To explain further why there were so few people with African ancestry, Bradstreet added that the birth rate of slaves in the colony was very low, no more than five or six per year.[9]

Until the latter part of the seventeenth century, slaves and a small number of free blacks could be found almost exclusively in the port towns of New England: Portsmouth, Salem, Boston, Newport, New London, New Haven, Middletown, Hartford, and even Springfield well up the

Connecticut River. The enslaved lived in the homes of prominent officials, wealthy merchants, and pious ministers, such as Governor Theophilus Eaton and the Reverend John Davenport of New Haven Colony. To a certain extent they signified the wealth or prestige of their owners, but more important they provided the hard work that maintained those households. Slaves cooked, cleaned, served, repaired, built, carried, tended to animals, tilled soil, sailed, fished, and performed the varied tasks assigned to them. Often living under the same roof as their owners, they might experience a relationship that bordered on friendship or, at times, the cruelty that came from uncaring people and dysfunctional families. When not working, they could leave the premises—at least during the day—and have some control over their lives.[10]

In some ways African slaves in the seventeenth century were a novelty, but in others they simply were a dark version of indentured servants, the key difference being the length of servitude. Few laws differentiated them from other subordinate parts of the population. The Massachusetts legislature in 1652 required that "all Scotsmen, Negers, & Indians inhabiting with or servants to the English" must train in militia drills, and then in 1656 it reversed itself by removing Indians and people of African descent from eligible participants; it precluded white servants as well but didn't specifically name them. Africans probably served in Connecticut militias as late as 1660, but by the end of the century, every New England colony barred blacks from militia duty. The restriction didn't prevent New England African Americans from fighting in every colonial war.[11]

Boston, fearing the dumping of sick or idle persons, in 1658 demanded that any person who freed his servant must secure employment and protect the town from any expense. The statute applied to both indentured servants and slaves but, most likely, was directed primarily at slaves. Three years later, the town ordered Thomas Deane not to employ his slave as a cooper. This was not a general law prohibiting people of African descent from a skilled trade. Although the decree was ambiguous (Deane's slave was identified as "a Negro"), it appears that Boston authorities were more concerned about unfair competition from a slave than from an African American. That would change. Connecticut, apart from its militia eligibility requirement, had no other laws in the seventeenth century directed at slaves or free people of color, and New Hampshire had but two during the entire colonial era: a 1686 law that prohibited the selling of alcoholic beverages to blacks, and a curfew issued in 1714.[12]

The rights, privileges, and treatment of people of African descent had its elements of ethnocentricity, but generally relationships between blacks and whites—though separated by wealth, status, and power—were relatively benign during New England's first century. Whites recognized black people's humanity and treated them as persons, within the context of hierarchical societies. African Americans married, could baptize their children, and bought and sold property. They often received basic education in reading, writing, and arithmetic. Their legal rights—trial by jury, suing on their own behalf (even for their freedom), legal counsel, testifying as witnesses for or against anyone—were equal to those of whites. There, nevertheless, is no record of a person of African descent voting, serving on a jury, or holding office.[13] That was true as well for all women and children and for a substantial number of white men. Subordinate status as servants, slaves, and children, poverty or small property holdings, and gender—not place of origin or complexion—determined a person's political rights.

The same pattern could be seen within New England churches. African Americans were eligible for church membership, and in 1641 a slave woman of the Reverend John Stoughton satisfied the congregation's requirements and became a member. Few other people of African descent followed her example during most of the colonial period. Those who did or who simply attended services found themselves seated well back in the meetinghouse. Peter Swinck, a free black, arrived in Massachusetts Bay by 1650. He was the first person with African ancestry to live in western Massachusetts. Springfield's First Church assigned him a seat next to a white neighbor, and, of course, his seat was located in the rear.[14] But he didn't sit in a black section. There was no black section. Instead he sat where people of his status, as determined by the church's seating committee, were expected to be.

The small number of African Americans, whether free or enslaved, and societies still dominated by a hierarchical worldview determined the place of people of African descent in seventeenth-century New England. To be sure, the ripples of individualism in the forms of Protestantism, early capitalism, and nascent democracy wore upon the shores of hierarchy, but erosion was slow. The accepted order had men above women, adults over children, masters over servants and slaves, wealthy over the poor, leaders above the multitude, Christians over heathens, Protestants above Catholics, English speakers above non-English speakers. As John Winthrop in 1630 put it: it was God's plan that "some must be rich some poore, some highe and eminent in power and dignitie; others meane and in subieccion." This was the world Africans encountered. Vulnerability, availability, and ethnocentrism—not racism (the belief that human beings constitute different physical types and that some types are superior to others)—brought Africans to New England shores as slaves. People of African descent were at the bottom because they were slaves or poor, because they for the most part were viewed as heathens, and to a certain extent because they were not English.[15] Perhaps had there been larger numbers of black people, white fears might have triggered racist practices sooner. Peter Swinck might have sat in a black section of the Springfield meetinghouse.

There is nothing magical about the year 1700. After all, it's a convention; depending on the culture, it just as easily could be 1 or 678 or 23,402 or any other number. But 1700 was a threshold for New England and relations between people of European descent and people of African descent. The number of Africans and African Americans climbed dramatically in the last years of the seventeenth century and exploded in the eighteenth. Although different historians have arrived at slightly differing tallies, they uniformly agree that the increase was substantial and faster than the population as a whole. Ira Berlin, whose estimates are on the high end, accounts for 470 slaves in all of New England as of 1680; 1,680 in 1700; and 10,982 in 1750. Although the number of free blacks was small, it enlarged the total number of people of African descent. Boston, as usual, offers an example, not typical of Massachusetts Bay as a whole but perhaps suggestive of numbers in other port cities. On a regular basis the town required its free African American men to serve several days a year on highway repair. In 1708, it identified thirty-two different individuals, with names covering the range from "Tom Cowell" to "a fellow came from Charles T [Charlestown]." Free women and children would have augmented this group. If Boston is any gauge, the number of free people of color stayed flat, if not slightly diminished, while the slave population surged. In 1715, the total of all free black men in Boston totaled twenty-five, and in 1721 twenty-six.[16]

Part of the growth of the enslaved came from births within New England, but most of the increase came from the slave trade. In the latter part of the seventeenth century, Great Britain with first the Royal Adventurers and then the Royal African Company seriously entered the slave trade between Africa and the Western Hemisphere. When Parliament curtailed the Royal African Company's monopoly in 1696, new opportunities opened for New England entrepreneurs. With trade already a key part of the New England colonies' economy, commerce in persons simply expanded the possible revenue. New England quickly became the leading colonial section in the slave trade, and in the eighteenth century, Rhode Island, particularly its port city of Newport, led New England. Most of the commerce was with the plantation colonies of the South and the Caribbean, but there was a steady demand for slaves in New England as well.[17]

Although slaves could be found throughout New England—in roughly 100 towns and villages in Massachusetts alone—they were most heavily clustered in the large port cities and in towns along the major rivers.[18] This basically was the same pattern as in the seventeenth century.

What differed was the tremendous growth and density in the Narragansett region of Rhode Island (the southern part of the colony west of Narragansett Bay) and in eastern Connecticut. Where the typical New England slaveholder owned one to three slaves, the Narragansett and eastern Connecticut owners usually possessed from five to forty-two slaves and sometimes exceeded fifty. Rhode Island governor William Robinson held twenty slaves, and Robert Hazard owned at least twenty-four (he named them in his will); Godfrey Malbone of the township of Brooklyn was the largest slaveowner in Connecticut with fifty to sixty slaves, and the Newport merchant and Narragansett landowner Abraham Redwood as of 1766 held a grand total of 238 slaves (an astounding number even in the South). In most of New England, people of African descent represented 2 to 3 percent of the total population—a few urban centers having higher densities, many villages lower; in the Narragansett and eastern Connecticut they constituted as much as one-third to one-half of the total. New England slaves individually and in small groups continued to work at a broad array of tasks. In the Narragansett district and eastern Connecticut, they also worked in large gangs raising stock, dairying, and growing tobacco. This small section of New England fit the description of a slave society, and its plantations looked surprisingly similar to those in the Chesapeake and the Carolinas. On the eve of the Revolution, Connecticut held more slaves than did any other New England colony, and Rhode Island had the densest population of Africans and African Americans.[19] These differences had consequences.

Throughout New England, there was concern about the growth of the black population, but the most adamant expressions and actions came from the areas with the highest concentrations of people of color. "The Numerousness of Slaves at this day in the Province," Samuel Sewall wrote in a pamphlet against slavery, "and the Uneasiness of them under their

Slavery" prompted him and others to question whether the institution of slavery was on a firm foundation. A successful Boston merchant, an esteemed jurist (even as a former "witchcraft" judge who had repented), a member of the governor's Council, a landowner with extensive property including portions of the Narragansett area, and one of the wealthiest men in New England, Sewall had a prominence that few could match. His tract, "The Selling of Joseph," published in June 1700, was one of the earliest antislavery documents written in North America.[20]

Sewall's message had layers of meaning. First and foremost, it condemned slavery as an affront to humankind and to God. Sewall anchored his proposition on the premises that all men are sons of Adam and entitled to equal liberty and comforts and that God had "made of One Blood, all Nations of Men." Such surprisingly Jeffersonian principles quickly were undermined by similarly Jeffersonian equivocations. By providing specific reasons why Massachusetts should abandon slavery, Sewall revealed a racism that contradicted his premises. White indentured servants with fixed terms of service would serve the colony better than would "Slaves for Life," who with no hope for freedom make "Unwilling Servants." White servants, moreover, had the advantage that they could serve in the militia and "might make Husbands for our Daughters." If we give Sewall the benefit of the doubt, we might allow for the possibility that he was referring to the condition of slaves and not to any inherent differences. But even that possibility was dispelled when he wrote: "And there is such a disparity in their ["Negros'"] Condition, Colour & Hair, that they can never embody with us, and grow up into orderly Families, to the Peopling of the Land: but still remain in our Body Politick as a kind of extravasat Blood."[21]

Sewall avoided claims of African inferiority, but he argued that the differences of condition and physical appearance between blacks and whites were so great that they could not together form families, societies, or states. People of African descent were aliens in Massachusetts, strangers in a strange land. The dilemma for Sewall was determining what course of action should be taken. He genuinely believed that slavery was wrong, but he also felt deeply that assimilation was impossible. He never quite called for slavery to end where it already existed. At the very least (and perhaps at the very most), he wanted "man stealing"—the slave trade—to end.

John Saffin, the following year, took a much harder line in reply to Sewall's tract. Saffin—a Boston merchant, jurist, politician, slaveowner and slave trader, and a foe of Sewall—parried that although all men may be sons of Adam that did not make them equal. "God . . . hath Ordained different degrees and orders of men," Saffin wrote, "some to be High and Honourable, some to be Low and Despicable; ... yea, some to be born slaves, and so to remain during their lives." The hierarchical views earlier expressed by John Winthrop clearly still were alive in the early eighteenth century, and they were a potent rejoinder to demands for equality. Saffin then asked, if it were unlawful to deprive heathens [read Africans] of their liberty, why shouldn't it be even more unlawful to deprive Christians [read Europeans] "though but for a time" of theirs? White servants might be preferable to black slaves, but to deny them their liberty for any length of time was worse than enslaving heathens who at least would benefit from Christian teachings. Although Sewall was ambivalent in his attitudes toward people of African descent, Saffin was unapologetically racist as he demonstrated in a poem he inserted at the conclusion of his argument. Entitled "The Negroes Character," it began hatefully with "Cowardly and cruel are those Blacks Innate,/ Prone to Revenge, Imp of inveterate hate," and it didn't improve as it went on.[22]

Early on it appeared that Sewall's might be the dominant voice, but as the years passed, a series of resolutions and laws made clear that at least for prominent New Englanders the view of Africans and African Americans had changed. The ethnocentrism of the seventeenth century hadn't disappeared, but various forms of racism had augmented it.

A Boston committee in 1700 endeavored to slow the growth of slavery by placing a duty on imported Africans, but failed. The following year, Boston's selectmen encouraged the town's representatives to the Massachusetts legislature to promote the immigration of white servants and "to put a Period to negros being Slaves." Thus far, these were proposals that Samuel Sewall could enthusiastically support. When in 1705 the Massachusetts legislature passed a bill placing a duty of £4 on each imported slave, Sewall may have been pleased, but he was outraged by the overall act of which the duty was just a part.[23]

"An Act for the Better Preventing of a Spurious and Mixt Issue," as the statute was named, was confirmation of the sea change that had occurred and of the emerging caste system that would characterize New England for centuries. The first two sections made it a crime for people of African descent and people of European descent to have sex. In some ways they were similar to the old fornication law; each person would be whipped for the offense. But in the past there had been no differentiation between whites and blacks. Now, white mothers must maintain a child of a mixed union. If unable, such children would be placed in service. White fathers were fined £5 and were required to support the child. Black offenders, whether men or women, however, would be sold outside the province. Section three required that any African or African American who struck "any person of the English or other Christian nation" be severely whipped. Section four prohibited marriage between people of African descent and people of European descent. The officiator would be fined £50. Although there is no record of the province enforcing the marriage ban, Massachusetts Bay was the only New England colony to have such a law. Samuel Sewall had fought against it and had the modest success of removing Indians from the law as well as interjecting section five that no master "shall unreasonably deny marriage to his negro" and another black person.[24]

Other New England colonies followed Massachusetts' lead. Rhode Island required a master to accompany any slave being entertained by a free person (1708), placed duties on imported slaves (1711), and established special courts to try people of African descent who had been accused of stealing (1718). Connecticut enacted provisions that any "Indian, Negro, or Molatto-Servant, or Slave" disturbing the peace or striking a white person would be whipped up to thirty stripes (1708), created curfews for after nine o'clock at night (1708), and required servants, slaves, and "Free Negroes" to carry passes when they traveled (1690, 1708, 1750). Owners had to post security for freed slaves (1711), and all free persons were ordered not to buy or receive goods from servants or slaves without orders from their masters (1708). The lower house of the Connecticut legislature passed a bill prohibiting African Americans from purchasing land or from living with their families without a town's consent (1717), but it failed to be enacted. New Hampshire—with the fewest number of African Americans, particularly outside of Portsmouth—limited itself to putting a curfew on black people after nine in the evening (1714).[25]

Some New England towns placed their own restrictions on people of color, but none could match South Kingstown, Rhode Island (in the Narragansett area), or Boston; and Boston alone bore the distinction of being the most racist urban area in all of colonial New England. The most disturbing example came in 1723, when the town sent fifteen proposed laws for "Better Regulating Indians Negros and Molattos" to the Massachusetts legislature—a comprehensive Black Code. Six laws applied to slaves or servants, but over half were directed exclusively at free people. Among the proposals were restrictions on owning firearms and other weapons, on gathering in groups, and on possessing alcohol.

More unusual and heartless was the requirement that "every free Indian Negro or Molatto Shal bind out, all their Children at or before they arrive to the age of four years to Some English master, and upon neglect thereof the Select men or Overseers of the Poor Shal be Empowered to bind out all Such Children till the age of Twenty one years." Boston and other New England towns frequently forced poor residents to indenture some of their children to reduce the costs of poor relief, but this proposed law, which removed children regardless of the family's financial circumstances, was unprecedented. It appears to have been designed to prepare children for subservience—and offer cheap labor—rather than to trim the town's financial obligations. The legislature was unable to craft a bill that satisfied both the House and the Council, and the colony's first flirtation with Jim Crow died.[26]

Boston nonetheless continued to pass laws restricting the rights of African Americans. Most pertained only to slaves and servants, but some affected all black Bostonians. Concerned about large groups forming, particularly after dark, the town ordered in 1723 that "all Indians Negros and Molattoes shall be Buryed halfe an hour before Sun Set at the Least." Five years later, in 1728, it prohibited all African Americans from carrying sticks or canes. A special watch patrolled the streets to apprehend "all Negro and Molatto Servants" who were out after 10 o'clock at night. Penalties were imposed for loitering on the "Lord's day," and innkeepers and sellers of alcoholic beverages lost their license if they sold liquor to "Negroes or Molatto Servants."[27] And so it went.

It is difficult to know with any precision to what extent these particular laws represented general views. At the very least they expressed the attitudes of those who voted for them and probably large portions of those who lived in areas most heavily populated by people of African descent. But there still were significant numbers of white New Englanders who had little contact with African Americans and who probably thought little about them, either positively or negatively. Many of the laws, moreover, were similar to earlier statutes whose aim was to control people who lived outside the domain of family governance, such as single, young men. The Mayflower Compact, for one, was in part an attempt to control that potentially unruly segment of the new immigrants. Even the witchcraft cases were to some degree efforts to control single, older women who were not governed by fathers or husbands. But in contrast to the seventeenth century, these eighteenth-century laws referred only to people of color. There was the crucial difference.

White attitudes toward blacks had hardened. In the seventeenth century, people of African descent had been enslaved, had been prohibited from serving in militias, and had had to sit in the back of a church even when they were church members. In none of those cases had the subordination resulted from perceptions of physical attributes but rather had originated from their condition. They had been heathens and vulnerable before their enslavement, and afterward in New England they were servants or slaves, or at the very least poor. Ethnocentrism and perhaps xenophobia—attitudes nearly universal across cultures—justified the oppression of black New Englanders. Even so, white New Englanders didn't question Africans' humanity but viewed them as God's creations with souls. That didn't lessen the pain of enslavement. It did, however, open up the possibility of assimilation. As people of African descent became more English, opportunities for upward mobility should have occurred. Before 1664, in Massachusetts Bay a male African who was admitted to church membership should have been eligible to be a freeman.[28] An African American who became free and through hard work acquired a farm should have sat in front of white, unpropertied servants in meetinghouses. There is no record of either type of assimilation having occurred. Numbers of blacks—particularly those who were free— were small, and extant documents are incomplete, but there is the faint possibility that more than ethnocentrism and xenophobia tainted white New Englanders.

Some historians have argued that English people brought racism with them to American shores and that it preceded slavery rather than resulted from it. There can be little doubt that some Elizabethans harbored prejudicial, even racist, views of Africans. Shakespeare's *Othello* is proof of that. But as scholar Emily C. Bartels has astutely noted, only the lowlifes in the play—Iago, Brabantio, and Roderigo—held and promoted racist views of blacks, Othello in particular. Other, more upstanding characters admired Othello's courage, intelligence, and leadership. The tragedy comes from Othello, poisoned by Iago's suggestions, doubting that the white Desdemona could truly love and be faithful to his dark self. For the play to work, Shakespeare's audience would have to have recognized the existence of racist views in their society and also the falseness of them. Other scholars have independently concluded that prejudice against black people was present in seventeenth-century England but far from universal, and that eighteenth-century British lower classes were hostile to servants from the continent and positive toward blacks.[29] Racist attitudes were hardly uniform. Some seventeenth-century British migrants may

have been predisposed to prejudicial attitudes, but the racism of the eighteenth century came from their experiences in New England.

The rapid increase of African slaves contributed to the change. Where
once there had been a few hundred people—many who held non-Christian
beliefs and didn't speak English fluently, if at all—now there were thousands. Fears of outsiders and of possible insurrections surely increased
in the areas where large numbers of black newcomers were being held
against their will, and means of controlling and subduing them must have
seemed necessary. Slave traders and slaveowners needed to somehow
reconcile commerce in humans and indefinite bondage with their other,
more humane, values and the assumption that people of African descent
were inherently inferior to themselves would have helped. And their
daily experiences would have reinforced such racism. The only Africans
and African Americans white New Englanders ever would have encountered were slaves, servants, or the economically impoverished. It would
have been easy to conclude that people of color were slaves, servants, or
poor because they were people of color. Predispositions of prejudice may
have played a role, but it appears that the emergence of overt racism in
eighteenth-century New England primarily was the consequence of what
people experienced and constructed at the time.[30]

3

Emancipation and Free African Americans

DESPITE RACISM, DESPITE profits and status, slavery at some level grated on New England consciences. It seemed wrong to seize people from their native lands, to break up families, and to enslave them simply because Africans were vulnerable and not Christians. Try as they might to justify the institution, white New Englanders remained uneasy. Even the rationale of converting heathens to Christian beliefs didn't balance out the evils of the slave trade and perpetual bondage. In the years leading up to the Revolution, the metaphors of slavery to describe their own relationship to the British and British law had a hollow ring as long as they deprived African Americans of their freedom. With slaves being marginal to the economy and a small percentage of the overall population—with the notable exceptions of the Narragansett area of Rhode Island and of eastern Connecticut—it was politically easier to end slavery in New England than it would be in the newly forming states south of the region.[1]

When Vermont, where few slaves lived, wrote its state constitution in 1777, it banned adult slavery—although a small number of slaves could be found in the state for an additional quarter century. New Hampshire enacted a bill of rights in its 1783 constitution, but it did not explicitly abolish slavery. That would not occur until July 26, 1857, seventy-four years later. The bill of rights of Massachusetts' 1780 constitution was similarly vague as to the legality of slavery, even though it declared all men to be free and equal. In a series of cases between 1781 and 1783, together called the *Quock Walker* case after a slave who sued for his freedom, the Supreme Judicial Court of Massachusetts interpreted the constitution as intending to outlaw slavery. The decision freed Walker and, although "not widely reported," probably contributed to the rapid demise of slavery in Massachusetts. Years later, Charles Lowell would claim that the court had accurately understood the intent of the framers. His father John Lowell, who had been on the committee that had interjected the clause that all men should be free and equal, had done so, Lowell reported, "for the express purpose of settling the question about slavery in the State." Connecticut and Rhode Island, each in 1784, provided for gradual emancipation. Any child born of slave parents in Connecticut would become free at the age of twenty-five. In 1797, the legislature reduced the age to twenty-one, and in 1848 it abolished slavery entirely. The Rhode Island legislature freed all children born after March 1, 1784, but their parents remained enslaved as long as their masters wished.[2]

If we look only at New England laws, the death of slavery was excruciatingly slow. But if we analyze population data, the story is quite different. In 1770, there were 14,892 African Americans in New England. The vast majority were slaves; but because census records before the federal census of 1790 don't differentiate between those who were slaves and those who were free, it is impossible to know with precision the exact number. What can be known is that after the Revolution, the number of slaves plummeted rapidly. There were 3,870 slaves in 1790, 1,339 in 1800, 418 in 1810, 145 in 1820, and 45 in 1830. Slaves were not randomly distributed across the region but tightly clustered primarily in Rhode Island and Connecticut. Massachusetts, by comparison, had 4,754 slaves in 1770 but none listed in the 1790 census. Even these declining numbers exaggerate how vigorous slavery was. Of the forty-five New England slaves identified in the 1830 census, twenty-four were age fifty-five or older (nineteen of them women), and four were younger than ten.[3] Owners almost certainly kept older slaves rather than relegating them, if freed, to the likelihood of severe deprivation.

By contrast, there were 13,059 free black New Englanders in 1790, 17,313 in 1800, 19,488 in 1810, 20,782 in 1820, and 21,224 in 1830. All New England states by 1790 had more free people of African descent (significantly more in all but Connecticut) than slaves.[4] Although the laws gradually abolished slavery and although the pace was painfully slow for those still enslaved, the predominant dynamic for New England society was the sudden emergence of a substantial, free African American population.

Just as the rapid growth of slavery in the early eighteenth century prompted a shift in the attitudes of many whites toward blacks, so too did the quick growth of the number of free, black New Englanders in the late eighteenth and early nineteenth centuries. Racism and laws regulating African Americans had appeared in the early eighteenth century, but major control rested in the hands of slaveowners. When slavery became a dying institution in the late eighteenth century, that control shrank and all but evaporated outside of Connecticut and Rhode Island.

An even more virulent racism and a Jim Crow environment materialized in its place. Segregation in schools, churches, transportation, housing, and public venues appeared, while what rights there were—such as voting in Connecticut and Rhode Island—and employment opportunities declined or disappeared. A whole genre of derisive entertainment, in the form of "bobalition" broadsides and blackface minstrelsy, emerged that depicted African Americans as buffoons, half-wits, and thrillingly subversive of societal restraints. White New Englanders disapproved of slavery in their midst, but that didn't mean they approved of equal rights for former slaves. Popular opinion was a significant force behind the abolition of slavery in New England, but it also helped create the world that Hosea Easton and David Walker so hated.[5]

The racism and disdain that Easton and Walker experienced in Boston during the 1820s pervaded New England, particularly in cities and towns where there were the largest concentrations of people of color, but there were variations in the expressions of prejudice and even pockets where near-equality existed. Of the 1,319 cities, towns, village, hamlets, and smaller settlements the 1830 Federal Census identified in New England, only 694 (53%) had African American residents. The northern tier of states—Maine, New Hampshire, and Vermont—had the smallest numbers of African Americans and the most towns populated exclusively by people of European descent. Black New Englanders lived in only 100 of 380 towns in Maine, 91 of 224 in New Hampshire, and 90 of 245 in Vermont. Portland, Maine, with 312 black residents, was the only city in all of upper New England with 100 or more African Americans. By contrast, black New Englanders resided in 250 of 306 towns in Massachusetts, 132 of 133 in Connecticut, and 31 of 31 in Rhode Island.[6]

Eight cities, all adjacent to the Atlantic or navigable rivers, each had black populations of 300 or more and together constituted one-quarter of all African Americans in New England. The remaining thirty-one towns and cities with black populations of 100 or more (six in Massachusetts, five in Rhode Island, and twenty in Connecticut) roughly equaled the same combined number of African American inhabitants as did the top eight (see Appendix 1). The remaining half of black New Englanders

FIGURE 3.1 *Bobalition of Slavery*, 1832, one of a series of broadsides mocking African Americans—in this case a celebration of the end of the slave trade. (Library of Congress).

Table 3.1 1830 New England Population

States	Population	African American Population	African American %	Slaves
Connecticut	299,012	7,982	2.7	26
Maine	400,448	1,187	0.3	0
Massachusetts	608,834	7,002	1.2	2
New Hampshire	269,137	606	0.2	3
Rhode Island	96,363	3,569	3.7	13
Vermont	280,603	878	0.3	0
Total	1,954,397	21,224	1.1	44

lived in settlements ranging from having slightly fewer than 100 African Americans to those with only a single person of African descent. Numbers mattered. In a city such as Boston, black residents could support one another with their own institutions and mutual aid associations. If their children encountered harassment in the classroom, they had the option of creating their own schools. If churches segregated them in rear pews, they could form their own churches. If white shopkeepers wouldn't serve them, they could patronize black establishments. Where there was a sufficient number of people of African descent, they could build communities. The largest cities provided their own types of humiliation and despair, but the black community at its best offered a haven to the legally free and a shield to fugitive slaves.[7]

The smaller the number of African American residents in a settlement, the fewer options black people had. Accommodation and assimilation were more essential, but not necessarily possible. If children experienced racist remarks or behavior from classmates and teachers, the only option might be to stop attending school. If white neighbors snubbed or avoided them, friends would have to be found in other towns. If racism became intolerable, they might have to move to a town with an established black community. And fugitive slaves would be conspicuous in a town with a small black population and might have to find permanent residence elsewhere. Places with few black residents, however, were less apt to be overtly racist. According to Elise A. Guyette, Hinesburgh, Vermont, with

Table 3.2 New England Cities with 300 or More
African Americans in 1830

1. Boston, Mass.—1,876 (3.1% of population)

2. Providence, R.I.—1,205 (7.3% of population)

3. New Haven, Conn.—530 (5.5% of population)

4. Newport, R.I.—439 (5.5% of population)

5. New Bedford, Mass.—383 (5.0% of population)

6. Hartford, Conn.—338 (4.8% of population)

6. South Kingston, R.I.—338 (9.2% of population)

8. Portland, Maine—312 (2.5% of population)

a population of 1,660, including nineteen black residents, was such a place. Shubael and Violet Clarke were members of the Hinesburgh Baptist church, and Shubael served on several committees that investigated the purported transgressions of white members. Their children were literate and, Guyette speculates, must have attended school. They had friends among their white neighbors as well as with other African American residents of central and northwestern Vermont. Shubael and Lewis Clarke, Samuel, Prince, and Josephus Peters, and William Langley paid taxes and voted in state and national elections. Some members of the Clarke and Peters families owned property. Hinesburgh was not an aberration, but neither was it typical.[8]

Some New England towns had few black residents by design. There was no employment for people of African descent in the textile mills, and few African Americans lived in the mill towns. Lowell, Massachusetts, for example, had a total population of 6,474 people but only eleven African Americans (five of whom lived in households headed by whites). Waltham, Massachusetts, had an overall population of 1,857 and not a single black person. Three other Massachusetts mill towns—Oxford, Pawtucket, and Rehoboth—offered similar patterns of few black residents, at least half of whom in each town dwelled in white households. People of African descent in 1830 remained outside the industrial revolution in the country's most industrialized region.[9]

The racism and Jim Crow laws and behavior in New England suggest a large African American presence, but people of African descent formed a small part of the overall population. Constituting only 1.1 percent of the total, black New Englanders were less than one-half of 1 percent in the northern tier of states and were barely above the regional average in Massachusetts. Rhode Island and Connecticut had small averages, with just 3.7 percent and 2.7 percent, but they were distinct from the other New England states (see Appendix 2). Averages, as is often the case, could be deceptive. Only 3.1 percent of Boston's population were people of African descent, but there were pockets—such as Ward 6 with 13.4 percent and Ward 7 with 7.8 percent—with significantly heavier concentrations and a vibrant black community. Despite representing a small part of Boston's overall citizenry, the 1,876 black Bostonians—8.8 percent of all black New Englanders—contributed a substantial number of the leaders seeking African American equality. Conversely, Ervings Grant, Massachusetts, was such a small settlement that with African Americans forming 7.5 percent of the village's population they still numbered only thirty-four, and every one of them lived in white-headed households. For the most part, however, cities and towns with relatively large black populations also had concentrations well above the region's average. The number of free African Americans, distributed most heavily in coastal and river towns and in the Narragansett area of Rhode Island and in eastern Connecticut, was large enough to incite racist fears but too small normally to be an effective political force in areas where they could vote.[10] These were obstacles to overcome in the struggle ahead.

There is one additional caveat to add in describing the world of Hosea Easton and David Walker. Emancipation did not necessarily provide autonomy from direct white control. There could be a progression between slavery and free nuclear households. Many former slaves first lived in white-headed households or institutions. The great majority were domestic servants, old retainers, and children, but some were prisoners, residents of almshouses, and boarders. No matter what the circumstances, they remained under close scrutiny by white adults, frequently their former owners. As of 1830 when Massachusetts, Vermont, and Maine had less than one-quarter of their African American populations living in white-headed households and institutions, roughly one-third of black residents in Rhode Island, Connecticut, and New Hampshire lived in a household or institution headed by a white person. New Hampshire is the anomaly. Rhode Island and Connecticut with their comparatively large numbers of black residents might be expected to be exemplars of paternalism and control, but New Hampshire, it

Table 3.3 1830 New England Residential Distribution

States	Family #	Family %	Black Household #	Black Household %	White Household #	White Household %	Alone #	Alone %
Connecticut	4,162	52.1	971	12.2	2,784	34.9	70	0.9
Maine	728	61.3	231	19.5	192	16.2	36	3.0
Massachusetts	3,477	49.7	1,676	24.0	1,727	24.7	115	1.6
New Hampshire	217	35.8	152	25.1	226	37.3	11	1.8
Rhode Island	1,289	36.1	1,104	30.9	1,135	31.8	41	1.1
Vermont	395	45.0	269	30.6	207	23.6	7	0.8
Total	10,268	48.4	4,403	20.7	6,271	29.5	280	1.3

would seem, should have been more like Maine and Vermont. The difference apparently was that, no matter the state, in towns and villages with five black residents or fewer, the likelihood that most or all would live in white households was exceedingly high, and New Hampshire stood alone in the number of towns with five or fewer persons of African descent.[11]

Most African American New Englanders lived in households headed by a black person (see Appendix 3). Some were boarding houses, houses sectioned off as small apartments, or dwellings for extended families or multiple, related nuclear families living under the same roof. Years later, William Brown reminisced about his own experience as a boy in 1820s Providence. He lived next door to a sailors' boarding house. "There were two rooms upstairs arranged the same as below," he wrote. "When we first moved in we occupied the upper rooms, until the family below could vacate their rooms, which was some six months after we moved in. Two rooms was considered quite a genteel tenement in these days for a family of six, especially if they were colored, the prevailing opinion being that they had no business with a larger house than one or two rooms." Approximately half of African Americans in New England lived in two-generation nuclear families in single dwellings, as William Brown's family eventually did. There were variations—one parent, a boarder, or an elderly grandparent—but the norm was two parents and children. The nuclear family, the sole occupants of a house, offered the greatest autonomy and provided proof of the family's higher status within the black community.[12]

No matter where a person of African descent lived—a town with a large black population or a small hamlet, in a city or in the countryside, in a vibrant black community or as a member of the only black family in the entire village—he or she inhabited a world restricted by racism. There might not be lynchings as in the post–Civil War South, and there might be some civil rights, such as voting in Massachusetts, but there were limited employment opportunities, the likelihood of poverty, and the near certainty of regular insults and humiliations. Black New Englanders drifted in a sea of whites; their numbers were small and their problems were great. The world depicted by Hosea Easton and David Walker would not change without white cooperation or at least grudging acquiescence. How to alter that world, how to attain that cooperation, was the question.

PART II

Girding Up

4

Unity and Uplift

THE LIKELIHOOD OF free African Americans reversing racist laws, attitudes, and behaviors during the colonial years was near impossible. Their numbers were too small, and poverty and rudimentary education at best kept their focus on sustaining themselves and their families rather than on transforming New England society. Even after the Revolution with the dramatic increase of free people of color, prospects for equal rights appeared grim. Whites dominated government at all levels; they organized religion, social and educational institutions, and all areas of the economy; and they seldom were inclined to support black advancement, let alone equality.

There were exceptions, to be sure. Lemuel Haynes, born out of wedlock to an African slave father and a Scottish servant mother in 1753, served as the minister of a white Congregational church in West Rutland, Vermont, from 1788 to 1818. Despite his compromised early status, he had been fortunate. Bound out as a servant to David Rose of Granville, Massachusetts, he had been raised almost as a member of the family. Mrs. Rose, in particular, grew strongly attached to Haynes. His upbringing provided love, education, and devout religious beliefs. Following his service as a soldier in the Revolution, he became a certified Congregational minister in 1780 and was ordained in 1785. Two years earlier he had married Elizabeth Babbit, a white schoolteacher who had proposed to him. At first he had hesitated to enter such a controversial alliance, but after several ministers had offered their support for the union he happily married her. Although racist views barred him from more prominent pulpits, the shortage of Congregational ministers in western Vermont made possible his leading a white congregation. Thirty years is a long time to serve a congregation, and there must have been tensions—some connected to his African heritage—along the way. Haynes' relations with his church, nonetheless, were amicable, respectful, and, perhaps, even affectionate, but in 1818 the congregation dismissed him. He was sixty-five, set in his ways, and now bitter. He concluded that racism had been the cause, that the people of his church "were so sagacious that at the end of the time they found out he was a nigger." That may have been true, but it wasn't the whole story. His age and an evolving congregation quite likely also contributed to his departure, and his politics probably were more central still. He was an outspoken Federalist in an increasingly Republican age. No matter the cause, the pain of rejection didn't disappear during the fifteen years of life remaining to him.[1]

Even more successful was Paul Cuffe. Born in 1759 on an island off the coast of Massachusetts near New Bedford to a West African father and a Wampanoag mother, he became one of the wealthiest African Americans in New England. When his father died, the teenaged Cuffe began maritime life on ships engaged in the Caribbean trade. During the Revolution he owned his own boat and ran British blockades between the mainland and Nantucket. After the war he joined his brother-in-law in shipbuilding and captained many of the vessels himself. His wealth grew and so did his identity with Africa and his antipathy to American racism. His birth surname had been Slocum, and he changed it to Cuffe, his father's African first name. He led all-black crews, and he became increasingly concerned for Africans and American slaves. His becoming a Quaker in 1808 reinforced his commitment to Africa, particularly to former slaves in Sierra Leone. By his death in 1817, he had become an advocate for the colonization of African Americans, and he was an early supporter of the American Colonization Society. His hope was for the abolition of slavery, but despite his own success he had doubts that the United States was a place where people of African descent could thrive.[2]

Cuffe was not the first black New Englander to propose emigrating to Africa nor the last. In 1787, more than seventy-five Bostonians—led by the former slave, skilled leatherworker, and equal rights activist Prince Hall—petitioned the Massachusetts legislature for assistance in moving to Africa. Some of them were Africans who wished to return home, but others were African Americans who believed they would be better off in Africa than in the United States. At this same time, Rhode Island, the New England state where the slave trade had continued the longest, held a substantial number of people of color with close ties to Africa who wished to emigrate. Few succeeded. By the mid-1790s, following the revolution led by Toussaint L'Ouverture, some African Americans shifted their gaze to

Haiti as a potentional homeland. Africa and Haiti would continue to hold appeal, but in the years after the termination of the international slave trade in 1808, the attraction was less to return home and more to escape oppression. And there was always the neighbor to the north, Canada.[3] Its close proximity to New England and its similar cultural patterns without the traditions of slavery and racism made it a much more realistic and, for many, desirable destination than either Haiti or Africa. It also provided a haven for fugitive slaves, when New England no longer felt safe.

For the vast majority of black New Englanders, including Prince Hall, emigration was a pipe dream, a last resort alternative. They much preferred improving where they already lived than moving to an unknown land. If whites treated them as a separate caste, they would create their own churches, schools, and fraternal organizations. They would build their own communities. And yet, they were Americans deserving of equal treatment, equal rights, and equal opportunities. Separate institutions might be necessary way stations or even worthy objectives, but they should be a choice, not an imperative.

Hosea Easton and David Walker captured the sentiment of black New Englanders in the 1820s when they called for unity and uplift as means for achieving equal rights. Working together would be more effective than pursuing disparate individual initiatives, particularly when their numbers were so small. But there was a fine line between unity and separatism. The goal was full and unimpeded participation in American society, not the creation of an autonomous African American world. An underlying question, connected to self-identity, was, who was being united? They were former slaves or descendants of slaves, they were people with an African heritage, they were objects of scorn and denigration to many whites, and they were Americans, but they were not a biologically distinct group inferior to other human beings. So far there was agreement.

These various articles of identity emerged in the debate of what to call themselves. In some ways it was easier to eliminate names they didn't want than to form a consensus on a common descriptor. "Negro" and its hateful spin-off "nigger" were rejected. Hosea Easton saw the two as one. "Negro or nigger," he wrote, "is an opprobrious term, employed to impose contempt upon them as an inferior race, and also to express their deformity of person." "Blacks" and "Mulattoes" were inappropriate, for, as one black Bostonian put it, they "sow among them the seeds of discord and strife, jealousy and hatred, and to hinder the advancement of the whole." There was some ambivalence about the term "African." The American

Colonization Society and its state branches poisoned the word for many black New Englanders because of its attempt to "return" former slaves to Africa. They considered themselves Americans, and Africa was no more their home than was England and other parts of Europe for whites. They were people of African descent, and Africa was a bond that connected them to each other. For the most part, they preferred other markers of identity. The African Baptist Church of Boston, founded as such in 1806, changed its title to the First Independent Church of the People of Color in the 1830s. But there were exceptions, such as Boston's African Methodist Episcopal Zion Church that originated in 1838.[4]

"A Subscriber," writing to *The Liberator* in 1831, had an alternative designation. Almost certainly African American himself, as were most subscribers to *The Liberator* at that time, he discarded "Negro" as insulting, "colored" as an "offensive distinction of color," and "African" as a denier of their being American. He suggested "Afric-American" or "Africamerican," because such a term recognized American citizenship and African heritage. The editor of *The Liberator*, William Lloyd Garrison, agreed. He regretted that any "distinctive appellation" was needed, but under the circumstances preferred "Afric-Americans" or Africo-Americans." Despite the endorsement, "colored people" or some variation, such as "people of color" or "Colored American," were the terms that most black New Englanders favored in the mid-nineteenth century. That nomenclature was the most all-encompassing and had the fewest detriments.[5]

Whatever name they chose, black New Englanders still encountered barriers to unity within and across their own communities. Shades of darkness prompted prejudice among African Americans, with lighter skinned people typically having higher status and being more likely to hold leadership positions in black institutions. During the period when slavery thrived, Election Day—when people of African descent in the larger cities elected their own "governors"—transcended the differences. It was a day of role reversal when slaves could act out their aspirations and let loose. These annual festivals brought together diverse people of color, if only for a day. Emancipation in New England terminated the need for mock civic participation and awakened a desire for the real thing. Election Day lost its allure. To replace it with a different celebration, to raise expectations for equal rights, and to unify black communities, African American leaders created events commemorating the end of slavery. Parades and mass gatherings with food, music, and speeches were joyous and even defiant occasions. They trumpeted what had been accomplished, they shouted the message that people of African descent deserved respect and equal rights, and they sang out hopes for themselves and their children. But these were only whispers if something didn't prompt white New Englanders to change their attitudes and behavior.[6]

Black New Englanders experimented with a variety of tactics. In 1831, property-owning people of color in Providence petitioned the state legislature. They requested that they be exempted from taxation or be allowed to vote and to send their children to public schools. They argued from strong and traditional ground—no taxation without representation—but to no avail. One state legislator, E. R. Potter, lamely explained that he and others had rejected the petition because it was so difficult to determine who was black, and he was afraid that people would claim the distinction in order to avoid paying taxes. *The Liberator* scoffed that "a black skin is too unpopular for any white man to claim, even to escape from taxation." More to the point its editor asked, "What have shades of color to do with a question of right?"[7] The petitioners, but a minority of a minority, certainly had the stronger argument, but justice alone, as is often the case, could not vanquish prejudice.

African Americans held endless meetings and issued innumerable remonstrances against slavery and inequality. The "colored citizens of Boston" on February 15, 1831, for example, met and passed resolutions objecting to the Massachusetts Colonization Society. Their prime objective may have been to reprimand clergymen who were advocating the removal of free blacks from the United States, but they were no more effective than the Providence petitioners. At best, such meetings strengthened black communities and organizations and gave a sense of purpose and accomplishment in place of despair, but in the short term they didn't change the status quo. Some preferred direct action. In 1836, a group of African American women invaded the chambers of the Massachusetts Supreme Court and rescued two women charged with being fugitive slaves.[8] Here was a concrete result, but such isolated episodes were no substitute for a far-reaching strategy for equal rights.

The prevailing strategy for this stage of the equal rights movement was to lift up people of African descent. The idea that African Americans needed to improve themselves so as to reduce white prejudice as well as for their own well-being was not new, but it received increased support in the late 1820s and the 1830s. Hosea Easton and David Walker were neither the first nor the last to call on blacks to seek education, work hard, and lead upright lives. By assuming the values of the middle class, they might elevate themselves. Maria W. Stewart, the first American woman to lecture on political subjects before mixed audiences of men and women, reiterated these themes in a lecture at Franklin Hall in Boston on September 21, 1832. "Were the American free people of color to turn their attention more assiduously to moral worth and intellectual improvement," the twenty-nine-year-old Stewart exhorted, "this would be the result:—prejudice would gradually diminish, and the whites would be compelled to say,—Unloose those fetters!" In an address at the African Masonic Hall on February 27, 1833, she implored young African Americans to refrain from gambling and dancing. There was nothing wrong with dancing, she acknowledged, but "we are poor, and have no money to throw away." Better to spend their meager incomes on "schools and seminaries of learning for our children and youth."[9]

What followed such advice was an explosion of institutions designed to educate, lift up, and inspire. In short order there emerged in Boston alone the Afric-American Female Intelligence Society, the American Union, the Adelphic Union Library Association, the Boston Minors' Exhibition Society, the Young Men's Literary Society, the Juvenile Garrison Independent Society, the Histrionic Club, the African Humane Society, and the Boston Mutual Lyceum. Most of these were open to whites as well as to blacks, and most of them had as a major instigator, William Cooper Nell. Only a teenager when he helped create these organizations, he was a major voice for uplift, black pride, and equal rights throughout his fifty-eight years. Nell, whose father was an associate of David Walker, learned young the iniquities of racism. An excellent student at Boston's segregated school in the basement of the African Meeting House, in 1829 he was denied the Franklin Medal—an award given to outstanding Boston students—and an invitation to the dinner honoring them, because of his African heritage. He attended the dinner, nevertheless, but as a waiter. Such an experience would have embittered and demoralized most people, but instead it drove Nell to a life committed to combating the oppressions of Jim Crow.[10]

In certain ways the efforts of the American Colonization Society could be viewed as white attempts to promote black uplift. Although colonizers' main objective purportedly was to end slavery, they believed there would be residual benefits for former slaves and Africans alike. Their underlying premise was that racism was so entrenched in American society that slaveowners would be reluctant to free their slaves for fear of dire consequences and that all free African Americans would be forever oppressed. Their solution was to promote the emigration of American people of

William C. Nell

FIGURE 4.1 *William C. Nell*, by an unknown photographer. (Collection of the Massachusetts Historical Society).

color to Africa. In their minds former slaves and their descendants were only returning home. Everybody would win. White Americans would live in a land free of an African presence, Africans would be converted to Christianity and civilized ways, and people of African descent would have rights and opportunities not possible in the United States. The American Colonization Society may never have issued formal statements declaring blacks inferior to whites, but there can be little doubt that its members were as infected with racism as was America in general.[11]

African Americans, with such exceptions as Paul Cuffe, rejected colonization. By the late 1820s, they vigorously opposed any attempts to transport themselves to Africa, voluntarily or not, and they viewed such efforts as a means of depriving them of rights and civic status that they deserved. They were Americans of African descent, not Africans who happened to be living in America.[12]

Most whites didn't understand this perspective—in part because they rarely heard African Americans discussing public affairs—nor did they want to. William Lloyd Garrison was different. Born in Newburyport,

Massachusetts, in 1805, Garrison grew up in poverty with an alcoholic father, who abandoned the family in 1818, and a deeply religious, Baptist mother. At the age of thirteen he apprenticed at the *Newburyport Herald*, and in the 1820s he edited a series of newspapers, all of which failed. When Benjamin Lundy, a fellow antislavery advocate, invited him to co-edit *The Genius of Universal Emancipation* in Baltimore, he found his voice and his calling. Never before had he lived in the midst of an African American community, and Baltimore's, which made up one-quarter of the city's population, was substantial. Here he heard criticisms of colonization first-hand and reversed himself to become a fierce adversary of the American Colonization Society. After two years of valuable experience and of building a reputation among an emerging group of abolitionists, he moved to Boston ready to start his own newspaper. Having abandoned his support for colonization, he had taken up the demands for immediate emancipation of slaves and for equal rights for free people of color. Shaped by his passionate religious beliefs, he held that slavery was not only wrong but also a sin, that all human beings were members of the same divine family, and that change should be brought about by peaceful, non-political means. He believed in the perfectibility of all humanity and supported a broad spectrum of reforms.[13]

His first task was to create a viable newspaper. One lesson he learned in Baltimore was how important the African American community was in sustaining a newspaper dedicated to the abolition of slavery and to equal rights for all, and he set out to win the confidence and the support of black Bostonians. An obstacle was his earlier backing of colonization, but his two years as co-editor of an abolitionist newspaper, his forty-nine days spent in a Baltimore jail for editorializing that the prominent merchant Francis Todd was a "murderer" for participating in the slave trade, and his comfortable social relations with blacks convinced Boston people of color that he could be trusted. *The Liberator* went to press with its first issue on January 1, 1831, because black leaders produced enough subscribers to cover the costs of production. Their support was essential, and *The Liberator* could not have survived its early years without it. Black agents solicited subscriptions in more than a dozen cities, and the vast majority of subscribers for many years were people of African descent. In 1834, three-quarters of the 2,300 subscribers were African American, and most of its advertising revenue came from black sources.[14]

Garrison kept up his side of the bargain. The first issue made clear that its twin purposes were to advance the cause of immediate emancipation

FIGURE 4.2 *William Lloyd Garrison*, 1833, an oil on wood portrait by Nathaniel Jocelyn. (National Portrait Gallery, Smithsonian Institution; bequest of Garrison Norton).

FIGURE 4.3 *Masthead of The Liberator*, January 5, 1833.

and to elevate blacks to their rightful place in American society. "To Our Free Colored Brethren," he wrote. "Your moral and intellectual elevation, the advancement of your rights, and the defence of your character, will be a leading object of our paper." *The Liberator* became a voice for African Americans. It published articles and poetry by black authors, it promoted community events, and it printed obituaries of deceased people of color. During its first months it set a radical tone by devoting substantial space to commentary on David Walker's *Appeal*. Such services may have held back the development of an independent black press in Boston, but at the time it provided exposure of black perspectives when no other vehicle existed.[15]

The Liberator was not confined to an African American audience. With its intent to promote change in the larger society, it couldn't be. Although its number of white subscribers was small in the first few years, its white readership continued to grow. Elizabeth Buffum Chace remembered in later years when her father, Arnold Buffum, brought a copy of the paper to her home in Fall River, Massachusetts. She questioned whether "it would be quite safe to set the slaves free all at once." After having read pertinent articles in *The Liberator* and holding conversations with Garrison, Buffum assured his daughter that all would be well, and "from that hour we were all Garrisonians."[16]

Enthusiasm and converts grew at such a pace that in early 1832, Garrison and others created the New England Anti-Slavery Society. A small group wrote a preamble and constitution, and on January 6, twelve men founded the society, and sixty others joined them in signing the constitution of the organization. No African American was among the founders, but roughly one-quarter of the signatories were of African descent. The preamble to its constitution laid out the society's principles: slavery was wrong and unjust, all human beings were entitled to natural rights regardless of "complexion," and they will use only "peaceful and lawful means" and "give no countenance to violence or insurrection." Quickly, local antislavery societies, often with a separate women's auxiliary, proliferated throughout New England. Within a few years the regional society disbanded in favor of the national American Anti-Slavery Society and state societies. By 1838, every New England state had its own organization, and local societies abounded: Connecticut, 46; Maine, 48; Massachusetts, 246; New Hampshire, 79; Rhode Island, 26; and Vermont, 104.[17]

These societies were the heart of the antislavery movement in New England. They supported agents in the field and the publication of *The Liberator*, they sponsored speakers and proselytized their neighbors, they raised funds, and they petitioned Congress and their state legislatures. Equally as important, they provided a community for like-minded people and validation of their beliefs. Despite their growing numbers, it wasn't popular to be an abolitionist. Maria Weston Warren, a prominent member of the Boston Female Anti-Slavery Society, wrote of the social and professional cost of advocating immediate emancipation in 1835: "It has occasioned our brothers to be dismissed from the pastoral charge—our sons to be expelled from colleges and theological seminaries—our friends from professorships—our selves from literary and social privileges." The Boston physician, Henry Ingersoll Bowditch, similarly felt ostracized. "[George] Ticknor's pleasant literary coteries were no longer accessible," he later reminisced. "Captain Oxnard, one of my father's old and respected friends, who had always greeted me with a smile when, as a youth, I met him in State Street, would even stare and scowl without speaking when we met after I had openly declared myself as one of the hated Abolitionists."[18]

Many of the societies fittingly had both black and white members. Blacks might hold leadership positions but were still a minority of the membership. Such cooperation was a valuable example to the outside world and a challenge to most participants. This was new ground with few precedents. Blacks and whites may have been members of the same congregations but had seldom sat in the same or adjacent pews or had social interactions. They may have provided services or goods to each other, but conversations rarely went beyond the transactions. For the most part, antislavery society members were middle class, and that may have eased early encounters. African American members came from the elite of black communities with such occupations as ministers, barbers, and tailors, while people of European descent may have ranged from workingmen to wealthy entrepreneurs but generally filled the broad middle. Try as they might, there still were tensions. No matter the twin goals of antislavery and equal rights, whites tended to be more concerned with terminating the institution of slavery than with elevating free African Americans, which frustrated their black counterparts who desperately wanted both.[19]

And then there was the issue of racism within the ranks. For some white abolitionists, there was no question that people of African descent and people of European descent were equals, but others had difficulty shedding the racist presumptions they had long held. Many recognized their own failings and worked to eliminate their prejudices. In 1837, for example, the New England Anti-Slavery Convention resolved "not only to educate and elevate the free people of color, but also to eradicate from among our white population, and especially from abolitionists themselves, the remains of that irrational, unnatural and unchristian prejudice." The convention was reacting to such incidents as occurred among the members of the Female Anti-Slavery Society of Fall River, Massachusetts. Elizabeth Buffum Chace related that she and her sister Lucy visited some young African American women who had come to their meetings and invited them to join the society. Some of "the leading members" were so outraged that the group nearly dissolved. "They said they had no objection to the women attending the meetings, and they were willing to help and encourage them in every way," Chace wrote, "but they did not think it was at all proper to invite them to join the Society, thus putting them on an equality with ourselves." Despite those objections, the society admitted the women. This was an advance, though most likely grudging, as reformers tried to confront and overcome lifelong prejudices.[20]

Some were more successful than others, and most maintained ambivalence toward treating blacks as social equals. The prominent and influential Unitarian minister, William Ellery Channing, published a book in 1835 condemning slavery while at the same time holding the belief that "we ought never to have permitted our colored brethren to unite with us in our associations." The distinguished public servant John Quincy Adams could attempt to curtail the "gag rule" on antislavery petitions to Congress, defend the *Amistad* captives, and protest the annexation of Texas and the ensuing war with Mexico, and yet write in an essay on Shakespearean plays that "the great moral lesson of the tragedy of *Othello* is, that black and white blood cannot be intermingled in marriage without a gross outrage upon the law of Nature, and that in such violations, Nature will vindicate her laws." The minister and fiery reformer Theodore Parker could befriend Frederick Douglass, have leading African Americans in his congregation, literally fight for fugitive slaves, and counsel John Brown, and still use the language of race to explain why Anglo-Saxons had advanced more rapidly than Africans.[21]

The belief that there were different biological types of human beings—some better than others—long preceded the word "race" having such meanings. People had talked of the "human race" or had used the word to distinguish between cultural and national groups, such as the "Irish race." Those distinctions could have pejorative meanings, but they weren't referring to physical types. During the antebellum period the use of the word "race" increasingly became connected to the racism that had long existed. Anthropologists and scientists were making "scientific" studies of humans much as eighteenth-century zoologist and botanist Linnaeus had typed the range and variety of all living things, and their language and meanings spread to the general public. Theodore Parker was not unusual when he referred to the "Anglo-Saxon race" and the "African race" as two groups of people with inherently dissimilar biologies and intellects.[22] In a country so laden with racist beliefs, it is all the more remarkable that there was a William Lloyd Garrison.

Garrison, unlike almost all white Americans in the nineteenth century and most white Americans in the twenty-first century, recognized that the language and meaning of race was no more than an arbitrary convention—an intellectual construct—and that it was false. In *Thoughts on African Colonization* (1832), a tract criticizing the American Colonization Society, he reasoned that colonizationists to be consistent should just as logically be able to justify "why all our tall citizens should not conspire to remove their more diminutive brethren, and all the corpulent to remove the lean and lank, and all the strong to remove the weak, and all the educated to remove the ignorant, and all the rich to remove the poor, as readily as for the removal of those whose skin is 'not colored like my own.'" Privately as well as publicly he sounded the same theme, as in a letter to Gerrit Smith. "I wish to see every man respected and elevated according to his merits and abilities," he wrote, "without any reference to his height, his bulk, or his complexion."[23] In short, any distinction that led to prejudice was wrong and arbitrary. It was just as mistaken to oppress a person for his height as for his color and, he implied, just as capricious.

There was a disagreement with Frederick Douglass, however, that led some contemporaries and later historians to question whether Garrison was free of all racism. In 1851, Douglass wanted to form his own newspaper, and Garrison tried to dissuade him in what could be interpreted as a condescending manner. Douglass went ahead with the *Frederick Douglass' Paper*, and their deteriorating relationship sputtered and then grew heated both over important and petty issues. Douglass resented any impediment to his command of his own enterprises, and Garrison feared that competition to *The Liberator* might factionalize the movement further and imperil the newspaper's viability. Disputes over the best means to end slavery and promote equal rights made matters worse. Charged with animosity toward black "manliness," Garrison retorted that "a 'black man' is to be criticized, rebuked, and 'denounced' as well as a white man, according to his position, failings or errors; and it is very absurd to make any outcry about it." The estrangement was over real issues, but it may have been exacerbated by an ego clash of a strong individual wanting an expanded role and an old leader demanding due deference. Neither man was without flaws. Some African American leaders sided with Douglass, but most remained loyal to Garrison, even when the split disappointed them.[24]

5

Advanced Education

WHEN WHITE REFORMERS in the 1830s considered ways for people of color to attain equal rights, they, like black reformers, almost always gravitated to uplift. The prejudice of their times, they thought, would disappear as African Americans acquired education and middle-class values. In words that could have been written by David Walker, Hosea Easton, or Maria W. Stewart, one white essayist in *The Liberator* wrote: "Next to good conduct . . . knowledge and mental cultivation are essential in the descendants of Africa, if they wish to rise to an equal station in society with the other inhabitants of this country." Education was indispensable, and issue after issue of *The Liberator* displayed advertisements for Sunday schools, evening schools, writing schools, and other schools for black children and occasionally for black adults. Almost all of the founders and teachers were white, and sometimes an endorsement from *The Liberator* was required to allay parental distrust. For the most part, black communities welcomed the assistance.[1]

These schools filled a need, but black and white leaders agreed that more advanced education was essential to prepare African Americans for all spheres of American life. John B. Russwurm had graduated from Bowdoin College in 1826. He was the exception, for at the time no other New England college was admitting people of African descent. Even high schools were in short supply. There was widespread discussion of creating institutions of higher learning for African Americans, and in 1828 colonizationists formed a school in Hartford for the training of black missionaries who would minister to Africans. Their planning was haphazard, pupils were scarce, and the school quickly failed.[2] African Americans, for their part, wanted advanced education for their children who would remain in New England and become pillars of their communities, not for those who

would abandon their homeland for Africa. Still, the very fact that colonizationists supported black education was promising.

In 1831, black New Yorkers took matters into their own hands and
formed an association to establish a high school. Their initiative reminded
Simeon S. Jocelyn of a more far-reaching idea. Jocelyn, a white abolitionist,
was the minister of the African American Temple Street church in New
Haven. He had been part of a group two years before who had presented
a proposal for a "school of high order for colored youth" to a "body of literary men" in New Haven. Nearly all had approved. Since then there had
been delays, but in May 1831 they resumed their plans. They contacted
the New Yorkers and suggested they combine forces for the creation of "a
college on the manual labor system, connecting agriculture, horticulture,
and mechanic arts, with the study of literature and the sciences, at New-
Haven." Securing their enthusiastic support, Jocelyn persuaded Arthur
Tappan, a wealthy merchant and reformer who had a summer residence
in New Haven, of the plan's merits, and Tappan convinced William Lloyd
Garrison to travel with them to Philadelphia to present their ideas for the
college to a convention of black leaders who were meeting there.[3]

Although only fifteen delegates from five different states attended this
first national convention of African Americans in June 1831, they firmed
up relationships for future actions, compared notes on tactics and strate-
gies, and graciously agreed to hear Jocelyn, Tappan, and Garrison. The
three white abolitionists made a strong case for a manual labor college
to a highly receptive audience, and the convention appointed a committee to meet with them for further consideration and to report back. To no
one's surprise, the committee recommended that a college for young men
of color be established as soon as $20,000 was raised. Such a large sum
might have caused alarm, had they not revealed that a "benevolent individual" (Arthur Tappan) promised $1,000 if the remaining $19,000 was
given within a year. The additional arrangement that four of the college's
seven trustees would be African American also heightened the delegates'
enthusiasm.[4]

The most controversial part of the report was where the college should
be located. Jocelyn, Tappan, and Garrison recommended New Haven, as
then did the committee. Their reasons ranged from vague platitudes to
practical benefits and included one or two assertions that would prove
disastrously wrong. The city provided a "healthy and beautiful" environment, and its citizenry were "friendly, pious, generous, and humane." Its
laws were free from racist distinctions. It was centrally located particularly

in relation to Boston, New York, and Philadelphia. Cheap land was available for agriculture, and its variety of manufacturing enterprises could augment instruction. Professors from Yale and a variety of seminaries could teach classes and would reduce the necessity of employing a broadly trained—and seemingly, full-time—faculty. Housing was cheap and provisions good. Last, New Haven's trade with the West Indies was extensive, and the wealth of free people of color of those islands was enormous. Blacks in Jamaica alone owned "property valued at thirty millions of dollars—equal to the entire capital of the United States Bank," and they would send their sons to the college.[5]

What they didn't mention was that Connecticut was a haven for colonizationists who loathed abolitionists and were, at best, paternalistic racists, and that New Haven with the largest population of African Americans in Connecticut and the third largest for all of New England was a hotbed of colonizationist sentiment. In the best of times, New Haven was a questionable location for a black college, but its selection roughly six months after *The Liberator* began publication with its constant attack on the American Colonization Society couldn't have been much worse, and yet it would be. Jocelyn, Tappan, and Garrison had all been colonizationists, but had converted to promoting immediate emancipation and equal rights. Connecticut colonizationists, the most active of any New England state, feared that the proposed college would become a center for abolitionism, a magnet attracting people of African descent, and a seedbed for "amalgamation"—the social and sexual mixing of whites and blacks.[6]

To a certain extent Jocelyn played into colonizationists' hands, and he misjudged the views and behavior of New Haven's elite and its working people. He apparently believed that the earlier plans to train black missionaries and the efforts to create a primary school and high school for New Haven African American children were indications of support for the advancement of all free people of color and, like most people, was inclined to hear what he wanted to hear. Jocelyn thought that opening the college to all young men of color, particularly to sons of wealthy West Indians, would be a boon to New Haven commerce, but the citizens of New Haven viewed the potential influx of outsiders as a threat. They might be supportive of educating New Haven's African American youth, as long as those students were in segregated schools, but they didn't want to encourage more people of color coming to their city. Jocelyn believed that manufacturing enterprises in New Haven were an asset, for they would provide practical instruction to the college's students. He didn't seem to understand how destabilizing industrialization had been to older ways or that preparing black men for industrial occupations would be perceived by white workingmen as imperiling their livelihoods. Upon his return to New Haven after the successful discussions at the convention in Philadelphia, he was so elated and so optimistic that he freely discussed his hope that the college would become a center for liberation worldwide.[7] Again he miscalculated.

As unfertile as the ground in New Haven was for the planting of a college for people of African descent, it became absolutely toxic when residents of the city learned of Nat Turner's insurrection in late August. Hurriedly, mayor Dennis Kimberly called for a town meeting to halt the proposed college before plans went any further. On September 10, approximately 700 townspeople met, and it was clear from the beginning that nearly all opposed the creation of a college for young men of color. Prior to the meeting, an elite committee drew up resolutions, and it preempted general discussion by immediately presenting them to the conclave. The preamble to the resolutions stated that the college would be committed to the immediate abolition of slavery in the United States, and the resolutions made plain that the citizens of New Haven opposed such a course. They argued that slavery was a state matter and that there should not be outside interference with the institution. They also indicated that somehow the college would undermine Yale and other local seminaries and schools. And they concluded, "We will resist the establishment of the proposed College in this place by every lawful means." The debate was overwhelming one-sided, and the vote was 700 in favor of the resolutions and four opposed—one of the opponents being Simeon Jocelyn.[8]

Supporters of the college, hoping that the people of New Haven could be persuaded to reverse themselves, tried to distance the proposed institution from antislavery. Samuel E. Cornish, who had been appointed general agent for raising funds by the convention in Philadelphia, countered in a newspaper article that the exclusive purposes of the manual labor college were to promote "habits of industry" and to prepare the students for mechanical or agricultural professions "while pursuing classical studies." He denied that there was any connection with "immediate emancipation, insurrection, or interference with the internal concerns and laws of the South." Perhaps trying to dissociate the college from anything Jocelyn might have said, Cornish added: "Whatever independent views individuals of the Convention or friends of the college may entertain we do not pretend to say, nor do we intend to account for." On October 1 in the *New Haven Advertiser*, Jocelyn reiterated and enlarged Cornish's remarks. Not only had the college "no necessary connexion with the subject of slavery," he protested, but some of its financial backers were slaveholders. Attempting to refute the claims of the town meeting, he provided a short history of how the plans for the college developed and then elaborated on the benefits to New Haven—ranging from potential financial gains resulting from increased trade with the West Indies to the "pious and industrious" behavior of the town's African American population.[9]

Whatever hopes that the proposed college could be salvaged were dashed later in October. On a Friday night in mid-October, a group of men—purported by *The Liberator* to be southern medical students—assaulted Arthur Tappan's New Haven house with obscene words and stones, and shortly thereafter Tappan sold the house. That attack with its racist undertones was intended to stop the college, but it sparked a broader racist offensive. Some New Haven whites confronted and insulted African Americans on the streets, and one night soon after the stoning of Tappan's house, a crowd tore a black person's house on Mount Pleasant—sometimes called Sodom Hill—to the ground. Days later, a vigilante group descended on New Haven's predominantly black enclave, New Liberia, which was pocked with brothels and dance halls as well as residences. There they "arrested" four white women and fourteen white men in their crusade against amalgamation. And late in the month, a letter-writer to the *New Haven Register* called on the town's selectmen "to prevent an increase of the colored population" in the city.[10] That ended any possibility of New Haven being the site for a manual labor college. For now the forces of reaction had won.

Nearly a year and a half later, *The Liberator* published an advertisement for a high school for "young Ladies and little Misses of color" to be held in Canterbury, Connecticut. William Lloyd Garrison proclaimed it "a seasonable auxiliary to the contemplated Manual Labor School for Colored Youth."[11] That frightened the respectable citizens of the village, for it wasn't supposed to have developed that way.

When Canterbury's elite residents had encouraged Prudence Crandall to form a boarding and day school, they had envisioned a female seminary that would offer instruction to their daughters and the daughters of other well-regarded Connecticut citizens "in several higher branches of education not taught in the public district schools." They knew and trusted the twenty-seven-year-old Crandall who, although born in nearby Hopkinton, Rhode Island, had lived in Canterbury from the age of ten until she went away to the New England Friends' Boarding School in Providence. At the time of the invitation, she was a teacher in Plainfield, Connecticut, a neighboring town.[12]

There wasn't much outward difference between the two villages. They both were situated in eastern Connecticut where slavery once had thrived, but by 1831 there were no slaves in all of Windham County and very few in adjoining counties. Canterbury had a total population of 1,881, including 70 African Americans, while Plainfield was slightly larger with 2,289 residents, including 77 people of color. They were both agricultural communities, with a scattering of domestics, artisans, shopkeepers, physicians, ministers, and lawyers. But Canterbury was where the unmarried Crandall's family still lived, and its townspeople were offering her the opportunity to lead her own school.[13]

The site would be the old Paine mansion, located at the intersection of the two main roads and next to the village green. With its four over four layout and an additional ell extension, it was much grander than anything the new headmistress had previously experienced. How she was able

FIGURE 5.1 *Prudence Crandall,* an engraving by C. A. P. (Collection of the Massachusetts Historical Society).

to afford such a stately dwelling, one of three in the village with the distinctive "Canterbury" style, remains a mystery, as does the nature of her indebtedness to others. Some of the leading citizens may have subsidized the purchase in some manner or made the terms of the mortgage particularly attractive, but acquire the property—debt and all—she did.[14]

Crandall's first year was quite successful. Twenty girls and young women attended the school, they and their parents appeared pleased with the education, and the arrangement was proving financially viable. As the fall term in 1832 began, all looked promising for another rewarding year. And then in September Sarah Harris asked if she might be admitted to the academy. Harris previously had attended the district public school with several of Crandall's current students and was a member of the community congregation. She was respectable, "a professor of religion, and daughter of honorable parents," as Crandall described her. Her father was a farmer in Norwich where he was the agent for *The Liberator*. She wanted the advanced education so that she might teach "colored children," and she herself was African American. Here was a potential problem that tore at Crandall's conscience. Her Quaker upbringing taught her that all people were God's children with the spark of divinity within them, yet the admission of a person of color might jeopardize her school. She postponed an answer. After additional conversations Crandall determined that Harris

FIGURE 5.2 *Elisha Payne House*, July 16, 1940, a photograph by Stanley P. Mixon of Crandall's school. (Historic American Buildings Survey, Library of Congress).

was a serious student and with full awareness of potential consequences admitted her to the academy.[15]

Repercussions came quickly. None of the students complained—at least publicly, but several parents objected to Sarah Harris' attendance, and a few removed their daughters from the school. Prudence Crandall was not so much alarmed by the controversy as awakened to prejudice in American society, particularly in her own community. She began reading *The Liberator* and other abolitionist publications and reflected on what more she might do. With enrollment declining and her concerns for equality rising, she began contemplating the possibility of transforming her school to an institution exclusively devoted to the education of African American girls and young women. She recognized that "high-minded worldly men would oppose the plan" but thought that as "christians" they would restrain themselves from further action. Her chief concern was whether her school could attract enough young women of color to pay the bills. There certainly weren't a sufficient number locally who were qualified, interested, and had parents who could afford $25 per quarter for tuition, washing, and board. Under the guise of surveying other schools and purchasing school materials, she traveled to Boston in January 1833. There she met with William Lloyd Garrison and inquired whether such a school was feasible. In his mind it was, and with his assistance she believed there would be enough students to sustain the academy.[16]

Crandall kept preparations secret for fear of scaring away her current students before she was confident the transformation could occur. On February 24, she was ready and notified her "white scholars" that they would have to transfer to another institution, because hers beginning April 1 would be open only for African Americans. The reaction was quick and angry, and it expressed a combination of racism and a sense of betrayal. That very evening four of Canterbury's most prominent citizens—Daniel Frost Jr., Andrew Harris, and Rufus Adams who were on the school's Board of Visitors and Richard Fenner who was a merchant—met and decided to try to persuade Crandall to change her mind. The next morning they sat with her and explained how improper it was to have a school for female people of color in their midst. Such an institution would break the natural order of whites over blacks, lower property values, and might even lead to mixed marriages. Crandall should have known not to take the bait and should have assured them that "amalgamation" was not the purpose of the academy. But she was inexperienced, high-minded, and strong-willed. She confirmed their worst fear by retorting "Moses had a black wife." Receiving no satisfaction the self-created committee shot back that then they would force the school to close.[17]

The reaction of some of the parents and townspeople was more complicated. These were people who had supported the school from its beginning, and, in the case of the parents, had kept their daughters in the institution after Sarah Harris began attending classes as a regular student. Months had passed, and now they were being told that Sarah Harris could continue but that their daughters couldn't. Whether they eventually would have withdrawn their daughters because it had become an integrated school cannot be known, but it should be no surprise that they became dismayed and bitter. There is another imponderable. What if Prudence Crandall had not dismissed the white students? Was there any possibility that her school could have continued with a mixed student body of girls and young women from only the New England states or even just from Connecticut? The likelihood of such a compromise working was extremely small. It would have had to overcome the various levels of prejudice held by the residents of Canterbury and the stubbornness of Prudence Crandall who already had set her course. And no one suggested that they try.

A week later compromise had become impossible. On March 2, *The Liberator* printed an advertisement for the "Canterbury, (Conn) Female Boarding School" which would serve "young Ladies and little Misses of color" beginning April 1. Fifteen men endorsed the ad and offered themselves as references in New York City, Philadelphia, Brooklyn (Connecticut), Middletown (Connecticut), New Haven, Boston, and Providence. They were leading abolitionists who supported immediate emancipation and equal rights and who opposed slavery, discrimination, and colonization. Seven of them—Joseph Cassey, Samuel C. Cornish, James Forten, William Lloyd Garrison, Simeon S. Jocelyn, Arthur Tappan, and Peter Williams— had been leading proponents of the manual labor college.[18] At this point, the nature of Prudence Crandall's school was no longer merely a local issue. It now pitted townspeople versus outsiders, colonizationists versus abolitionists, and supporters of caste versus advocates for equal rights.

The following morning before Sunday services at the Congregational church next to the village green, Andrew T. Judson, the town clerk, posted a notice for a town meeting to be held on March 9 for the purpose of waylaying the school. A state attorney for Windham County, a director of both the county bank and insurance company, a former state senator, an aspirant to the governorship, and a neighbor (his new home was across the road from the academy), Judson rapidly emerged as the school's most aggressive antagonist. Before the town meeting took place, Crandall began receiving insults and threats of violence should she persist. Because of her gender, she could not present her case at the meeting, and she asked Samuel J. May—a minister in the adjoining town of Brooklyn, an endorser of her advertisement, and an abolitionist— to speak on her behalf. Apparently believing in the overall decency of the people of Canterbury and their sense of justice, she wanted him to explain why her plans for the school had changed and to offer to move it to a location on the outskirts of the village, should equitable financial arrangements be possible.[19] Why she didn't ask her father, a resident of the village, to make the presentation is not known, but by selecting May she opened herself to the charge that she was being manipulated by outside abolitionists.

Arnold Buffum, vice president for the New England Anti-Slavery Society and its chief agent, and George and Henry Benson—two abolitionist brothers from Providence—accompanied May to the town meeting. Crandall had also given a note to Buffum requesting that he be allowed to speak on her behalf. There may have been two or three "stout Negroes" who supported the school there as well. The meetinghouse had balconies on three sides and, all told, could hold approximately 1,000 people. When May and friends arrived, they were astonished to find the building nearly packed. They nudged their way up a side aisle and conspicuously sat in a wall pew near the deacon's bench. The only order of business was two resolutions: one condemning the school and the other appointing a committee to deliver the town's displeasure to Crandall and to try to persuade her to "abandon the project." Rufus Adams, one of the men who first visited Crandall and possibly the father of one of the dismissed students, moved their acceptance. He appeared as much concerned by outside influences as by the transformation of the school.[20]

Andrew T. Judson then took the floor. He told of the ruin that would come to the village's sons and daughters and of the threat to property should an African American academy be established. As May characterized his performance, he "twanged every chord that could stir the coarser passions of the human heart." One protection, Judson suggested, was the old law that empowered the town to "warn out" outsiders, and it should be used against the incoming students. He concluded with an appeal to the townspeople's xenophobic and populist leanings, first by alluding to the "foreign influence" represented by May and friends and then by an attack on outside monied interests. "Are we to be frightened," he questioned, "because Arthur Tappan of New York and others are worth a few millions of dollars, and are going to use it to oppress us? No. I know you will answer no."

Once Judson concluded his remarks, May and Buffum approached the moderator and gave him the slips of paper from Prudence Crandall asking that they might speak. The moderator in turn handed them to Judson who immediately exploded with invectives—invectives that embarrassed even Judson so much that two days later he visited May and half-heartedly apologized. Judson shouted that such a request was unprecedented. This was the first time ever that persons from other towns and states had attempted to "interfere" with deliberations of the Canterbury town meeting, and he peppered his attack with "foreign power" and "foreign influence." Judson may have had a legitimate point that could have been made dispassionately, but the tone of his outburst inflamed the meeting. Other townspeople jumped to their feet, yelled insults, and shook their fists at the seated abolitionists. In the midst of full-scale commotion, the moderator called for a vote on the resolutions, which passed unanimously, and quickly adjourned the meeting.

As people began to depart, May rose and pleaded: "Men of Canterbury, I have a word for you! Hear me!" Somewhere between one-third and one-half of those in attendance stopped and listened. May tried to allay concerns raised by the evening's speakers. The purpose of the school was to educate young women of color; it was not to be a center of abolitionism. The students would have high character and would not disrupt the community nor come as paupers dependent upon community assistance. After those brief remarks May gave way to Buffum who addressed the lingering crowd for about five minutes before trustees of the church demanded they leave. They complied without incident.

On March 14, representatives of the village met with Crandall. They conveyed the resolutions passed in town meeting and tried to persuade her to stop the enterprise. She, as they expected, refused, but they had come with a backup offer. So that she would not be a financial loser in the affair, they would purchase the house at full value, on condition she would not open a school for African American girls and young women elsewhere in the township. Again she declined.[21]

And so matters stood. Prudence Crandall wanted to promote social justice by providing advanced education for young women of African descent. She was surprised, hurt, and defiant of the actions taken by her childhood hometown. Abolitionists from New England and beyond, including the leaders of the failed manual labor college project, rushed to her side. They wished to support a fellow abolitionist engaged in a worthy endeavor, but they also wanted to defeat colonizationists and win greater public support for immediate emancipation and equal rights.

Opponents of the school were even more multi-layered in their objections. Townspeople who had assisted the school from its origin and parents of expelled students felt betrayed and angry, regardless of their racist proclivities. White residents of Canterbury held a range of racist views that allied them with the female seminary's opposition. The school would increase the village's African American population and by providing advanced education for people of color would disrupt the traditional caste system. Students would be disorderly and, were they poor, could bring additional expenses to the town. Their presence would lower property values. Then there was the typical fear of mixed marriages—but with a twist. Ordinarily there was alarm that black men would wed their white daughters, but here there was the concern that the "sable belles" would be "a palatable morsel for our white bachelors." Wedged within this prejudice was the unintended and contradictory acknowledgment of the beauty, social graces, and intelligence of African American women; for why else would the students be potential marriage partners? Xenophobics dreaded the introduction of foreigners from beyond Connecticut into their village as well as the influence of outside, agitating abolitionists. At this point, local and broader issues commingled. Colonizationists and abolitionists were in a bitter struggle in the North, particularly within New England, and to a certain extent Crandall's school was the chosen battleground for those rivalries.[22]

April 1 came, and Crandall's school opened with just two students— Sarah Harris and a boarder Eliza Glasko from Griswold, Connecticut, a town adjacent to Canterbury. Despite the meager initial enrollment, the village held a town meeting that evening. With less conflict than at the previous meeting, the town's citizens voted in favor of a petition to the state legislature requesting enactment of a law "deprecating the evil consequences of bringing from other towns, and other states, people of color for any purpose, and more especially for the purpose of disseminating the principles and doctrines opposed to the benevolent colonization system." They also passed a motion to request other towns to send similar petitions to the legislature.[23] The heavy emphasis on colonization may have been necessary to capture the requisite votes in the legislature and it certainly reflected the views of town leaders, such as Andrew

T. Judson, but it hardly represented the concerns of the general populace who continued to focus on local concerns and prejudices.

Much to Prudence Crandall's relief, students trickled in throughout the spring and summer. On April 12, the first out-of-state student—seventeen-year-old Eliza Ann Hammond from Providence, Rhode Island—arrived; on April 13, justice of the peace Rufus Adams served her with a writ warning her out of town. She had violated an old law common to New England towns since the early seventeenth century but long unenforced. Such laws originally had had a dual purpose: to keep undesirable people out of the community, and to free the town from any financial obligations to support an indigent person. Over time it became less common to force a person from the town and merely became a way to protect the community from financial responsibility for transients, no matter how long they resided there. There were penalties that could be applied. In Canterbury, a warned-out person was required to pay $1.67 per week. If unable to pay, the person was subject to a whipping, "not exceeding ten stripes." Hammond refused to leave, and a week later the town fined her $1.67 and issued a writ against Prudence Crandall "for receiving Miss Hammond as a pupil." This was all to no avail. Hammond remained, and six new students from New York arrived to begin their studies. Outside the school, the town tried to make life as unpleasant as possible for Crandall, her assistant and sister Almira, and by late May her thirteen students. Insults greeted them whenever they left the school grounds, and townspeople began withholding supplies and services, requiring regular trips to Norwich and Providence for provisions.[24]

The state of Connecticut, as the town had hoped, weighed in on May 24 with what was called the "Black Law." The law prohibited establishing any kind of educational institution that admitted out-of-state African Americans unless a majority of the town's authorities approved. Although the legislators wrote the law in general terms, no one doubted that its specific target was the Canterbury Female Boarding School. The town celebrated that night with the ringing of bells and the firing of a cannon. The question now was how soon Prudence Crandall would be arrested and arraigned for trial. In the meantime, Andrew T. Judson and Rufus Adams threatened Crandall's family and supporters that they would be heavily fined if they visited her at the school.[25]

Her arrest came on June 27, and she was arraigned that morning before Judges Adams and Bacon. They set her trial for August, when she would appear before the Superior Court at its next session in Brooklyn,

Connecticut. Should she wish to avoid jail, she would have to post bail. Days before her arrest, she had discussed a strategy with her friends Samuel May and George Benson. So as to publicize the injustice of the law, she would go to jail, at least for a night. May and Benson then contacted those friendly to the cause, told them of the plan, and asked that they not post bail. May also requested that the jailer tidy the room and allow him to replace the bed and mattress. The previous occupant had been a murderer, Watkins by name, and May wanted to alleviate the impending odious experience as much as possible. On the afternoon of the arraignment, a messenger on behalf of the town informed May that the sheriff was on the way to take Crandall to jail, and he begged that bail be posted so as to spare Canterbury the embarrassment. May rushed to the jail and pulled Crandall aside before she entered. He inquired whether she was sure she could endure the ordeal. Bail was available, if not. But she was strong and, almost cheerfully, informed him that her only fear was that "they will not put me into jail."[26]

The following day, friends from nearby Norwich posted bail, and Prudence Crandall was released. Her incarceration had been only for a single night, but she won sympathetic newspaper coverage. Her courage, however, didn't alter the behavior of her detractors. Local merchants persisted in refusing to sell her food or clothing. A committee from the Congregational church reprimanded her for taking her students to Sunday services. Vandals threw eggs at the walls of the school, and a large stone shattered a downstairs window. Even so, the student body continued to grow with seventeen students by July 6 and nineteen by mid-August. As important, Arthur Tappan wrote her that he would pay for her legal defense and hire outstanding lawyers.[27]

The trial began on August 23. The prosecution, after the state attorney and lieutenant governor both found themselves too sick to serve, consisted of Johnathan A. Welch as ostensible lead counsel joined by Andrew Judson and Ichabod Bulkley. Their task was to prove the state's "black law" had been violated by Prudence Crandall, in that she conducted a school with out-of-state African American students. Such a seemingly simple undertaking proved difficult when several students and the Baptist minister of Crandall's church refused to testify. Eventually, a student—after first declining to speak, then being threatened with time in jail, and last being advised by friends to cooperate—told the court that young women of color from outside Connecticut were attending school. That was all the prosecution needed. The defense, composed of Calvin

Goddard, William Wolcott Ellsworth, and Henry Strong, countered that the law was unconstitutional and therefore invalid. The United States Constitution stated that "the citizens of each state shall be entitled to all the privileges and immunities of citizens in the several states." In short, citizens of Pennsylvania, New York, Rhode Island, and Massachusetts were as entitled to attend Crandall's academy as were citizens of Connecticut. The case then hinged on whether the students were citizens of the states from which they came. The prosecution took the position that because of their African ancestry they were not citizens, and the defense offered evidence that they were. Despite the court's charge to the jury that the law was constitutional, five of the twelve jury members disagreed. Without a verdict, the case was deferred to the December session of the Superior Court.[28]

In response to a request by the prosecution, the trial was moved up to October 3, and Chief Justice Daggett of the state's Supreme Court presided. Again the central questions were whether the "black law" was constitutional and whether free people of color were citizens, thus entitled to all the rights and protections of the United States Constitution. After both legal teams repeated their arguments from the first trial, Daggett instructed the jury that free blacks were not citizens with constitutional rights. Even if they were, he suggested that Connecticut's law was constitutional, though he wasn't fully certain on the point. He did everything but directly tell the jury to find Crandall guilty and offered the caveat that if they were mistaken, the verdict could be appealed. This time the jury unanimously agreed that Crandall had broken the law.[29]

The defense immediately appealed, but Connecticut's Supreme Court would not hear the case until July 22, 1834. In the intervening nine months the school continued to operate. Enrollment remained at about twenty students. But harassment continued as well. Locals pelted one of the instructors, Charles C. Burleigh, with eggs. After administering to a sick student, the physician and school opponent Andrew Harris stated that it was the last time he would provide services for anyone at the school. Months later, he kept his word when he refused to cross the road from his house to the school to help a student "who was suffering severe pain." Crandall and others had to purchase all supplies outside of Canterbury. And in January 1834, the building caught fire "under such circumstances as lead to the belief that it was the work of an incendiary." The flames were quickly extinguished and the damage was minor, but the incident reminded Crandall, her staff, and students how perilous their venture had become.[30]

The decision handed down by the state's Supreme Court in late July left the situation muddled. Both legal teams repeated their arguments in great detail. Rather than attempt to resolve whether the Connecticut law was constitutional or whether free people of African descent were citizens, the court overturned Crandall's conviction on the technicality that Windham County's state attorney had presented defective information and therefore there was no need to answer the larger questions.[31]

No longer willing to wait for a legal process to close the school, some local residents seized the iniative and escalated the violence. Whatever joy Prudence Crandall may have experienced in August when she married the Baptist minister Calvin Phileo of New York was short-lived. On August 12, Phileo called upon Andrew Judson with the offer that they would leave the village if they could get a fair price for the school property. To what extent Prudence Crandall was in agreement is unknown, but Judson refused to talk with him. Soon someone tried to set the building on fire for the second time that year. The blaze was quenched without doing serious damage, but the incident led to the discussion of whether students should be exposed to such ongoing danger. For the time being, Crandall decided to keep the school open. But on September 9, another attack occurred. Assailants armed with iron bars and heavy clubs destroyed five windows and ninety panes of glass. Downstairs rooms were "hardly tenantable," and several of the young women barely escaped flying glass. The next day, Prudence Crandall Phileo, her husband, staff, and Samuel May reluctantly concluded that with local officials refusing to investigate or protect them they must close the school. They summoned the students together and informed them that for their safety they must return to their homes. Prudence and Calvin Phileo left Canterbury shortly thereafter. May wrote Garrison that he "felt ashamed of Canterbury, ashamed of Connecticut, ashamed of my country." Years later in his *Reminiscences* he added, "ashamed of my color."[32]

Despite such setbacks in New Haven and Canterbury, New England supporters of "uplift" remained convinced that improved educational opportunities were an essential foundation in the struggle for equal rights. The New England Anti-Slavery Society, meeting on nearly the same day that Sarah Harris first approached Prudence Crandall in 1832, resolved that a manual labor school for young people of color must still be created, and it should be open to "both sexes." In addition to instruction in literature and the sciences, the institution should offer training in "agriculture and the mechanic arts" for males and in "domestic concerns" for females. The society committed itself to raising $50,000 for the enterprise.[33]

Perhaps the Prudence Crandall episode distracted it members, but two years later the society had raised little more than $1,500 and there were no concrete proposals for where and when to construct the school. There was debate at the society's annual convention of whether the better move was to focus attention on integrating existing educational institutions rather than creating something new. But led by "several colored persons" the attendees concluded that as important as desegregation was the process would be lengthy and would not serve African American youth who were in immediate need of advanced education. Words and hope were not enough. They needed a school now.[34]

An opportunity arose in June 1834 when the state of New Hampshire chartered the Noyes Academy in Canaan. Sixty persons, including the prosperous farmer and Revolutionary War veteran Samuel Noyes for whom the school was named, had contributed to building "a neat and handsome edifice," and among the leadership were several abolitionists. The original intent apparently was to provide education to the white children of the area, but during that summer a small group conceived the idea that the Noyes Academy should be open to all qualified students, regardless of descent. The proprietors met on August 16 and debated whether to adopt the proposal. Thirty-six of the fifty-one present voted in support and then elected a board of trustees. Here they connected with the Anti-Slavery Society, selecting David Child, Samuel E. Sewall, and other abolitionists from Boston and elsewhere. At least one of the original proprietors was unhappy with the new direction, and he called a town meeting with the hope of blocking the introduction of African American students. Three hundred citizens of Canaan came forward that evening, but only eighty-six supported a resolution opposing an integrated academy in their midst. Taking the vote as a positive sign of village sentiment, the board of trustees moved forward to recruit students and select an instructor for a March 1 opening.[35]

In many ways, situating an academy in Canaan, New Hampshire, was an odd choice for this experiment in advanced education. The village in western New Hampshire was remote from large population centers. As of the 1830 census, it had only 1,428 residents in a county where the largest village housed but 2,361 souls. Only one person of color lived in Canaan, and she—a girl or young woman somewhere between the ages of ten and twenty-four—resided in a white household, the home of George

Kimball, one of the instigators of Noyes Academy. Enfield immediately to the south had 1,492 residents—all white, as was Dorchester to the north and Orange to the east. Hanover, directly west of Canaan and bordering the Connecticut River and Vermont, had the distinction of Dartmouth College, but its total population numbered fewer than 2,500 people, only twelve of whom were people of African descent. All of Grafton County numbered only twenty-nine African American persons.[36] Like Prudence Crandall's school, the Noyes Academy would have to seek students of color from outside the area.

Notwithstanding these disadvantages, forty-two students were present when the school opened. Fourteen were African American; of the thirteen young black men, Alexander Crummell, Henry Highland Garnet, and Thomas Paul would become prominent leaders, as would Julia Williams, a refugee from the Canterbury Female Boarding School. The first few months promised success. There were no incidents inside or outside the school. No insults, no eggs to dodge, no provisions or services withheld. As the trustees' report stated: "the school went on in peace and prosperity."[37]

And then the rumors began. None commented on the actual students, but they revealed other deep-seated fears. Canaan soon would be "overrun with negroes from the South." Slave huts would line the streets, and "paupers and vagabonds" would abound. Distrust of outsiders—black and white—fueled imaginations. On July 4, several hundred misguided "patriots" gathered, and sixty to seventy of them brandishing bludgeons and other tools of destruction marched on the academy. There was an attempt to force open the door, when the figure of a magistrate appeared in a second-story window. He ordered them to disperse and began taking names. Reluctant to leave, the crowd nonetheless shortly skulked away. A week later there was a repeat performance—an assembly of some discontented townspeople and others from neighboring Enfield, half-hearted threats against the school and its supporters, and then dispersal.[38]

John Harris in his report for the Noyes Academy board of trustees lamented that calm would have returned to Canaan and the Noyes Academy had it not been for "the opportune visit of some slavers from the South," who apparently played on the unease in general and the wariness of abolitionists in particular. As fits the pattern, local officials accordingly called a town meeting for July 31, at which a Superintending Committee was appointed to remove the school. The committee took its directive quite literally. On the evening of August 10, roughly 300 people, including residents of Canaan and neighbors from Enfield and other surrounding villages, along with 90 to 100 oxen destroyed the school's fences and dragged the building about a mile until they reached the common near the Baptist church. There it remained a beacon of liberty, as the school's opponents called it, or "a monument of violence and ruin," as described by the academy's trustees.[39] Advanced education for African American youth had suffered another blow.

6

Intimidation, Assaults, and Riots

THE REACTIONS TO the proposed manual labor college in New Haven, the Canterbury Female Boarding School, and the Noyes Academy in Canaan reflected widespread anxiety throughout New England over such initiatives, particularly between 1831 and 1838. *The Liberator*'s call for immediate emancipation and equal rights and its disdain for the colonization movement, the formation of antislavery societies often with black and white members working together, the mounting unity of African American communities, the emergence of national connections between black leaders, and the frequency, intensity, and growing success of antislavery meetings in towns and villages in all parts of New England alarmed conservatives from all strata of society.

Factory owners, factory workers, sailors, captains, financiers, entrepreneurs, and stevedores might not support slavery, but they depended on healthy relations with slaveowners. They opposed disruptions to markets undergirded by the institution. Their livelihoods, particularly of those engaged in textile production, were fundamentally intertwined with the southern economy. Besides that, the business elite might have long-term friendships with slaveowners that dated back to their days in school and college and to vacations at Saratoga and other watering holes of the wealthy. White workers might fear emancipation as they imagined hordes of former slaves moving north and competing for their jobs and their place in the social order. Members of colonization societies resented the relentless attack by abolitionists on their efforts. Defenders of the Union, the Constitution, and the status quo resisted demands for emancipation and equality that they believed could sever the whole. And underlying all of these uncertainties, fears, and suspicions were long-established foundations of racism, a racism that increasingly viewed equality as synonymous to promiscuity, mixed marriages, and mixed offspring.[1]

Mob attacks on abolitionists became a regular feature of New England life in the 1830s. Their primary purposes were to silence antislavery voices and mollify the South. Occasionally a crowd's anger would focus on particular abolitionists with the possibility of violent assault, but generally the disrupters were satisfied by breaking up a meeting. There were few events before 1833, but from then on, antislavery speakers could expect dissidents—often southern students attending New England colleges—in their audiences. Antislavery agent Arnold Buffum reported such an incident at New Haven. As he was about to speak in a local church, a few young men began to "groan, and cry out, and make disturbances." Several women quickly left, and as the commotion grew louder most of the rest there that evening rose as if to leave. Buffum paused, then asked the audience whether he should continue. Some urged him to proceed, and people returned to their seats. Despite efforts of the dissidents to interrupt—hissing, stamping their feet, and swearing—he spoke for nearly an hour. In Middlebury, Vermont, Orson S. Murray endured "scraping of feet, frequent showering of corn over the room, and other disturbances," yet he too was able to complete his remarks. Again in New Haven, a few constables quelled an outbreak so that the Reverend Mr. Phelps and a Mr. Thorne could present their case for antislavery. More violent was a mob in Norwich, Connecticut, who stopped a Presbyterian minister at an abolitionist meeting, threatened him with tar and feathers, and drove him from town.[2] And so it went until October 1834, when British abolitionist George Thompson reached New England soil. Then it became worse.

For the next thirteen months, Thompson was the center of an unrelenting storm. Although he may have had abolitionist stirrings earlier, he had become a professional activist only in 1831 when he answered an advertisement in a London newspaper for a position as an antislavery agent. His oratorical skills served him well, and he rapidly rose as an electrifying and effective speaker. William Lloyd Garrison met Thompson on a trip to Great Britain in 1833, and recognizing how well he might advance the antislavery cause in the United States, Garrison solicited an extended visit by Thompson. In America, Thompson immediately became a lightning rod. New Englanders either loved or hated him. In his first weeks he was applauded and threatened. The day after he gave a stirring address at the Maine Anti-Slavery Convention in Augusta, "five gentlemen" approached

FIGURE 6.1 *George Thompson*, a lithograph by E. W. Bouves. (Collection of the
Massachusetts Historical Society).

him, called him "a foreign emissary, an officious intermeddler, &c.,"
and instructed him to leave town. On the advice of friends, Thompson
departed, only to give an antislavery lecture in neighboring Hallowell. At
both Concord, New Hampshire, and Lynn, Massachusetts, mobs threw
eggs and stones as he spoke. There were at least five mobs in 1835 alone
who threatened him and his audiences. In Abington, Massachusetts, after
a lecture, "sober and upright citizens" shouted insults and threats, and one
of their number threw a stone that struck him on the side of the face. But
he was a hero to the members of the Boston Female Anti-Slavery Society,
and they invited him to be the featured speaker at their third annual gathering on October 14, 1835.[3]

The ugly incidents overshadow the fact that Thompson was giving
antislavery lectures eight to ten times a week, the vast majority without
disruption. The odds should have been that it was unlikely there would be
an attack. Boston, however, already was primed for an assault on abolitionists, and Thompson provided a worthy target. Little more than a month
before, 1,500 of Boston's most reputable citizens met at Faneuil Hall to

demonstrate to southern slaveholders—some of whom had been invited to witness the spectacle—how protective of their interests the city was. As the meeting moderated by Mayor Theodore Lyman Jr. made clear, abolitionism was a menace that must be contained, or better yet curtailed, so that the Union and they themselves would prosper. The crowd left Faneuil Hall—the site of previous revolutionary activity in the "cradle of liberty"— ready to act. Soon thereafter, William Lloyd Garrison awakened to find a gallows constructed outside his home. If that had not been warning enough of brewing trouble, only one suitable venue was willing to lease its auditorium for the Female Anti-Slavery Society's event. After several of Boston's newspapers denounced the impending meeting, the owner of Congress Hall at the last minute demanded a bond of $10,000 to insure against possible damages that might ensue. The abolitionist women had no choice but to postpone the affair. A crowd appeared outside Congress Hall anyway, and, believing that the meeting had moved to Ritchie Hall, inadvertently disrupted a gathering of the Ladies Moral Reform Society that was meeting there.[4]

The Boston Female Anti-Slavery Society soon rescheduled for Wednesday, October 21, at 3:00 in the afternoon. With no other site available, the members settled for the hall at 46 Washington Street—the home of the Boston Female Anti-Slavery Society, the Massachusetts Anti-Slavery Society, and the office of *The Liberator*. In its advertisement inviting all interested women to attend, the society carefully refrained from naming speakers. The situation was so perilous that the preferred lecturer, George Thompson, on the advice of friends had left the city on October 20. His absence, verified by Mayor Lyman, didn't stop detractors from posting scurrilous handbills just hours before the meeting was to commence. "That infamous foreign scoundrel THOMPSON, will hold forth this afternoon, at the Liberator Office," it bellowed. "The present is a fair opportunity for the friends of the Union to snake Thompson out!" Should that not stir up a sizable and frenzied crowd, it offered a reward of $100 for "the individual who shall first lay violent hands on Thompson, so that he may be brought to the tar kettle before dark."[5]

When Garrison and his fellow abolitionist Charles C. Burleigh arrived at the building at approximately 2:00, many young men already were inside. Garrison and Burleigh went upstairs to Garrison's office and locked the door. Ten minutes later, about twenty-five members of the society climbed up the increasingly crowded stairway. There were the usual insults, but except for one or two African American women who "were rudely pushed into the hall," none of the others was touched. As many as 100 additional women had planned to attend. Only about five more, however, were able to squirm their way through the hostile crowd that by then filled the staircase and the area in front of the hall's door. Garrison came out of his office at one point and tried to persuade the young men to leave, but they were immovable. When he entered the hall at 2:40, he estimated that roughly 100 people were congregated at the street door or opposite the building. Before the end of the afternoon he thought the number of "genteel ruffians" had grown to 4,000 or 5,000.[6]

Garrison had planned to speak, but after conferring with the society's president and recognizing how dangerous the crowd was becoming, he left the hall hoping that his departure would quell the disturbance. He intended to leave the building, but finding the stairway impassable returned with Burleigh to his office and again locked the door. At 3:00 the president called the meeting to order and offered a prayer. By the time the secretary tried to read the annual report, the clamor had grown so loud that it was impossible to conduct further business. Outside, Mayor Lyman informed the multitude that Thompson was not in the building and asked them to clear the street. They remained and became even louder. Days later Garrison concluded that "it proves that the object of the 'respectable and influential' rioters was to put down the cause of emancipation, and that Mr. Thompson furnished merely a pretext for five thousand 'gentlemen' to mob thirty christian women!" Having no success with the unruly crowd, the desperate mayor entered the hall and attempted to convince the women to leave. Inside the building the crowd tried to break down the temporary barrier between the landing and the hall and kicked out the lower panel of the door to Garrison's office. The women realized that it was fruitless to go on. The president adjourned the meeting, and the members arm in arm left the building with as much dignity as possible. As they walked the seven blocks to the home of Maria Weston Chapman where they resumed the agenda, other women swelled their number to fifty. Their understanding was that Garrison had safety preceded them.[7]

In fact, he was still at the headquarters with Burleigh and at least two other abolitionists, Samuel E. Sewall and John R. Campbell, who had come to support the cause. But it was Garrison that the crowd wanted. Mayor Lyman had hoped that when the women left, the crowd would break up. Instead, shouts of "Garrison! Garrison! We must have Garrison! Out with him! Lynch him!" filled the air. Temporarily the sign with the words "Anti-Slavery Office" that was hanging on the outside of the building diverted their attention. With the mayor's consent, Henry Williams and John L. Dimmock—two respectable citizens of Boston—tore the sign down, threw it to the ground below, and watched as the crowd broke it into small pieces that they prized as tokens of their achievement. Garrison understood that the mayor had allowed the destruction as a means of calming passions, but there was no event of that entire day that more disturbed his equanimity. Weeks later, he still ranted at its memory. The obliteration of the sign was only an interlude, and immediately the frenzied cry for Garrison returned. Mayor Lyman and the abolitionists agreed that Garrison should leave through the rear of the building.[8]

John Campbell proposed that he and Garrison jump from a second story window onto a shed and then hurry down Wilson's Lane to safety. All at first went well, despite their nearly "falling headlong to the ground." As they scurried through a carpenter's shop to Wilson's Lane, however, some of the crowd spotted them. The workmen closed the shop and tried to keep the intruders at bay. Garrison thought it futile to prolong the chase and was ready to surrender to the crowd, but the others convinced him to hide in a corner on the second floor where Campbell and a carpenter's assistant placed boards to camouflage him. In a matter of minutes, "several ruffians" gained entry and briefly held Campbell. Although Campbell refused to divulge where Garrison was, Garrison's blind was inadequate and he was captured. Coiling a rope around his body, his captors led him to a window for the crowd to see. Garrison thought they were going to heave him out, but he was allowed to remove the rope and descend to the ground floor where two other men, Daniel and Buff Cooley, seized him.[9]

The Cooley brothers were two burly truckmen. Whatever their politics and beliefs, they wanted to spare Garrison from harm. As they skillfully escorted him down Wilson Lane to State Street and from there past the site of the Boston Massacre to the Old State House where city hall was located, they called out: "He shan't be hurt! You shan't hurt him! Don't hurt him! He is an American!" Others along the way took up the cry, "He shan't be hurt!" Only as Garrison and his protectors reached the south door of city hall was there a serious attempt to recapture him, but the Cooley brothers successfully placed him inside. His hat was gone, his glasses broken, and his clothes were torn, but otherwise he had survived the gauntlet unharmed. The mayor—who had tried to assist Garrison into the building but had been pushed aside by the boisterous crowd—and his advisors concluded that the Old State House itself was endangered as long as Garrison stayed there. They suggested that there

be a sham arrest with Garrison spending the night in jail for his protection. Then he should leave town until tempers cooled down. Garrison
agreed to the plan, but there still was the issue of how to transport him
safely to the town jail. Kind individuals already had lent him clothing
to replace his own torn garments, and his appearance thus would be
somewhat disguised. Drivers brought two carriages up to the Old State
House—one to the north door, the other to the south. That helped to
confuse the crowd. Garrison dashed out the north door, and the driver
whipped his way on a circuitous route to the jail where Garrison arrived
unharmed and elated. Visitors that night commented on his "high spirits" and how well he looked, and Garrison later reflected that he had a
tranquil night's sleep and awakened refreshed. In the morning, after the
judge dismissed the faked charge against him, he and Helen Garrison
left for a short visit to Connecticut. When he returned to Boston two
weeks later, it was as if the town had collective amnesia. He walked the
streets as before—safe and secure.[10]

As threatening as the entire episode was, what is surprising is how little
harm occurred. The only property damage—a demolished sign, a kicked-
in panel on a door, and other inconsequential nicks and scrapes—was
minor. The crowd insulted, pushed, jostled, tore clothing, and temporarily
held various abolitionists, but they didn't throw eggs or stones, strike, beat,
wound, stab, shoot, hang, or perform any other hostile act. The Cooley
brothers could not have stopped the massive assemblage had even a small
part truly wanted to kill Garrison. The crowd's rage had bounds. Perhaps
part of the reason for restraint was because so many of the 5,000 angry
Bostonians were recognizable. Maria Weston Chapman recalled, as she
walked down the staircase of the antislavery headquarters and through the
streets, seeing "the faces of those we had, till now, thought friends." Most
observers referred to them as "wealthy and respectable" and as "gentlemen of property and standing." Many were elite Bostonians, and they may
have been the chief instigators. Garrison believed that to be so, but he also
noted that the antagonists came from all strata of Boston society. The only
group missing was people of African descent.[11] The key reason that there
was no greater violence is that, like the Faneuil Hall Meeting in August,
this was a performance piece, intended in part to discourage abolitionists and in part to convince southerners of the solidarity between the two
regions. Had George Thompson, the foreigner, been present rather than
Garrison, the native-born Boston resident, the results might have been
different.

More vicious than the attacks on abolitionist meetings were the 1830s riots in Providence and Hartford. The violence on Olney's Lane and the adjacent Snow Town section of northern Providence had similar sources as those of the Hardscrabble riot of 1824. The residents, black and white, were poor and could not afford to rent in more well-kept parts of town. Saloons, brothels, and dance halls with their noise, drunkenness, fights, and crime dotted the neighborhood. Sailors on shore leave or from nearby boardinghouses were prominent customers. Residents had complained about these conditions to local authorities for years, but being poor, they had no clout. The key difference from Hardscrabble was that these houses and buildings had white owners.[12]

The sad series of events began in an Olney's Lane saloon ordinarily enough with a fight between sailors, in this case complicated by the fact that one crew was black and the other white. Seamen of diverse ancestry had a long history of working well together, even brawling side-by-side as in the Boston Massacre. But whatever underlying tensions there might have been exploded on this occasion. The black sailors were victorious and drove the white steamboatmen away. The following night—Wednesday, September 21, 1835—at 8:00 P.M., six or seven of the defeated whites accompanied by about 100 allies returned for their revenge. At the foot of Olney's Lane they encountered a group of five white sailors—George Erickson, William Hull, Jack Smith, William Henry, and a tar named Tom—out "on a cruise" for fun and perhaps mayhem. Whether the cruising sailors meant to join the fray or simply tagged along for the spectacle is unclear, but they walked with the singing and shouting crowd up the lane. Suddenly stones were being thrown from the "vicinity of the houses occupied by blacks" and guns were fired, while simultaneously stones were thrown from the crowd at the houses. The official report that the city issued later stated that the initiator of the outbreak couldn't be determined. Most of the crowd retreated back down the lane, but the five sailors were undaunted. When they arrived close by a blacksmith's shop, another gun fired. William Henry "put his hand to his face and said he was shot." Erickson and Hull kept going toward a house where an African American man holding a gun—one account identified him as a bartender—ordered them to keep moving. The two sailors rejoined their fellow "cruisers" and continued to walk for about 100 feet, where they stopped and were joined by three or four other men. The man with the gun again shouted at them to be on their way or he would fire. "Is this the way the blacks are to live," he angrily cried out, "to be obliged to defend themselves from stones."

The sailors refused to move, and George Erickson contemptuously hollered back, "fire and be damned." Those were the last words he ever uttered. After two failed attempts to fire his weapon, the black man finally succeeded. Erickson fell with a large shot to his chest (he would linger for half an hour), and William Hull and John Phillips suffered minor wounds. The now enraged and enlarged crowd retaliated by pulling down two houses and breaking windows and furniture in others and then departed.[13]

By the next day word had spread that "a white man had been shot by the blacks" and that a crowd would tear down more houses that night. Hoping to prevent further bloodshed and damage, the sheriff, accompanied by deputies, constables, and the town watchmen, arrived early. He immediately ordered the crowd to disperse and, when there was no response, arrested seven men. And then the vicious dance commenced. The crowd began destroying houses; the sheriff and even Governor Lemuel H. Arnold ordered them to desist and made arrests; the crowd temporarily halted its activities, rescued those who had just been arrested, and then resumed its attack. This cycle repeated three or four times. In frustration and after several of his men had been struck by stones, the sheriff requested military force. By midnight Captain Shaw and twenty-five soldiers from a state militia company came to stop the riot. As before, stones and brickbats were the throng's response. Governor Arnold and Captain Shaw huddled and agreed that rather than fire on the crowd the military should leave. With no authorities left to stop the destruction, the emboldened multitude demolished six houses on Olney's Lane and then went to Snow Town where it pulled down one house, "overturned" another, and damaged two more. By then it was four in the morning, and as dawn approached the wrecking crew—tired and elated—concluded its work.[14]

Friday, September 23, was another day for rumors, this time that an attempt would be made to free the seven prisoners. The city council and the sheriff asked the governor for military assistance, and he told the leaders of five state militia companies to be on alert. Local magistrates, in the meantime, questioned the prisoners, discharged four of them, and arraigned the remaining three who then posted bail and were released. Thirty to fifty men, nonetheless, stood outside the jail for a few hours that evening. They made some threats, huffed and puffed, and then with their cause for action preempted went home.[15]

Although authorities may have hoped that the riot had ended, they still commanded the five militia companies to form at their armories by 6:00 P.M. on Saturday. At 8:30 that night the sheriff went to Snow Town where he found a large crowd throwing stones at houses. As soon as he left, the crowd began dismantling structures. The sheriff met with the governor and requested the five militia companies; the governor immediately ordered them to Snow Town, and soon thereafter 130 armed soldiers and officers confronted the rioters. Most likely remembering how ineffective the militia had been two nights before, the crowd shouted insults, threw stones, and even attacked individual soldiers, trying to wrestle muskets away. The sheriff and governor in turn ordered the crowd to disperse and warned them that the soldiers' weapons were loaded. Justice of the Peace William S. Patten then stepped forward and read a riot proclamation, requiring rioters to desist and informing spectators that they would be subject to the same penalties as rioters should they not leave. The sheriff called out that they had five minutes before the troops would fire upon them. The crowd answered with stones and shouts of "fire and be damned." After both the governor and the sheriff demanded that the people leave the area, the troops fired their muskets into the air. The rioters derided the effort to intimidate them. Having played all but their last card, the authorities reluctantly had to decide whether to order the militia companies to leave and allow the destruction to continue or to command the soldiers to fire into the crowd. Doing nothing left the troops exposed to serious injury. The sheriff directed the captain of the infantry company to fire. The captain yelled out, "ready." The crowd increased the intensity of its attack. The captain looked to the sheriff, who told him to complete the command. "Aim-Fire," the captain ordered, the troops discharged their muskets, and four men fell to the ground, dead or dying. The riot was over.[16]

The behavior at Olney's Lane and Snow Town clearly was a race riot, but it was more than that. Fights between sailors, usually drunk, were a common feature of all port towns. The particular fight that sparked the riot could have been merely a fight between two men who then were joined by their shipmates; it could have been a fight between mariners from two different ships or two different types of ships—a sailing vessel and a steamship; it could have been a fight between a group of black men and a group of white men; or it could have been some combination of causes. When the steamboat men returned after their defeat, they were spoiling for a fight in an area that had white and black residents and was lined with saloons and brothels. The African American residents as typified by the bartender with a gun perceived the sailors and their compatriots as a particular threat to people of color. Once the bartender shot and killed the white sailor, the riot took on another dimension. A black man had killed a white man. The Thursday night attacks with a reported thousand spectators took place within that context, but they were also an assault on disreputable establishments about which local residents had complained for years. For the most part the attacks throughout the riot, as described in the town report, were on buildings, not persons—except for the soldiers who had been placed in jeopardy. William Brown, an African American memorialist, later claimed that the rioters "warned the better class of colored people to move out" before they began their destruction. And unlike the Hardscrabble Riot, the owners of the destroyed buildings—with one possible exception—were white.[17] The perpetrators were white, the owners of the buildings were white, and the five dead men were white. This was a most peculiar race riot.

At Hartford—seventy-five miles to the west— there was a constant undertow of violence, punctuated by occasional riots stemming from racial tensions. Following a six-month tour of the United States in 1834, the Englishman Edward Strutt Abdy concluded that no city of similar size in the entire country treated its black population so unkindly as did Hartford. "One man assured me," Abdy wrote, "that he never ventured out after daylight, without some weapon of defence about him. No young woman of that race, if she would avoid insult, dare pass through the town in the dusk of the evening, without a man to protect her. To pelt them with stones, and cry out nigger! nigger! as they pass, seems to be the pastime of the place."[18]

One Hartford correspondent to *The Liberator* in 1831 believed that "all the riots in this place" came from "a strong connexion [that] exists between our colored women and white men." A large-scale street fight one night in April that left seven or eight white men injured, several severely, substantiated the writer's claim. It began when some African American men found some young black women in the company of white men. Whether the white men were attempting to seduce the women or vice versa is unclear. Whether the black men were attempting to rescue the women or were jealous of the relationship is equally murky. The result in any case was a bloody brawl and the arrest of two men of African descent. Three nights later a white crowd formed to tear down the black men's houses. Apparently not as skillful as the Providence rioters, they only managed to break some windows. Hartford authorities investigated the incident and placed one of the participants "under bonds for good behavior." One of the city's councilmen received a crank letter stating that there was no point trying to curtail the riots because they would continue "until every negro was driven from the city." Fortunately it was an empty rant, and the riots stopped for the time being.[19]

Hartford experienced a more vicious race riot in 1835. One Monday evening in June a "gang" of white men wielding clubs stationed themselves outside a black family's home and dared the residents to come out. Whatever the source of the gang's displeasure, it was not enough to detain them for more than an hour or two. The next night the men "made a disturbance at the African Meeting House," and then went down the street to wait for the family's appearance. As soon as the assault began, a fellow congregant rushed to his nearby house, loaded his gun, and on his return struck down one assailant with the weapon itself and, upon firing, wounded two others. Authorities arrested the gunman, and that same night the gang with additional support destroyed his home. The rioters increased their numbers the following night and demolished two more houses inhabited by people of color. On Thursday the sheriff ordered out the Governor's Guard, but the 200 rioters settled for "hallooing and hooting." Authorities arrested seven "ringleaders," and peace temporarily returned to Hartford. Three months later arsonists burned down an "African Church," whose minister possibly was Hosea Easton who had lived in the city since 1833.[20]

The peak year for such assaults in New England turned out to be 1835. After that date, although individual insults and taunts continued, mass attacks on African American neighborhoods and on abolitionists of every hue tapered off and then all but disappeared. A backlash to the violence developed. Some people—through shame, embarrassment, or perhaps just a curiosity sparked by dramatic events—gave a second look to emancipation and equal rights. In 1838, the Connecticut legislature reversed itself and overwhelmingly repealed the "black law" prohibiting out-of-state students of color from attending school within its borders and granted jury trials to people presumed to be fugitive slaves.[21] That might be cause for hope, but any dispassionate assessment of the decade of the 1830s had to conclude that the rights of black New Englanders were no better in 1840 than they had been in 1830. Unity and uplift were not enough.

PART III

Toward Equality

7

Riding the Rails with Jim Crow

THE EQUAL RIGHTS movement in New England functioned best at the local level. The broad voice of *The Liberator* and the loose connections between antislavery societies helped shape public opinion against injustices and supported efforts to promote equality, but in the 1840s, the initiative came from individuals and small groups, almost always led by African Americans. Unity and uplift remained important, but increasingly tactics shifted toward direct action. Constituting only a small portion of the overall population, activists could not overturn segregation and racism by themselves. They believed—they almost had to—that most New Englanders were decent people who, when aware of injustice, would want it eliminated. Others might need economic or political persuasion. Sit-ins, boycotts, petition drives, political maneuvering—all with specific reforms as targets—became the means for change. Abolitionists were divided over whether they should create or participate in political parties, but even Garrison and his allies—who contended that the political process was inseparable from corrupt compromises—joined in efforts to sway legislators.[1] Soon they would become aware that despite so many indicators to the contrary, the public tide, ever so gradually and incompletely, was moving with them.

One of the first targets was discrimination on public conveyances. Stagecoaches and steamships long had been sources of frustration for people of color. Part of the problem was how arbitrary the oppression was. There was no official policy of differentiated treatment; but if a driver or captain or white passenger objected to the presence of an African American in a stage compartment or a ship's dining room, the person of color would be ejected or required to travel on top of the stage or on the ship's deck. If there were no complaints, there was no discrimination. The experience in

1834 of Boston schoolteacher Susan Paul—a member of one of the city's
most prominent black families—exemplifies the uncertainty of travel. She
had hired three coaches to transport her and her school's choir to Salem.
When the stages arrived and the drivers "discovered that the children were
somewhat darker in complexion than themselves, they got into a rage, and
profanely declared that 'they would be d—d if they were to carry a load of
niggers in the best coaches in Boston.' " Paul quickly secured other coaches,
whose drivers were "very accommodating," and she and her students successfully made the trip to Salem. Conversely, one day in 1836, William
Lloyd Garrison climbed into a stage at Thompson on the way to Worcester
and found "a very neatly dressed colored female" among the passengers.
No one protested her presence, and there were no incidents.[2]

The Paul and Garrison experiences were self-reported anecdotes during the decade of the 1830s. Far more prevalent, but still anecdotal, were
newspaper accounts. In 1831, one clergyman of color who had already paid
for his passage from Boston to New Bedford was stopped from entering a
stagecoach because one of the passengers demanded the action. Another
black clergyman, his wife, and two other women of color, traveling to New
Bedford from Nantucket, were forced to leave a ship's cabin and "sit in the
rain upon deck until the steward made preparations for them in the fore-
castle," because "a gentleman refused to sit in the cabin with them." The
December 10 issue of *The Liberator* in which the second story appeared
claimed that such treatment was typical. It's hard to know. In the 1830s
there were more than thirty stagecoaches that connected Boston and
Salem each day. All of New England must have had hundreds. Each coach
typically had room for eight people inside. Estimates of the annual number of passengers between Boston and Salem alone were 77,500.[3] How
many of these travelers were African American and how often a person of
color was deprived of passage or humiliated simply cannot be known. But
the possibility of discrimination and insults on coaches and steamers was
constant. Whatever the probabilities, black New Englanders could only
have approached public conveyances with dread.

Segregation and the promotion of caste was a matter of policy on some
railroads, and the passenger cars of the Eastern Railroad, the New Bedford
and Taunton Railroad, and the Boston and Providence Railroad officially
introduced "Jim Crow" to New England. Other New England railroads,
such as the Boston and Worcester, which initiated passenger service in
the region in 1834, did not practice segregation. The most notorious Jim
Crow railroad was the Eastern. When its directors first approached the

Massachusetts legislature for incorporation in 1836, they intended the line only to connect Salem and Boston. The legislature, however, demanded that it extend all the way to the border with New Hampshire and provided $500,000 in state scrip to assist the expansion. An additional $90,000 of scrip was issued before the project was completed. Like railroads that would follow, this was a private/public venture. The directors of the Eastern reasoned that if they were going to extend to the New Hampshire border they should keep laying track until they reached Portsmouth.[4]

Gangs of Irish laborers working long and hard hours for relatively little pay completed the section of track between east Boston (passengers had to take a ferry from the station in Boston to the terminal across the harbor) and Salem by 1838. The task then was to convince people that a train was a better form of transportation than stagecoaches. Steam engines were dirty, noisy, and liable to explode, and a derailment at the unheard of speed of thirty miles per hour risked serious injury and even death for passengers. To compensate, the Eastern offered cheaper fares than stagecoaches ($.50 for first-class passage between Boston and Salem as compared to $1.00 for the stagecoach), quicker trips—just thirty-five minutes to forty minutes between the two cities, including ferry travel across Boston harbor— and more luxurious accommodations. Early passenger cars consisted of the equivalent of three stagecoach compartments placed on four wheels. The Eastern Railroad replicated the innovative design of the Boston and Worcester Railroad by placing a passageway from one end of the car to the other, thus allowing all twenty-four passengers to face in the same direction and to walk the length of the car. The seats were "very commodious, of ample height and dimensions" and covered with haircloth for comfort. Eastern cars also were the first to have "a ladies' room" and a toilet room. Second-class cars were not as nice but were about one-third cheaper than first class. The railroad quickly became more than a novelty. Passenger usage exceeded expectations as businessmen, shoppers, and occasional travelers found the advantages of compressed distances.[5]

The Eastern Railroad not only was an initiator of railroad accommodations but also was a leader, as a matter of company policy, in segregating people of color. On each of their trains, the railroad designated one of its second-class passenger cars as restricted to African Americans and prohibited free people of color from riding in other cars. Slaves were the exception, for they sat near their masters in first class. Initially the common name for the African American cars was "dirt car," apparently describing the condition of the conveyances (as a forward car, they were particularly

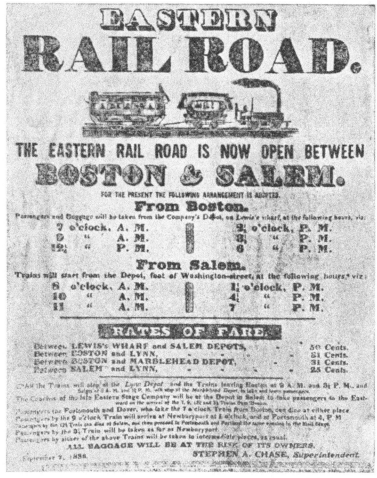

FIGURE 7.1 *First Timetable of the Eastern Railroad*, September 7, 1838, from Bradlee, *The Eastern Railroad*, frontispiece.

vulnerable to soot and smoke) as well as attitudes toward people of color. By 1839—just a year after the Eastern Railroad first began providing service—the popular term had become "Jim Crow car." Jim Crow derived from the white entertainer Thomas D. Rice's blackface performances of "Jumping Jim Crow," beginning in 1832. It was only a short leap to apply the demeaning caricature of black people to segregated railroad cars and soon to other forms of segregation, first in New England and years later in the post–Civil War South. No later than 1842, the Eastern Railroad created one additional segregated car, the "paddy car"—restricted to Irish passengers and twelve and a half cents cheaper than the Jim Crow car for the run between Boston and Salem. Irish travelers without much difficulty could "pass" and ride in a first-class car should they wish, but free people of color could neither travel in first class nor in a paddy car.[6]

Although segregation was company policy, the Eastern Railroad did not publicize that their trains had Jim Crow cars and that they prohibited African Americans from riding in any other car. When in 1839 William Reed and William Ford purchased first-class tickets at the Salem station, they expected "to enjoy the same privileges that other people do." Much to their dismay and embarrassment, as they boarded the train the conductor informed them that they must sit in the Jim Crow car. Their complaints that they held first-class tickets and were entitled to ride in a first-class car were met with "abuse and insult," and they spent the journey to Boston in the "extremely dirty" Jim Crow. The correspondent who brought the incident to the attention of the *Lynn Record* readers entreated people to speak out against such injustice. "It is very easy to declaim against oppression in an Alabama slaveholder," he observed, but it required much more "moral courage . . . to confront the monster face to face." He singled out the railroad's superintendent Stephen A. Chase, a Quaker, as a particular hypocrite. Reformers should petition the legislature to repeal the Eastern Railroad's charter, he suggested, for that governing body never granted the "right to make rules whereby they may trample with impunity upon the rights and privileges of our citizens."[7] It was a shrewd tactic to attack the privileges and arrogance of a corporation, but for the time being it went nowhere.

Nearly a year and a half later in March 1841, the Nantucket representative to the Massachusetts legislature, George Bradburn, resurrected those objections. The issue before the House was the Eastern Railroad's request to extend its wharves farther into Boston Harbor. Bradburn, an abolitionist and former Unitarian minister, in a speech before the legislature stated that he had enthusiastically championed the railroads before, but this time he was going to vote against the bill. In his estimation, the behavior of the Eastern Railroad toward people of color disqualified it from further assistance. The state—representing the labor and capital of all its citizens—had provided critical financial support, and yet the railroad continued to discriminate against one portion of the population "as though they came not within the pale of humanity." Bradburn, moreover, thought it hypocritical that slaveholders could bring their "degraded slaves" into railroad cars, stagecoaches, and steamboat cabins where free people of color were prohibited from sitting. Bradburn's impassioned address didn't prevent the legislature from granting the Eastern Railroad's request, but it helped raise public awareness of the issue.[8]

Whether through frustration, seething outrage, or the awareness of a political tool for change, later in 1841 African Americans developed a new tactic in their struggle for equal rights: the sit-in. They sat in first-class passenger cars and refused to move until they were forcibly sent to the Jim Crow car or ejected from the train. Most likely the first sit-ins were spontaneous acts—much like Rosa Parks more than a century later—but soon they became intentional provocations with the hope of pressuring the offending railroads to eliminate their segregation policies. Shadrach Howard, the thirty-one-year-old grandson of Paul Cuffe and a resident of New Bedford, apparently initiated the practice with a sit-in on a train of the New Bedford and Taunton Railroad Company. After being cast out of a first-class car, he sued the railroad but lost. David Ruggles, among others, took notice.[9]

Ruggles, though born in Norwich, Connecticut, in 1810, had lived during the 1830s in New York City where he became a leading abolitionist and reformer. He established the first African American bookstore, the first black printing press, and the first African American magazine, the *Mirror of Liberty*. The center of a dispute with other New York reformers and the victim of ill health and deteriorating eyesight, he recently had moved to Northampton, Massachusetts. On June 19, 1841, he took the steamboat *Telegraph* from New Bedford to Nantucket, and that is when the trouble and the solution began.[10]

On board when the call came for passengers to pay their fares, Ruggles approached the captain's office and asked the price of the voyage. For $1.50 a passenger must stay in the forward deck, but for $2.00 the person was "entitled to all the privileges of the Boat." Ruggles chose to pay the $2.00 fare, but Captain Lot Phinney told him he must pay the lesser amount and not leave the forward deck. Ruggles insisted on full privileges and argued that "no man or body corporate has a right to decide for another person what he or she shall purchase" and that no one should be required to buy what he doesn't want. The captain, infuriated at his audacity, assaulted him and took his private papers. Ashore in Nantucket without his papers and his hat, Ruggles was unable to conduct the business that had prompted the trip. On his return, Captain Phinney accepted his $2.00 for full privileges, and there were no further unpleasant incidents. When New Bedford's African American community learned of Ruggles' treatment, it called a meeting and passed a resolution condemning the attack and supporting

Ruggles. A fugitive slave who then lived in New Bedford and was quickly gaining prominence, Frederick Douglass, chaired the meeting.[11]

When he boarded a New Bedford and Taunton train on July 6, Ruggles was ready, even eager, for a confrontation. He already had paid the $2.00 for a first-class ticket from New Bedford to Boston, and the ticket agent had taken his money without signifying any restrictions. Ruggles entered a first-class car and sat down. Almost immediately one of the conductors rushed in and ordered Ruggles to take a seat in the Jim Crow car. Ruggles refused "on the ground of his right to hold and enjoy what he had purchased." The conductor took no action himself but reported the problem to the railroad's superintendent. Not wishing to enter a debate with the recalcitrant traveler, the superintendent gathered several railroad employees and together dragged Ruggles from the car, tearing his clothes in the process. Stranded in the station Ruggles demanded that his trunk be removed from the baggage car and returned to him, but the railroad workers ignored his pleas and the trunk made the journey to Boston without him.[12]

Outrage and embarrassment went beyond the African American community this time, and New Bedford held a town meeting on July 12 and 13. The meeting invited Ruggles to recount his experience, and he provided the sorry details. A committee offered a resolution condemning the New Bedford and Taunton Railroad, but a vote was postponed until an investigating committee could report the following day. When the committee substantiated Ruggles' account, the town of New Bedford resolved "That as citizens of a free and enlightened community, and descendants of those revolutionary worthies who poured out their hearts' blood in the cause of our civil liberty, we do remonstrate in the most solemn manner against such inhuman proceedings as took place at the rail-road Depot in this town on the 6th of the present month, in expelling David Ruggles of New-York, from the car, for the unworthy cause of his having a color which the God of nature was pleased to give him."[13] Ruggles knew what he was doing. The railroad for the time being continued to force people of color into the Jim Crow car, but the citizens of New Bedford had become awakened to the injustices waged against African Americans.

Ruggles was not as successful in the Police Court where his attackers were tried on July 19 and 21. No one disputed the facts. The defendants, James A. Crocker, Benjamin West, Charles R. Sisson, and Peter McCollum, had assaulted David Ruggles. But Judge Henry A. Crapo, a stockholder in the New Bedford and Taunton, found them not guilty because "no assault and battery had been committed, on the ground that the plaintiff should have submitted to the rule of the rail-road company."[14] In other words, failure to comply with racist company policy removed the protection of the law.

Having learned of David Ruggles' use of the sit-in, Frederick Douglass began the practice in September 1841. Reminiscing years later, he remarked that because Jim Crow cars perpetuated the system of caste he "made it a rule to seat myself in the cars for the accommodation of passengers generally." On September 8, Douglass and John A. Collins—a white Boston abolitionist and general agent of the Massachusetts Anti-Slavery Society— purchased first-class Eastern Railroad tickets in Newburyport for a trip to Dover, New Hampshire, where they were to attend the annual meeting of the Strafford County Anti-Slavery Society. They boarded a "long car" and sat down together with Collins nearer the aisle. A conductor—most likely a former stagecoach driver, whom the Eastern favored because of their experience with the general public—quickly approached Douglass and ordered him to the "forward car," a euphemism for the Jim Crow. Collins and nearby passengers objected, and no one on the car complained of Douglass' presence. When Collins inquired why Douglass must leave, the conductor pulled down a placard from near the door and showed him a statement of the company policy authorizing conductors to place passengers where they wished. The conductor then asked Collins to leave his seat so that he could more easily "snake" Douglass to the Jim Crow. Collins refused and "coolly remarked, 'if you haul him out, it will be over my person, as I do not intend to leave this seat.'" The conductor sullenly retreated but soon returned with "four or five of the Company's minions." They grabbed Douglass, pulled him over Collins, and dragged him to the Jim Crow car. Douglass' clothes were damaged in the scuffle, and Collins was bruised and scratched. George Foster, a fellow abolitionist and passenger, entered the Jim Crow to bear witness "against this proscription against colored people" but was ejected because he "was not black enough to ride there."[15]

Douglass and Collins repeated their protest later in the month. On September 28, the two men planned to travel on the Eastern Railroad to Newburyport for the annual Essex County Anti-Slavery meeting. Collins left from his home in Boston and met Douglass as well as James N. Buffum and a woman abolitionist at Lynn from where they would continue on to Newburyport. They sat close together—Douglass and Collins again side by side, the woman directly before them and Buffum immediately behind—on "very luxuriant and beautiful" first-class seats. As they must have suspected, the very same conductor—as Collins described him: "a small, spare and feeble looking man"—shakily demanded that Douglass go to the Jim Crow car. Buffum asked if he could accompany him to continue their conversation but was threatened with expulsion from the train should he venture into the segregated car. Douglass merely observed "there are but very few in this car" and questioned why he must leave. Most of the passengers must have been abolitionists, for first one and then another called for a vote on whether Douglass could stay. Douglass repeated his question of why he was being ordered to the Jim Crow. Others echoed the inquiry. Eventually the exasperated conductor blurted out "because you are black." By this point the conductor was ready to use force and he asked the woman in the seat in front of Douglass to leave the area so that she wouldn't be injured. Upon her refusal he pulled her by the arm to the far end of the passenger car and called for eight or ten other railroad employees to remove Douglass. Five or six of them made for Douglass who quite literally declined to give up his seat. They grabbed Douglass, who held onto the seat with all his strength, and yanked him and the attached seat out of the car and onto the station platform. They left Collins who had suffered a blow to the head, a cracked lip from a fist to his face, and a sore back from a kick while he was lying on the aisle. Leaving Douglass at the Lynn station Collins traveled as far as the Salem station where the Quaker superintendent of the Eastern Railroad, Stephen A. Chase, ordered him off the train. To prevent further disruption, Chase soon instructed that no train would stop at the Lynn station until Douglass had departed the town.[16]

These were the types of dramatic events that raised awareness of segregation on New England railroads and sparked demands for its termination. Douglass and Collins—speaking at antislavery meetings, regaling newspaper editors with juicy details, and inspiring African Americans throughout New England to resist caste and prejudice and to demand equal rights—publicized the episodes as frequently as possible. The Middlesex County Anti-Slavery Society, the Worcester County North Division Anti-Slavery Society, and Plymouth County Anti-Slavery Society passed resolutions calling for boycotts of the offending railroads and urging their members and others to sign petitions to the Massachusetts legislature demanding prohibition of segregated cars. The town of Lynn joined New Bedford and the antislavery societies in expressing its outrage. The citizens held three, "overflowing" town meetings where they passed resolutions condemning the Eastern Railroad and calling for its reform. James N. Buffum, a respected citizen of Lynn and one of the abolition-ists who had witnessed the mistreatment of Douglass, was heartened that the events had convinced a substantial proportion of the town—white and black—that they could no longer "look on with silent acquiescence."[17] Abstract principles remained important, but tales of specific injustices captured hearts and shaped opinion.

Two days after Douglass' Lynn confrontation with the Eastern Railroad, the sit-ins resumed. On the morning of September 20, Mary Newhall Green with her five-month-old baby in her arms boarded the first-class car at Lynn. She was an abolitionist and the secretary of the Lynn Female Anti-Slavery Society, but her purpose was to travel on the train, not to pro-test the Eastern's discriminatory policy. Having straight hair and a light complexion, she—almost certainly being perceived as white—had ridden in the long cars previously without incident. This time, when railroad employees still were on edge, was different. No sooner had she sat down but the conductor, a Mr. Shepard, commanded her to leave the car. Her refusal—based both on her distaste for the condition of the Jim Crow car and her resentment of segregation— politicized the event and enraged Shepard. The conductor gathered five railroad workers and ordered them to drag Green off the car. They left her on the platform, with an injured knee and shoulder and a severely cut finger. Her husband, as he waited for the train to depart, heard her cries and rushed to the car but was beaten as well.[18]

That evening a second assault occurred on an Eastern Railroad train at the East Boston station. Once again it began with a clash between a con-ductor, George Harrington, and an unnamed person of color (at the police court trial that ensued all that was divulged about him was that he wasn't Frederick Douglass) seated in a general car surrounded by five white abo-litionists and sympathizers. When Harrington told the black man to leave the train, he didn't answer and didn't move. Those around him strenu-ously objected; and as Harrington and his cohorts attempted to drag the man from the car, they tried to obstruct the action, placing their bodies in the way and holding onto the unfortunate passenger as best they could. But to no avail. Much to their surprise, Harrington, shouting "Drag out every damned one of them!," and his men returned and threw three or four of them off the train. One of them, a Boston dentist, Dr. Mann, filed suit for assault and battery against the conductor Harrington, and the trial took place in October. Mann had determined to make the trip after learning of the mistreatment of Mary Green earlier in the day and on the ferry boat from Boston to the East Boston station had argued with another passenger about the Eastern Railroad's segregation policy. He apparently planned to take the train to Lynn with the hope of protecting any African American who dared sit in first class. The others—including the twenty-seven-year-old abolitionist, Joel Prentiss Bishop, who later became an important legal scholar—were traveling to Lynn to attend one of the town meetings protesting the recent actions of the Eastern Railroad. Whether the incident was planned in advance or spontaneous can't be known, but the judge at the trial concluded that Harrington "was justified by the disorderly and unlawful conduct of Dr. Mann and his friends, in ejecting them from the cars" and dismissed the case.[19] Nonetheless, momentum was building.

On Saturday, October 21, 1841, H. Cummings and J. W. Alden were returning to Boston from Fall River on the New Bedford and Taunton Railroad. At the Taunton train stop, they encountered an acquaintance Dr. Thomas Jennings (or Jinnings) Jr., a dentist, who had been at New Bedford and also was returning home to Boston. As the train left the station, they continued their conversation on the platform at the end of one of the long cars. After a while Cummings and Alden invited Jennings to sit with them inside. There were few other passengers in the car, and the three friends sat at one end apart from the others. The conductor walked through and took their tickets. All was well until the next stop at Norton. Then the conductor burst into the car and ordered Jennings—who was a person of color—to sit in the Jim Crow car. Cummings and Alden instantly told the conductor that Dr. Jennings was "a highly respectable, well educated colored gentleman of Boston" and a friend of theirs. "I don't care who he is, *damn him*," the conductor frothed, "he has abused me enough at New-Bedford, and he *must and shall go out*." After Jennings retorted that he wouldn't leave, a tugging match began. The conductor, soon joined by two brakemen, pulled Jennings toward the door while Cummings and Alden tried to protect Jennings from the onslaught. One of the brakeman jammed Cummings against a window and broke it. The violence escalated further when another train employee—a large, "two fisted fellow"—joined the melee. The match was a draw, until Jennings brought it to a halt by stating he would go. Days later, Cummings recounted the outrageous actions in a public letter to the editor of the *New-England Christian Advocate* and offered a remedy for such abuse: people should vote for legislators who will rescind the railroad's charter unless it curtailed its segregationist policies.[20]

This was the last sit-in that *The Liberator* described in its pages that fall, not because people of color didn't continue to resist Jim Crow on the railroads but because the equal rights movement had entered a new phase. The sit-ins had dramatized the injustice of segregation and energized advocates of equal rights and fair-minded citizens alike. Additional tactics now were needed for changing the railroads themselves. The focus became political and economic pressures on the railroads. In all of 1842, *The Liberator* only reported two incidents of conflict on the passenger cars, both involving the same conductor George W. Bird—one involved the brutal treatment of Shadrach Howard and Howard's drawing a knife for protection; the other began as a sit-in but ended with Richard Johnson and his daughter taking an alternative conveyance.[21] Each portrayed the unchecked and unjust behavior of a chartered corporation, and the Johnson episode highlighted the feasibility of boycotts.

Women may have had limited political rights in the nineteenth century, but they—often organized by female antislavery societies—were in the forefront of petitioners to the United States Congress and to state legislatures calling for social reform during the antebellum period. Year after year they pleaded for an end to slavery, the curtailment of the law prohibiting mixed marriages, and the recognition of the independence of Haiti. In late 1841, inspired by the wave of sit-ins, they petitioned the Massachusetts legislature to stop railroad segregation in their state, and thousands of men added their signatures. In response, the legislature appointed a committee to review the subjects of the petitions. On February 10, 1842, the committee devoted itself to the issue of the railroads, and beginning at 3:00 in the afternoon in the Representatives' Hall before an overflowing crowd, "consisting of the members of the two houses, and ladies and gentlemen generally," they heard the testimony of Wendell Phillips, Charles Lenox Remond, and Ellis Gray Loring.[22]

Phillips and Remond, among the most outstanding abolitionist orators of the day, were particularly well suited for the task. In many ways they were surprisingly similar. Both had been born in 1810 to prominent families, both belonged to the Garrison wing of abolitionists, both had a commanding presence, both found their calling as reformers, and both had attended the 1840 World Anti-Slavery Convention in London where they had supported women's participation. But there were some important differences as well, the most significant being that Phillips' ancestors were European and Remond's were African. Phillips opposed slavery and discriminatory treatment largely on moral grounds (they were sins and

FIGURE 7.2 *Wendell Phillips*, 1853–1860, daguerreotype by Mathew B. Brady. (Library of Congress).

unjust) while Remond—who didn't disagree with Phillips—also viewed slavery and prejudice as personal affronts. Those different perspectives were evident in their testimony.[23]

Phillips argued as if he were before a panel of judges and were offering a legal brief. He informed the committee that he appeared in their presence as a representative of the petitioners, and he quickly reviewed the problem of discriminatory treatment on some of the state's railroads. The petitioners, he reminded members of the committee, wanted legislation or some other means to curtail the practice of Jim Crow on the railroads. "There can be but two objections to such action on the part of the Legislature,"

FIGURE 7.3 *Charles Lenox Remond,* by an unknown photographer. (Collection of the Massachusetts Historical Society).

Phillips observed. "It might be said, first, that they have no right to take it; or, second, that it is not worth while." Here was where Phillips directed the bulk of his remarks. The legislature surely had the authority to take such action, for it had created and funded the corporations. Moreover, corporations were "public servants" and must operate within the laws of the land. In this case, the railroads should provide equal service to all the citizens of the state. The poor should have the same rights as the rich, and the black as the white. From there, he addressed whether the railroad's behavior was worthy of the legislators' attention, and he gave a resounding "yes." This was not a "trifling matter" without impact. "To the colored citizen, sir, it is not so, but one seriously affecting the every day interests of life." Before he sat down, Phillips gave some specific examples of prejudice in their society, and he shifted attention to the growing suspicion in New England that southern slaveholders had undue influence in the nation, some of it creeping into their own region. "The prejudice against color is said to be strong," he thundered. "I believe that it is wrongly named. It is, in its nature, deference to the slaveholder." He implied that Jim Crow cars did not necessarily reflect the will of the railroads but rather that of the South, thus offering cover to wavering legislators.[24]

Remond took a much more personal approach and offered a narrative rather than an intellectual discourse. In his first sentence he acknowledged that he was "the first person of color who has ever addressed either of the bodies assembling in this building" and he hoped that "this intelligent Committee" would give him "an impartial hearing." Prejudice against people of African descent was rampant in the land and had no "counterpart" in any other country. He had recently returned from a stay of nineteen months in Great Britain, and at no time had he been "insulted, or treated in any way distinct or dissimilar from other passengers or travelers, either in coaches, rail-roads, steampackers, or hotels," as was so common on American soil. He hastened to assure the Massachusetts representatives that he recognized "a marked difference between social and civil rights." Everyone should be able to determine their own social relations, but no one should have the power to define another's civil rights. He then resumed his own story. When he had returned from abroad and was boarding a train from Boston to his home in Salem, he immediately was reminded of the injustices of his native land by being relegated to the Jim Crow car. The following day he had business in Boston and again took the train. He met two friends at the station, and they asked if they might join him. Seated with him in the Jim Crow, one of them remarked, "Charles, I don't know if they will allow us to ride with you." Remond related that he had laughed at the absurdity of the situation, but nonetheless the conductor soon demanded that the two white men sit elsewhere. Such grievances must be redressed, he contended. People of color had not chosen to come to America. "If to ask at your hands redress for injuries, and protection in our rights and immunities, as citizens, is reasonable, and dictated alike by justice, humanity and religion," Remond concluded, "you will not reject, I trust, the prayer of your petitioners."[25]

Phillips and Remond made a powerful team, and their presentations—reinforced by the spontaneous applause of those in the audience—must have helped sway the committee. The structure, the substance, and even the wording of the report that the committee sent to the whole legislature were almost a duplicate of Phillips' comments. It declared that the discrimination of persons on railroad cars was a direct violation of the rights section of the state constitution. In a close paraphrase of Phillips' remarks, the committee wrote: "The only questions for consideration seem to be, whether this matter lies within the authority of the Legislature, and whether any interference on its part is called for." Following Phillips' logic, the committee explained why they gave a positive response to each question and then proposed "An Act Relating to the rights of Rail-Road Passengers." The act was even stronger than anything the petitioners had requested. First, railroads were prohibited from making distinctions between passengers based on "descent, sect, or color." Second, the act provided severe penalties for any railroad employee and accomplice who assaulted passengers for the purpose of segregation. Any person so convicted must serve between six days and six months in a county jail, pay a fine of $10.00, and be legally "answerable to the person assaulted." Although the House voted affirmatively, the Senate wasn't as sympathetic and it defeated the act.[26]

Advocates of equal rights had previously suggested the economic pressure of boycotting the offending railroads, and with the defeat of the bill they ratcheted up their efforts. Beginning on April 8, 1842, and continuing for nearly a year, the last page of every issue of *The Liberator* contained a "Travelers' Directory," where each railroad with a Boston terminal was evaluated: Boston and Lowell Railroad, "Humanity respected"; Boston and Worcester Railroad, "No exclusiveness"; Boston and Providence, Taunton and New-Bedford Railroad, "A vile complexional distinction, enforced by brutal assaults"; Boston and Maine Railroad, "Human rights not invaded"; Eastern Railroad, "An odious distinction on account of color, and a bullying propensity to carry it out, even to a Quaker Chase and overthrow of equity"; Western Railroad, "Equality of privileges"; Nashua and Lowell Railroad, "Equally free to all"; and Norwich and Worcester Railroad, "No unwarrantable distinctions." Readers offered their own suggestions, such as taking stagecoaches rather than the Eastern or, if possible where railroads had similar routes, taking the line that didn't practice segregation. A stockholder of the New-Bedford and Taunton Railroad and abolitionist, Nathaniel Barney, condemned the Jim Crow cars as well as all forms of prejudice and called on the railroad and his fellow stockholders to change the practice. Until that was accomplished he would neither sell his stock nor accept dividends so that he would not profit by the exclusion of people of color from equal rights. Such pressures as well as growing public disapproval must have had some affect, for the superintendent of the Eastern Railroad, Stephen A. Chase, reluctantly resigned.[27]

As the Massachusetts legislative session for 1843 approached, petitions once again flooded the chambers. This time the act passed the Senate but became bogged down in the House. Members attempted to waylay the bill in a variety of ways. Some claimed that the proposed legislation was

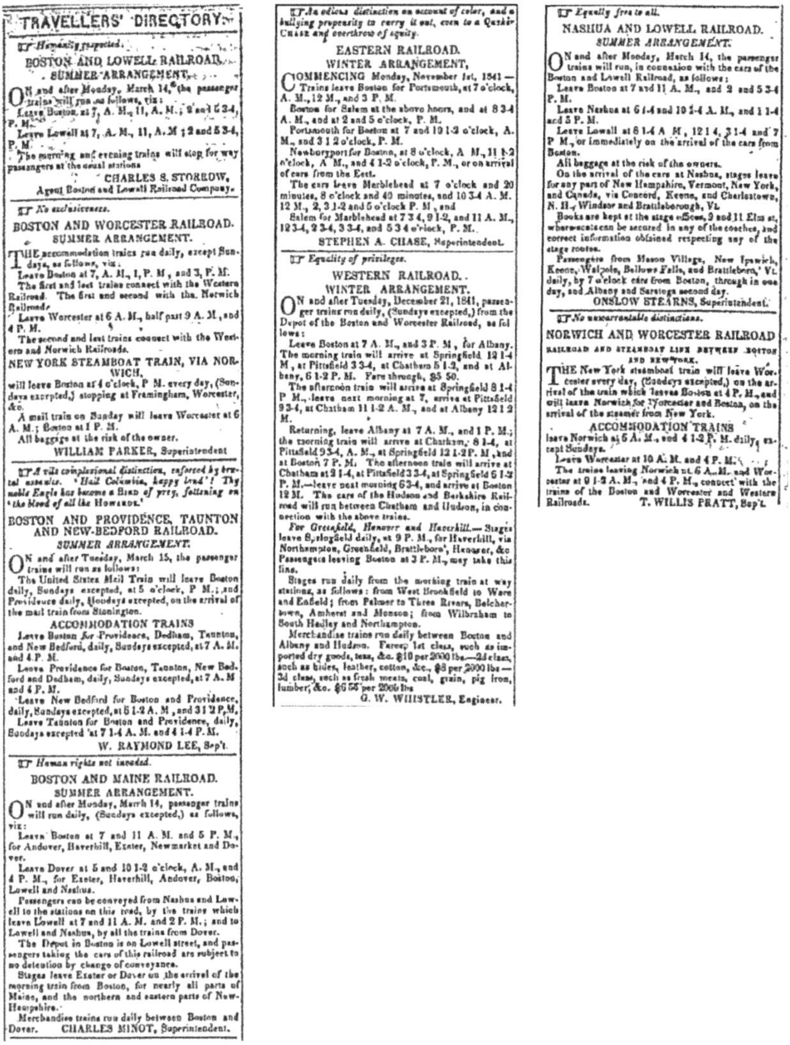

TRAVELLERS' DIRECTORY.

☞ *Humanity respected.*

BOSTON AND LOWELL RAILROAD.

SUMMER ARRANGEMENT.

ON and after Monday, March 14, the passenger trains will run as follows, viz:

Leave Boston at 7, A. M., 11, A. M.; 2 and 5 3-4, P. M.

Leave Lowell at 7, A. M., 11, A. M; 2 and 5 3-4, P. M.

The morning and evening trains will stop for way passengers at the usual stations.

CHARLES S. STORROW,
Agent Boston and Lowell Railroad Company.

☞ *No exclusiveness.*

BOSTON AND WORCESTER RAILROAD.

SUMMER ARRANGEMENT.

THE accommodation trains run daily, except Sundays, as follows, viz:

Leave Boston at 7, A. M., 1, P. M., and 3, P. M.

The first and last trains connect with the Western Railroad. The first and second with the Norwich Railroad.

Leave Worcester at 6 A. M., half past 9 A. M., and 4 P. M.

The second and last trains connect with the Western and Norwich Railroads.

NEW YORK STEAMBOAT TRAIN, VIA NORWICH,

will leave Boston at 4 o'clock, P. M. every day, (Sundays excepted,) stopping at Framingham, Worcester, &c.

A mail train on Sunday will leave Worcester at 6 A. M.; Boston at 1 P. M.

All baggage at the risk of the owner.

WILLIAM PARKER, Superintendent

☞ *A vile complexional distinction, enforced by brutal assaults. 'Hail Columbia, happy land'! Thy noble Eagle has become a* Bird *of prey, fattening on 'the blood of all the* Howards.'

BOSTON AND PROVIDENCE, TAUNTON AND NEW-BEDFORD RAILROAD.

SUMMER ARRANGEMENT.

ON and after Tuesday, March 15, the passenger trains will run as follows:

The United States Mail Train will leave Boston daily, Sundays excepted, at 5 o'clock, P. M.; and Providence daily, Mondays excepted, on the arrival of the mail train from Stonington.

ACCOMMODATION TRAINS

Leave Boston for Providence, Dedham, Taunton, and New Bedford, daily, Sundays excepted, at 7 A. M. and 4 P. M.

Leave Providence for Boston, Taunton, New Bedford and Dedham, daily, Sundays excepted, at 7 A. M and 4 P. M.

Leave New Bedford for Boston and Providence, daily, Sundays excepted, at 5 1-2 A. M., and 3 1-2 P. M.

Leave Taunton for Boston and Providence, daily, Sundays excepted at 7 1-4 A. M. and 4 1-4 P. M.

W. RAYMOND LEE, Sup't.

☞ *Human rights not invaded.*

BOSTON AND MAINE RAILROAD.

SUMMER ARRANGEMENT.

ON and after Monday, March 14, passenger trains will run daily, (Sundays excepted,) as follows, viz:

Leave Boston at 7 and 11 A. M. and 5 P. M., for Andover, Haverhill, Exeter, Newmarket and Dover.

Leave Dover at 5 and 10 1-2 o'clock, A. M., and 4 P. M., for Exeter, Haverhill, Andover, Boston, Lowell and Nashua.

Passengers can be conveyed from Nashua and Lowell to the stations on this road, by the trains which leave Lowell at 7 and 11 A. M. and 2 P. M.; and to Lowell and Nashua, by all the trains from Dover.

The Depot in Boston is on Lowell street, and passengers taking the cars of this railroad are subject to no detention by change of conveyance.

Stages leave Exeter or Dover on the arrival of the morning train from Boston, for nearly all parts of Maine, and the northern and eastern parts of New-Hampshire.

Merchandise trains run daily between Boston and Dover. CHARLES MINOT, Superintendent.

☞ *An odious distinction on account of color, and a bullying propensity to carry it out, even to a Quaker* Chase *and overthrow of equity.*

EASTERN RAILROAD.

WINTER ARRANGEMENT,

COMMENCING Monday, November 1st, 1841 — Trains leave Boston for Portsmouth, at 7 o'clock, A. M., 12 M., and 3 P. M.

Boston for Salem at the above hours, and at 8 3-4 A. M., and at 2 and 5 o'clock, P. M.

Portsmouth for Boston at 7 and 10 1-2 o'clock, A. M., and 3 1 2 o'clock, P. M.

Newburyport for Boston, at 8 o'clock, A. M., 11 1-2 o'clock, A. M., and 4 1-2 o'clock, P. M., or on arrival of cars from the East.

The cars leave Marblehead at 7 o'clock and 20 minutes, 8 o'clock and 40 minutes, and 10 3-4 A. M. 12 M., 2, 3 1-2 and 5 o'clock P. M., and

Salem for Marblehead at 7 3 4, 9 1-2, and 11 A. M., 12 3-4, 2 3-4, 3 3-4, and 5 3 4 o'clock, P. M.

STEPHEN A. CHASE, Superintendent.

☞ *Equality of privileges.*

WESTERN RAILROAD.

WINTER ARRANGEMENT.

ON and after Tuesday, December 21, 1841, passenger trains run daily, (Sundays excepted,) from the Depot of the Boston and Worcester Railroad, as follows:

Leave Boston at 7 A. M., and 3 P. M., for Albany. The morning train will arrive at Springfield 12 1-4 M., at Pittsfield 3 3-4, at Chatham 5 1-2, and at Albany, 6 1-2 P. M. Fare through, $5 50.

The afternoon train will arrive at Springfield 8 1-4 P. M., leave next morning at 7, arrive at Pittsfield 9 3-4, at Chatham 11 1-2 A. M., and at Albany 12 1 2 M.

Returning, leave Albany at 7 A. M., and 1 P. M.; the morning train will arrive at Chatham, 8 1-4, at Pittsfield 9 3-4, A. M., at Springfield 12 1-2 P. M., and at Boston 7 P. M. The afternoon train will arrive at Chatham at 2 1-4, at Pittsfield 3 3-4, at Springfield 6 1-2 P. M.—leave next morning 6 3-4, and arrive at Boston 12 M. The cars of the Hudson and Berkshire Railroad will run between Chatham and Hudson, in connection with the above trains.

For Greenfield, Hanover and Haverhill.— Stages leave Springfield daily, at 9 P. M., for Haverhill, via Northampton, Greenfield, Brattleboro', Hanover, &c. Passengers leaving Boston at 3 P. M., may take this line.

Stages run daily from the morning train at way stations, as follows: from West Brookfield to Ware and Enfield; from Palmer to Three Rivers, Belchertown, Amherst and Monson; from Wilbraham to South Hadley and Northampton.

Merchandise trains run daily between Boston and Albany and Hudson. Fares, 1st class, such as imported dry goods, teas, &c. $10 per 2000 lbs.—2d class, such as hides, leather, cotton, &c., $8 per 2000 lbs.—3d class, such as fresh meats, coal, grain, pig iron, lumber, &c. $6 55 per 2000 lbs

G. W. WHISTLER, Engineer.

☞ *Equally free to all.*

NASHUA AND LOWELL RAILROAD.

SUMMER ARRANGEMENT.

ON and after Monday, March 14, the passenger trains will run, in connexion with the cars of the Boston and Lowell Railroad, as follows:

Leave Boston at 7 and 11 A. M., and 2 and 5 3-4 P. M.

Leave Nashua at 6 1-4 and 10 1-4 A. M., and 1 1-4 and 5 P. M.

Leave Lowell at 8 1-4 A. M., 12 1 4, 3 1-4 and 7 P. M., or immediately on the arrival of the cars from Boston.

All baggage at the risk of the owners.

On the arrival of the cars at Nashua, stages leave for any part of New Hampshire, Vermont, New York, and Canada, via Concord, Keene, and Charlestown, N. H., Windsor and Brattleborough, Vt.

Books are kept at the stage offices, 9 and 11 Elm st, where seats can be secured in any of the coaches, and correct information obtained respecting any of the stage routes.

Passengers from Mason Village, New Ipswich, Keene, Walpole, Bellows Falls, and Brattleboro,' Vt. daily, by 7 o'clock cars from Boston, through in one day, and Albany and Saratoga second day.

ONSLOW STEARNS, Superintendent.

☞ *No unwarrantable distinctions.*

NORWICH AND WORCESTER RAILROAD

RAILROAD AND STEAMBOAT LINE BETWEEN BOSTON AND NEW-YORK.

THE New York steamboat train will leave Worcester every day, (Sundays excepted,) on the arrival of the train which leaves Boston at 4 P. M., and will leave Norwich for Worcester and Boston, on the arrival of the steamer from New York.

ACCOMMODATION TRAINS

leave Norwich at 6 A. M., and 4 1-2 P. M. daily, except Sundays.

Leave Worcester at 10 A. M. and 4 P. M.

The trains leaving Norwich at 6 A. M. and Worcester at 9 1-2 A. M., and 4 P. M., connect with the trains of the Boston and Worcester and Western Railroads. T. WILLIS PRATT, Sup't.

FIGURE 7.4 *Section of the Travellers' Guide in The Liberator*, April 4, 1842.

too narrowly constructed, others argued that there was no need for it, and John C. Park of Boston advanced an amendment to remove the word "railroad" from the bill so that the act would apply to all corporations. Park's amendment was a ruse to kill the bill, and it worked when Massachusetts members of the House tabled the amended act indefinitely. On the House floor before the vote was taken, representative Charles Francis Adams, son and grandson of American presidents, presciently warned the railroads that they would be wise to terminate their Jim Crow policies voluntarily before public opinion compelled them to do so.[28]

The Eastern Railroad and the New Bedford and Taunton Railroad listened, and by the end of the year both had discontinued the practice. Sit-ins, petitions, boycotts, appeals to regional distinctiveness, and economic and political pressure had won the day. The general population may not have abandoned its racism, but it no longer was willing to countenance all forms of segregation and prejudice either.

8

Forward Steps

THERE WERE OTHER victories in the first half of the 1840s—more than for any other five-year span during the antebellum period. More New Englanders became aware of the injustices heaped on people of African descent and were appalled to find the variance from the ideals they thought characterized their society. Reform in all its various coats became somewhat more respectable; even abolitionism seemed less threatening than it had during the previous decade. There were larger targets in the changing and often incomprehensible world in which they lived—particularly the Irish and the increasingly arrogant and belligerent South—at which New Englanders could hurl their anger. Most of all, African Americans were learning how to work the system, and they were taking the lead in fighting for equal rights. Prejudice was frustratingly persistent, but hope grew as some progress was made.

Political inequality had been integral to Rhode Island since its first charter in the seventeenth century. A man had to possess property of a certain value to be eligible to vote and hold office. Even with the democratic waves rolling from the Revolution, Rhode Island held firm, and in 1822 the state became even more restrictive when it disenfranchised people of color. At the time, not many African Americans had the wealth to vote, but this constraint eliminated the possibility for all black Rhode Islanders. By the 1830s, a growing number of whites and blacks—many of them working-class residents of Rhode Island's most urban and industrialized city, Providence—resented the unchecked power of the state's propertied and traditional elite. The black community became further aggravated when, late in the decade, the city of Providence imposed a property tax on its black residents—just as it always had on whites—but continued to deny them a voice in local governance. There were very few African Americans who owned real estate, but the idea that any person of color would have to pay taxes and not be eligible to vote violated basic American principles and highlighted the caste system. Providence blacks in response appointed a committee to make their case before the state legislature. The argument that there should be no taxation without representation was powerful, and some members of the House supported the proposition that African Americans should both be taxed and represented, but most members, particularly the delegation from Newport were adamantly opposed to expanding the franchise to the state's black citizens. One legislator made no attempt to hide his racist contempt for people of African descent: "Shall a Nigger be allowed to go to the polls and tie my vote? No, Mr. Speaker, it can't be. The taxes don't amount to more than forty or fifty dollars; let them be taken off." Rather than enlarging male suffrage, the Rhode Island legislature rescinded the tax.[1]

Disenfranchised white Rhode Islanders at this same period began to organize on their own behalf. In 1840 they rallied together and formed the Rhode Island Suffrage Association that in its constitution called for all native-born white men to have the vote. Quite consciously the document excluded people of color and the seemingly more threatening and certainly more numerous foreign-born immigrants. Still, the Suffrage Association offered a faint glimmer of hope for the ostracized black population. Thomas Dorr, one of the movement's leaders, had abolitionist and equal rights leanings. A son of a prominent and wealthy Providence family, a graduate of Harvard College, a lawyer, and a former state legislator, he was an unlikely partner in a working-man's cause, but somehow he had become a democratic reformer. Other members of the Suffrage Association may have been sympathetic to universal male suffrage in Rhode Island or they may cynically have given the impression of inclusion, but in either case they allowed blacks to participate in association meetings and elections, even voting, until October, 1841, when an extralegal convention drafted a constitution to replace the state's antiquated charter.[2]

Indications of trouble for the prospects of potential black voters had surfaced during the previous month at a Suffrage Association meeting. A majority of the executive committee nominated Alfred Niger, a barber and one of the leaders of Providence's African American community, to be treasurer, and a minority of the executive committee put forward Thomas Green who was of European descent. Thus far, in order to maximize its support among Rhode Islanders, the association had carefully walked the tightrope between equal rights and racism. The chairman of the association tried to finesse the situation by withdrawing Niger's nomination, but others prevailed. The vote took place, and Green won.[3] The message had been sent to voters statewide that the association championed would-be white voters and had little intention to promote rights for all. The stage had been set for their October convention.

The Suffrage Association had been their most likely ally, and black Rhode Islanders didn't want to abandon it if concessions could be won. Led by Alexander Crummell, the former Noyes Academy student and currently a Providence minister, a delegation of African Americans presented a petition calling for the removal of "white" from the suffrage clause of the proposed state constitution. In the debate following the reading of the petition, Thomas Dorr eloquently spoke of the need to remain true to their democratic principles, but others countered with visions of the political damage that might occur should the association be perceived as siding with people of color. The convention defeated the request by a vote of forty-six to eighteen, and the "People's Constitution" remained whites only. The possibility of a future referendum on black suffrage was dangled, but it would only transpire after the voters had approved the constitution. African Americans weren't fooled by such a bait and switch tactic, and they broke off from the Suffrage Association.[4]

Unfortunately, the alternative was no better. State authorities had their own convention and their own proposed constitution, and, as before, they excluded blacks. Their convention's constitution capitulated to political reality by abandoning traditional voting restrictions and providing that all native-born, white men could vote without any property requirements. Foreign-born white men could vote, if they owned real property worth at least $134. African Americans could not vote under any circumstances. At the twin referenda on the competing state constitutions, voters overwhelmingly supported the "People's Constitution" and in a separate vote narrowly defeated the "Legal Constitution." Rhode Island faced a dangerous dilemma. Was an extralegal constitution now the law of the land? Did the standing government whose constitution had been defeated still have legitimacy? The situation became more complicated when the Suffrage Party declared their constitution legal and called for elections to be held in April 1842. More than 6,000 Rhode Island citizens voted and elected Thomas Dorr governor. Rhode Island then had two constitutions and two governors.[5]

Fearing a military assault from Thomas Dorr and his party, Rhode Island officials looked to the black community in Providence for assistance. Although there is no tangible evidence of an agreement, there can be little doubt that a deal was made. African Americans had not accepted the promise of a referendum on expanding the franchise from the Suffrage Association, and it is unlikely that they would have supported the existing government without some near ironclad guarantees. Two hundred black residents of Providence, thereafter, planned to form a militia company; but one of their number, a barber named Patterson, cautioned them to be skeptical of government assurances, and they joined existing companies instead. When Dorr and his followers marched on a state arsenal, black soldiers helped patrol the streets of Providence and protected against fire. The Dorr Rebellion quickly flamed out (Dorr was captured and served time in jail before resuming his role as a democratic reformer), and state authorities retained their sovereignty. And they kept their word. In September 1842, the establishment's Law and Order Party held a convention and passed a clause providing the franchise to all native-born men, black and white, as well as to foreign-born men with sufficient real estate, and that shortly became state law.[6]

George Latimer had been in Boston for less than a week when he landed in jail. He was a young man in his early twenties with "a very intelligent and expressive countenance." Newspaper accounts consistently described him as light skinned. "He was whiter, and had straighter and lighter hair," one report went, "than many . . . who are classed as white men!" Few people passing him on a street would have recognized his African heritage. That, in part, made his case all the more dramatic to white Bostonians, for Latimer was a fugitive slave. He had escaped in early October 1842 from James B. Gray, the owner of a mercantile store in Norfolk, Virginia, where Latimer and two or three other slaves had worked. Arriving in Boston in mid-October, he was captured on October 19. Gray, tipped-off of Latimer's presence in Boston, had arrived the day before.[7]

Gray accused Latimer of stealing and convinced one of the Leverett Street jailers, a man named Stratton, to lock him up. The initial charge was that the theft had taken place in Boston, but the site of the crime soon was changed to Norfolk. Gray's attorney later claimed that it was an unintentional mistake. It is more likely that Gray had told Stratton that the theft occurred in Boston so that Latimer would be jailed without question. The Virginia merchant's goal, after all, was to retain Latimer long enough to have a court issue a certificate of removal for a fugitive slave. Being a

FIGURE 8.1 *George Latimer, 1840–1853.* (Collection of the Massachusetts Historical Society).

fugitive slave was not a crime in itself, and Gray had to offer some explanation for Latimer's incarceration. Norfolk was out of the jurisdiction of Boston officials, and it would have required a request from the governor of Virginia to justify holding Latimer for extradition. To sweeten the deal, Gray assured Stratton that he would pay for Latimer's board while he was in jail, and perhaps he promised more.[8]

Later in the afternoon Gray approached Elbridge Gerry Austin, the Boston city attorney, to retain him for the case. He informed Austin that he wanted his slave George Latimer to be returned to his possession and that Latimer already was locked up in the Court House on the charge of theft. Austin agreed to represent Gray and that evening filed a complaint against Latimer and gave a written authorization to Stratton to hold

Latimer as a fugitive slave. By then a large crowd, primarily composed of black men, formed outside the Court House. Austin, fearing that there might be an attempt to free the captured man, went before the angry protesters and promised that there would be no attempt to take Latimer away that night and that the law would be followed. At 8:00 P. M. Chief Justice of the Massachusetts Supreme Court Lemuel Shaw issued a writ of habeas corpus commanding Stratton to bring Latimer before him at 6:00 P. M. the following day. The jailer then took the prisoner to the Leverett Street jail without incident.[9]

After the United States Supreme Court decision in *Prigg v. Pennsylvania* (early 1842) in which the court struck down state laws prohibiting the return of fugitive slaves, Boston people of color established a Freedom Association and Vigilance Committee to collect funds for the assistance of fugitive slaves. Almost certainly representatives of the committee retained Samuel E. Sewall and Amos B. Merrill to defend Latimer. During the day of October 20, Latimer told his lawyers that Gray had held him as a slave illegally. He asserted that a previous owner had provided for his freedom in her will, but after her death her daughter had destroyed the document before it had been proved.[10] There, of course, was no way to substantiate his claim.

That evening the prisoner appeared before the full state Supreme Court in a courtroom packed with reporters and other interested parties. A large number of African Americans accompanied by a scattering of whites filled the area outside the Court House. Jailor Stratton brought the defendant into the courtroom and stated that he held Latimer as a fugitive of justice from the state of Virginia where he had committed a crime and as James B. Gray's fugitive slave. He added that he was Gray's agent for retaining Latimer. Merrill rose and objected to the fugitive of justice charge. He contended that the warrant was invalid because the governor of Virginia had not asked for extradition, as required by congressional legislation. The court took no action at the time. Austin then called two witnesses from Virginia who were "casually in the city as visitors," and they testified that Latimer was Gray's slave. The court decided that Latimer was legally in the custody of Stratton as Gray's agent, and the case would continue the following morning before a justice of the Police Court. As Stratton escorted the defendant back to jail, a commotion broke out resulting in the arrest of several participants.[11]

The Police Court met the following morning for the sole purpose of trying Latimer on the charge of theft. All counsels agreed, however, to postpone the hearing for ten days so that it first could be determined whether the defendant was a fugitive slave. When the judge ordered bail of $200, Austin had second thoughts. Latimer already was being held as an alleged fugitive slave, and bail for the charge of theft might muddy who had custody. Rather than risk having Latimer placed in the custody of his attorneys or any other supporter (thus opening the possibility of his disappearing), Austin moved that the charge of theft be dismissed; and Sewall and Merrill happily agreed. The only remaining business before the Police Court judge was a slander suit that Latimer had filed against Gray. The Norfolk merchant was arrested for claiming that Latimer had stolen from him and placed in his lawyer's custody. It had merely been a nuisance suit, and no one raised it again.[12]

Latimer appeared before United States Supreme Court Justice Joseph Story—serving in the capacity as a Circuit Court justice—on October 22. Austin applied for a certificate to return the defendant to Virginia as a slave and requested a delay to acquire evidence. Sewall countered that evidence already should have been prepared so as to justify retaining the prisoner. Judge Story decided that delays for the gathering of evidence were normal in such proceedings and set November 5 for the hearing. Latimer's defense team on October 24 made one additional effort to free him from jail by issuing a writ of personal replevin to the jailor Coolidge, who had replaced Stratton. The writ required Coolidge to release Latimer until January 1843, when a jury would decide the defendant's fate. Coolidge refused to accept it, and in a hurried hearing in the jailor's house, Chief Justice Shaw declared that despite his own sympathy for Latimer's plight, United States law superseded the Massachusetts law of personal replevin, making it void. The defendant had to remain incarcerated.[13]

During the legal interlude of the next week and a half, Latimer's supporters turned their attention to the battleground of public opinion. Boston people of color met as a great body on several occasions and in small committees nearly constantly. They expressed their outrage that Boston officials had participated in arresting and imprisoning George Latimer and had assisted a slaveholder in reclaiming a fugitive slave. More practically, they made plans to secure John Quincy Adams as the lead attorney in Latimer's defense for the November 5 hearing (Adams declined, stating he had neither the time nor the preparation, but volunteered to serve as a consultant if needed) and to raise funds for legal expenses. They also appointed a committee to circulate a request to the city's clergy to discuss slavery and Latimer's situation at Sunday services on October 30. A note from Latimer—at least he made his mark below the written words—accompanied the appeal asking for all Boston congregations' prayers. Agents for *The Liberator* kept tabs and reported, church by church, that twenty-nine read the note at least at one service and that twenty had declined, some vehemently. That very night a raucous meeting was held at jam-packed Faneuil Hall. Cheers and hisses greeted each speaker. Samuel E. Sewall chaired the meeting and he indignantly reviewed the course of events. Edmund Quincy and Wendell Phillips were able to complete their speeches—despite interruptions—excoriating slavery and a government that would support slavery and demand the return of fugitive slaves. They advocated a set of resolutions that called for prohibiting any government official in Massachusetts from participating in the rendition of fugitive slaves, repealing the clause in the United States Constitution requiring the surrender of fugitive slaves to their masters, and committing civil disobedience by ignoring the clause altogether. Charles Lenox Remond was not so fortunate. A segment of the audience tried to shout him down, and after seven minutes of ear-deafening clamor they succeeded. Somehow amid all the noise and confusion, the body of Boston citizens passed the resolutions by a voice vote.[14]

November 5 turned out to be a disappointment for Gray. The slave-owner had received the documents establishing his ownership of Latimer, and he hoped to conclude the legal process quickly and return to Norfolk with his slave. Judge Story was ill, however, and the hearing was postponed to November 7, when the district judge of the United States would preside in Story's place. At that hearing, Latimer's counsels, well aware of growing public disapproval of their client's predicament, asked for a delay so they could acquire evidence that Latimer had been freed by a previous owner. The judge granted their request and set November 21 as the new hearing date.[15]

The hearing never took place because on November 18, George Latimer became a free man. In the intervening week and a half, public sentiment—throughout Massachusetts and even New England—had grown increasingly hostile to Latimer's imprisonment and the state's complicity in assisting a slaveholder to capture and return a fugitive slave. *The Liberator* published articles about the Latimer case in every issue, three abolitionists created a newspaper—the *Latimer Journal and North Star*—dedicated exclusively to George Latimer and fugitive slaves in general, and abolitionists and other concerned citizens throughout the state held meetings to protest. All the while African Americans in

Boston made clear that they would resist any attempt to return Latimer to Norfolk, Virginia.[16]

Political pressures mounted on local officials. Suffolk County sheriff Joseph Eveleth, who had authority over the county's jails, felt the greatest heat, and on November 17 he composed a note for Latimer's jailer to release the prisoner the following day by noon. Coolidge informed Austin that he anticipated such instructions the next day, but no order reached the jailer the following morning. From Austin's perspective, Latimer's lawyers had produced a more serious threat when they requested a writ of habeas corpus to bring Latimer to the trial of the rioters who had been arrested on October 20. Sheriff Eveleth made clear to Austin that once Latimer left the jail—no matter what the reason—he, and any other future fugitive slave, would no longer be confined in a public cell. With few options remaining, Austin began negotiations. He conveyed to Latimer's attorneys that they could purchase their client's freedom for $800. Sewall and associates replied that such a sum could be raised. Before deliberations went any further, Coolidge informed Austin that "certain persons would pay the sum of $650." Austin, acting for Gray, readily accepted, and the transaction was set up for 7:00 P. M. No sooner had Gray's attorney with papers in hand arrived at the jail than "certain persons" told him that there was no deal. Those persons feared that it would send the wrong message to slaveholders, some at that very moment lurking in Boston, and besides they had learned of the sheriff's order about to be delivered to Coolidge. Giving the jailer the ownership papers and instructing him to get the best price possible, Austin then left in disgust. Within three hours, Coolidge concluded negotiations, and at 10:00 P. M. Nathaniel Colver delivered $400 to the jailer. On the condition that he would not sue for false imprisonment, George Latimer was free.[17]

Wasting no time to build on public interest in Latimer's case, abolitionists from throughout Massachusetts met on November 19 as the "Grand Convention of Massachusetts Freemen." Their main accomplishment was initiating "The Latimer and Great Massachusetts Petition," which called for the legislature to pass a series of laws: to prohibit all officeholders in Massachusetts, from the governor to local constables, from assisting in the capture, retention, and return of fugitive slaves; to forbid the use of jails and other public buildings from holding fugitive slaves; and to amend the United States Constitution so as to remove "the people of Massachusetts from all connection with slavery." The three editors of the *Latimer Journal*—Henry I. Bowditch, William F. Channing, and Frederick

S. Cabot—formed the Latimer Committee who oversaw the collecting of signatures. By February 1843 when the legislature received the document, 64,526 Massachusetts men and women had signed. At least 15 percent of the state's approximately 410,000 adults had taken a public stand. The petition itself was a symbol of resistance. It measured two feet wide, two feet in diameter, and half a mile long, and it weighed about 150 pounds.[18] This was a tremendous feat. Seldom has a citizenry spoken so clearly to its legislature.

The Boston African American community applauded the outcome of the Latimore episode, and it provided important support for the Latimer and Great Massachusetts Petition. On November 30, black Bostonians met to assess events of the previous two months and to plan ways to prevent a recurrence. They reasserted the values of the Massachusetts Bill of Rights, condemned the behavior of state and local officials, and praised the actions of their white allies, particularly Latimer's legal team. With perhaps a prescient unease they scheduled a second meeting for December 7. By then they had learned that James B. Gray had not given up his intent to re-enslave George Latimer. Upon his return to Norfolk, Gray swore an affidavit claiming that Latimer had stolen from his store and began the process to extradite Latimer to be tried in Norfolk. His charge of theft, as before, was simply a pretext for placing his former slave back in bondage. Public officials in Virginia cooperated, and on December 7, Lieutenant Governor John M. Gregory, in the governor's absence, sent a demand of extradition to Governor John Davis of Massachusetts. A large and vociferous crowd attended the second meeting of Boston's people of color. Those in attendance understood that "an impartial trial in a slave State is seldom, if ever, given to a colored man." And they were not going to allow Latimer to be placed in such jeopardy. They called on "all the citizens of Massachusetts to use all the means their consciences will allow, to prevent the delivery of our guiltless and persecuted brother to the power of slavery." They had served notice on Massachusetts officials that they would use any means available, including violence, to protect George Latimer. Governor Davis heard them, recognized public sentiment, and, perhaps acting from his own principles, wrote Virginia's lieutenant governor that there wasn't sufficient evidence and denied the request.[19] This time Latimer was truly free.

The Massachusetts legislature was listening as well, and prompted by the huge outpouring of signatures on the Latimer and Great Massachusetts petition, it appointed a joint committee of the Senate and the House to report back with recommendations. The committee, chaired by

Charles Francis Adams, clearly was sympathetic to the petitioners but was faced by the recent United State Supreme Court ruling in *Prigg v. Pennsylvania* that essentially gave a slaveholder the right to reclaim a runaway slave without due process. It recognized the constitutional basis for such a decision, but it asserted that there were other constitutional principles in conflict. Under the recent ruling, a free person of color might travel to a place where no one knew him, be seized and enslaved by an unscrupulous kidnapper, and have no recourse. "The burden of proof is completely transferred from the party claiming the man as property to the party struggling to be free," the committee wrote. "Thus the most fully established principle in the government of the United and the several States, that the man is presumed to be free until he is proved to be otherwise, is completely overturned." The country had reached this point, according to Adams and his colleagues, because the slave states had too much power. The committee then recommended an amendment to the United States Constitution and "An Act Further to protect Personal Liberty," thus meeting the demands of the petitioners and its own sense of justice. The proposed amendment would eliminate the three-fifths clause. In the future, representation and taxation would reflect the population only of free persons; slaves would not be counted. The personal liberty act prohibited all state and local judges from issuing certificates to return fugitive slaves and forbade all law enforcement officers from arresting, imprisoning in any state or local facility, or assisting the capture and rendition of fugitive slaves. Any local official who violated the act would be fined up to $1,000 for each offense or be imprisoned as long as a year in county jail. The Massachusetts legislature approved the committee's report, and the governor signed the law. Although the proposed amendment, as everyone knew in advance, would be unsuccessful, the personal liberty law protected fugitive slaves and free people of color until 1850 when the United States Congress passed the notorious Fugitive Slave Act. By the end of 1843, every New England state, except Maine where its Senate rejected a house-passed bill, had enacted personal liberty laws. And *The Liberator* proudly proclaimed: "George Latimer is still in Massachusetts, walking abroad in the majesty of freedom and manhood, and doing good service in the anti-slavery cause."[20]

The principles of a democratic society and racist beliefs clashed most openly over the issue of educating black New Englanders. By the 1830s, the larger cities of the region—Portland, Maine; Portsmouth, New Hampshire; Salem, Lowell, Worcester, Boston, New Bedford, and Nantucket, Massachusetts; Providence and Newport, Rhode Island; Hartford and New

Haven, Connecticut—had segregated, public schools. For the most part, these cities created segregated schools as a solution to promoting equal opportunities and maintaining caste simultaneously. In a few cases, such as Boston, an African American community had initiated segregation with the hope that schools under their own control would be better than the mistreatment of their children in integrated schools. Before long it was clear that despite rhetoric to the contrary, separate was not equal. Schools for people of color typically offered only primary education while white children could attend publicly funded high schools. African American schools generally were open for fewer hours per day and fewer days per year than schools available to whites. They were underfunded, inadequately maintained, often poorly staffed, and controlled by white school committees. African Americans in New Bedford refused to accept such conditions and successfully led the way to integrated schools in 1838. Elsewhere it took longer, but by the mid-1840s, all of New England north of Rhode Island and Connecticut, with the single exception of Boston, had integrated their schools.[21]

The process was arduous, and progress often came in spurts followed by setbacks until there was a final resolution, as was the case in Nantucket. Public schools initially came to the island in 1825 with the creation of four elementary schools for white children and one for children of color. As of 1830, African Americans numbered only 277 out of a total population of 7,202 and there were fewer than 100 school-age black children, so the ratio of the segregated schools seems heavily weighted toward children of African descent. The reason for the seeming discrepancy is that Nantucket children of European descent overwhelmingly went to private schools. Public schools were for the poor. In 1837 that changed. Cyrus Peirce, a graduate of Harvard College and an ordained Congregational minister who had found his calling in education, became principal of Nantucket's newly created high school. During the previous six years, he and his wife Harriet had led a private academy on the island. He was an innovator who eliminated corporal punishment and, even while he directed the academy, developed a plan for educating all of Nantucket's children through a four-tiered system. Peirce's popularity and the establishment of a public high school devastated Nantucket's private schools, leaving only one by the end of the year. His success caught the attention of educational reformer Horace Mann and the Massachusetts Board of Education, and in 1839 he left the island to become the initial principal of the Massachusetts State Normal School, the first teacher-training institution in North America.[22]

Among the students inspired during this period of reform and improvement was seventeen-year-old Eunice Ross. She was one of eighteen Nantucket students who passed the high school entrance examination in 1840, but because of her African heritage she was the only one denied admission. The merchant Edward Gardner soon offered a motion in town meeting to instruct the school board to admit children of color to all of Nantucket's schools, but it failed.[23]

For the next two years the segregated schools remained intact and unchallenged. Abolitionist and chair of the school committee Nathaniel Barney, a champion of ending segregation wherever it existed, found an opportunity in early 1842 to raise the issue in a town meeting when a fellow townsman offered an innocuous resolution that "no party consideration" should influence decisions affecting the island's schools. Barney rose in full agreement and cleverly proposed an amendment that "if, in either of our schools, there is any inequality or discrimination, every consideration of duty and justice requires of us to lay aside our party feelings and prejudices, and place the scholars in that school, and in the other public schools, with reference to their eligibility to said schools." Much to his delight the amendment and the resolution passed. Nantucket's schools

FIGURE 8.2 *African Society Baptist Church*, constructed in Nantucket by 1828 and used as a schoolhouse for African American children. (Historic American Buildings Survey, Library of Congress).

would be integrated. But quickly the intoxication of a victory for social justice evaporated. The following day the town meeting reconsidered its hasty decision and reversed itself.[24] Eunice Ross still was barred from Nantucket's high school.

Black Nantucketers had been silent, but the results of the town meeting so angered them that finally their years of resentment and anger burst out. At a meeting of the "colored inhabitants of Nantucket" held soon thereafter, they first passed two resolutions: one thanked those who had taken up their cause at the town meeting; the other claimed their right to have "their youth educated in the same schools which are common to the more favored members of this community." They then agreed to have an address to the school committee and to all of Nantucket be published in the island's two newspapers. Years of discontent poured out. The address made clear that their oppression was not simply a recent event but rather a long-standing wound. They were citizens of the Commonwealth entitled to all the rights and privileges, as were all other citizens. There were no laws excluding them from equal access to education because of their "complexion or symmetry." As a matter of justice and the state's constitution, their children had as much right to attend all of Nantucket's four layers of schools as did any other children. "We here submit these remarks to the inhabitants of the town of Nantucket," the article concluded, "hoping that the day is not far distant, when the good sense and christianity of this republic will proceed to make its distinctions in society on just and reasonable grounds, and not according to the color of the skin." So energized was the African American community that six members ran for the school committee in April. None won, as local segregationists triumphed once again, but they had sent a message that the rights of citizenship must be theirs—the sooner the better.[25]

While African Americans increasingly spoke with one passionate voice, white residents of Nantucket were deeply divided. In the early months of 1843, Nathaniel Barney repeatedly attempted to convince town meetings to integrate the schools. He and others used a variety of arguments, ranging from the expense of separate schools for children of African descent to the logical absurdity of creating a school "for all Children having Red Hair." Nothing convinced a majority in attendance, and all motions failed. The reformers had hoped to build a consensus supporting equal access to education, but they now controlled the school committee and could instigate the changes on their own. Fearing such an outcome, Nantucket segregationists called several town meetings, resulting in an instruction for the school committee "to resign, if they could not carry out the wishes of the town." The committee contended that its members were state officers obliged to carry out state law, which always had greater authority than town orders. It then prepared the way to open all schools to the island's children beginning in September. Attendance would be based on proximity of residence rather than descent. The African School—its name a billboard for caste and injustice—became the York Street School.[26]

Nothing came easily to Nantucket. The waters that pounded its shores could be both life sustaining and destructive. This year's bounty could be followed by next year's disaster. And so it was with equal access to education. In early 1844, a majority of Nantucket voters elected new town officials and a new school committee that opposed the integration of their schools. At a town meeting, 213 out of approximately 1,500 eligible citizens voted to restore segregation; 148 opposed the measure. As of April 21, children of color could only attend the York Street School. A meeting of Nantucket integrationists had issued a protest, citing state law and the Massachusetts constitution, financial considerations, and even Christian virtues, but was unsuccessful. Most African American parents joined by a few white parents boycotted the return of segregation and kept their children home. It was a peculiar tactic, more effective as an expression of frustration than as a means of promoting justice. To boycott a railroad could have economic repercussions that would contribute to eliminating Jim Crow, but a boycott of schools mainly deprived their children of education, no matter how inferior. It did shine a light on how grim the parents believed the conditions to be, but it required a citizenry that could be shamed or enlightened to be effective. One unexpected consequence was the integration of the York Street School when the school committee sent white children there to study with the small number of African American children whose parents didn't support the boycott.[27] But that was a temporary and one-way measure to justify keeping the school open. Children of color remained barred from all the other schools.

With little prospect of a change of sentiment among the voting citizens of the island, the African American community and white reformers in 1845 sent a series of petitions to the Massachusetts legislature requesting the rights to which state law seemingly entitled them. The segregationists of the island countered with their own petitions extolling separate but equal. State law already supported equal access to educational opportunities and prohibited districting on any basis other than geographical. The problem was that there were no penalties for a town violating those laws.

After heated debate, the Massachusetts legislature passed a compromise that apparently had teeth. The law stated: "Any child unlawfully excluded from common public school instruction in this Commonwealth, shall recover damages therefor, in an action on the case, to be brought in the name of said child, by his guardian or next friend, in any court proper to try the same, against the city or town in which such child has a domicil."[28] An optimistic interpretation might conclude that segregation in any form was unlawful and that offending towns would have to compensate children for violations. Even a dull lawyer, however, would have recognized major loopholes. It easily could be read that access to any common public school instruction was good enough, even if a child was segregated by descent and deprived of some features of public instruction. As often happens, the legislature shifted the burden to the courts.

Absalom Boston was ready to test the law when he sued Nantucket for denying his daughter, Phebe Boston, admission to the high school. Boston, like many on the island, began as a whaler, rising to the position of sea captain. He invested his income in property and a public inn, and his wealth grew. At the time of the lawsuit, he was sixty years-old, one of the most prominent leaders of the African American community, and an abolitionist. The town's segregationists prepared to fight. Despite the wishes of some citizens of Nantucket to settle out of court by integrating the schools, they convinced a town meeting to contest the suit. The case dragged on, as it was transferred from the Court of Common Pleas to the Massachusetts Supreme Court. Animosities flamed. Irresolution continued. Some black parents resisted, but others began to send their children back to school rather than deprive them of further education. Potential costs to the community mounted. A cloud hung over Nantucket. Finally the bulk of the population had had enough. In 1846 they elected an entirely new school committee with the understanding of bringing the crisis to an end. The committee integrated the schools. Absalom Boston dropped his suit. And at age twenty-four Eunice Ross became a student at Nantucket High School.[29]

The struggle in Nantucket had an impact throughout Massachusetts, if not all of New England, and nowhere greater than in Salem. In 1830, some members of Salem's black community challenged the town's long-held tradition of segregated schools after an African American girl passed the entrance test to high school and authorities denied her admission. They presented legal opinions that argued state law supported equal rights, and school officials allowed her to matriculate soon thereafter. Three years later, 176 white residents objected to her presence at East High School, and school officials reversed themselves and restored segregation. Why white racists waited so long to protest or why local authorities capitulated so easily is unclear. The protesters, 176 people out of a total population of nearly 14,000, were hardly an overwhelming force. The number of people of color as of 1830 was just 267 (a number smaller than in Nantucket and only 1.9 percent of the total population), and the number of school-age black children was no more than eighty at the time. One "Tax-Payer" in the *Salem Register* sputtered that the cost of meeting-space, desks, apparatus, and a teacher's salary was too high a price to pay to assuage the prejudice of a few. But prejudice won out. School officials preempted an African American counter-revolt by appointing William Dodge, reputed to be the best teacher in Salem, as the instructor for the town's children of color. He must have been an outstanding educator, for no protests arose from the black community—even to the fact that all their children were taught in a single room—until Dodge retired in 1842.[30]

Local authorities cut the salary of Dodge's successor and apparently got what they paid for. In the fall of 1843, a grandfather approached a school committeeman and told him that he wanted to place his two grandchildren into one of the town's primary schools. The rejection he received and awareness of events in Nantucket prompted demands for integration, a school boycott—attendance plummeted from sixty students to twenty-two—and a petition to the school committee. Salem's people of African descent were fortunate to have a town government sympathetic to their cause. Mayor Stephen Phillips supported the new school committee's decision to end segregation. A controversy immediately arose represented by the *Salem Register* applauding integration and the *Salem Gazette* demanding that segregation be restored. Phillips acted quickly before opposing sides could make reconciliation impossible and appointed the highly respected Boston lawyer Richard Fletcher to write an opinion. Fletcher, a former congressman and future member of the Massachusetts Supreme Court, reviewed the past as a guide to the present. He reminded townspeople of the tradition of free and equal education first begun by the "Pilgrim Fathers." Without the poor receiving the same educational opportunities as the rich, he reasoned, oppression would result. He concluded that "neither the constitution nor laws of this Commonwealth, make any distinction between a colored person and a white person. A colored person is a free citizen, with the same rights, privileges and duties as any other man, so far as the constitution and laws of this Commonwealth are concerned.

The children of colored parents are therefore, entitled to the benefit of the free schools, equally with others." Fletcher convinced the school committee of the rightness of its decision, and there was no further public outcry.[31] Salem had integrated its schools.

If only Fletcher's opinion, which was widely published and distributed, had convinced Bostonians as well. They would be the last in all of New England north of Rhode Island and Connecticut to integrate their schools. Even Boston's African Americans lagged behind other Massachusetts towns in trying to open all the schools to their children. William C. Nell, who was central to attacks on Jim Crow throughout the antebellum period, with others initiated efforts to curtail segregated schools in 1840 with a petition to the Primary School Committee calling for the elimination of the two blacks-only schools. The committee rejected the request, and there is no record of further action from Boston's people of African descent until 1844, the year Salem achieved integration and Nantucket's black community and other reformers were battling to achieve permanent equal rights on their island.[32]

Once again black Bostonians petitioned the school committee to end segregation and also to dismiss Abner Forbes, the principal of the Smith School, who, they charged, was mistreating their children. And again the committee denied their petition. Although it cleared Forbes of misconduct, it reassigned him to another school; but until it secured a substitute, Forbes would remain at Smith School. Boston African Americans in response determined to make their cause more public. In a series of meetings in May and June they passed resolutions asserting their rights under state law, condemning the school committee for violating those laws, recommending that parents remove their children from Smith School, and transmitting their proceedings to the city's newspapers for publication.[33] As was usually the case, they were dependent on the larger community to take the side of social justice and rally behind their cause. It was a harder case to win. White Bostonians could support George Latimer and a personal liberty law without changing their own lives in the slightest. They could oppose Jim Crow cars without having to sit next to an African American, and, for most, transportation on a railroad was an occasional event. But having children of color in the same classrooms as their own children raised more direct fears, including the bugaboo of amalgamation. Other Massachusetts cities had overcome racism and integrated their schools, but Boston with the largest African American population in New England would be more resistant.

The boycott of Smith School may have been a means to dramatize the inequities of segregation, but it mostly stemmed from the parents' conclusion that Abner Forbes was unfit to head the school and teach their children. That had not always been the case. When he was hired ten years earlier, the Williams College graduate had been an abolitionist; and he had been an effective and respected teacher during his first five years. More recently, he had soured. He had begun punishing children in ways that were unusual. The parents who had testified before the school committee believed that corporal punishment was legitimate for maintaining discipline. Forbes, however, had struck boys on the bottom of their feet, compelled children to stand on only one foot, pulled hair and ears, and pinched them, and he had administered the punishments arbitrarily. Forbes' offenses were serious and grounds for dismissal, but African American parents were willing to retain him, should he reform. What was at the heart of the parents' complaint was his disrespect for people of African descent, students and parents alike. Forbes expressed "opinions unfavorable to the natural capacities of the colored population as a race." Some parents, such as John Hilton who led the protest, sent their children to schools in other towns, but most parents faced the horrible choice of returning their children to the unhealthy environment of Smith School or depriving them of education until changes were made. By the end of the year, enrollment was down by 40 percent.[34]

When the school committee met in February, 1845, Henry I. Bowditch— one of its members—presented a petition from fifteen black Bostonians repeating their earlier requests that "the children should be allowed to go to any schools nearest their respective residences, and that the colored schools should be abolished." It was a simple and mild document, simply asking in effect that Boston follow the law as the state's Supreme Court had stated it. Rather than engage in an unwinnable debate, the committee tabled the motion. Bowditch angrily pursued the members after adjournment and vowed that he would raise the issue every three months at the quarterly meetings until a special committee had been selected. Much to his surprise, at a meeting only a month later, the school committee appointed a special, five-man committee, with Bowditch as its chair, to consider the petition. With one of its members away, it soon became clear that the group was evenly divided. Each side, not knowing whether they represented the majority or the minority, wrote a report. After a lengthy delay, R. W. Bayley returned and voted with the members opposing the petition, thus making theirs the majority report.[35]

Both reports came up for a vote at the school committee hearing on June 19. The majority report attempted to finesse the central issue of integrating the schools and proposed that the petition be denied because the "Grammar School Committee had not acted on the subject." That was it. There was no analysis of the merits or deficiencies of the petition. The minority report, by contrast, was substantive, and what debate there was—proponents of the majority report largely remaining silent—focused on its arguments. Citing morality and the law, Bowditch and his allies claimed that abolishing the segregated schools would reduce prejudice in the schools and in the greater society, would improve the morals of whites, would comply with the law, would save money, and all in "perfect safety," as exemplified by Salem and elsewhere. In a fifty-five to twelve vote, the committee adopted the majority report and blocked integration. The Reverend T. F. Norris, one of the editors of the *Boston Olive Branch*, gave a public sigh of relief. He asserted that the entire controversy was the work of some "agitators," whose aim was amalgamation. "May good men and heaven defend us from such a social intercourse of the two races," he intoned, "as might destroy the usefulness of our excellent schools, or lead to the abomination of the unnatural amalgamation of two races, *who God intended should ever be distinct*. There is as much propriety in negroes marrying with the OURANG OUTANG, as there is of the matrimonial amalgamation of the Saxon and the negro races; and motley schools are the forerunners and producers of such amalgamation."[36] As long as men and women like Norris populated Boston, social justice would be difficult to attain.

Despite such antagonists as T. F. Norris, once again members of Boston's black community in 1846 petitioned the school committee to abolish the blacks-only schools and to allow their children to attend schools that were close to their residences. As before, the school committee appointed a special committee that split three to two against the petition and issued a majority report and a minority report. What was different was that the majority report lengthily explained why it supported segregation, and the full committee broke its previous silence and engaged in vigorous debate.[37]

The majority report minced no words. The issue was not merely color but rather race. Boston's blacks and whites constituted two distinct races created by God. Based on that premise the report posed a rhetorical question: "Now if, in the opinion of the School Committee, there is a race, not only distinct in respect to color, hair, and general physiognomy, but possessing physical, mental, and moral peculiarities, which render a promiscuous intermingling in the public schools disadvantageous, both to them and to the whites,—what law of the Statute book is to prevent them from maintaining special schools for their instruction?" There it was, an unapologetic racist justification for segregation. The remainder of the report contained largely debater's points to counter anticipated objections to separate schools. Boston's schools were equal. On a per capita basis the city provided more funds for black students than for white. If African American schools were in any way inferior to other schools, the fault rested with the black community for not making them better. Keeping the schools separate protected the children from the inevitable conflict that would occur between them. Last, the majority report questioned whether the petition truly reflected the wishes of black Bostonians. It concluded that the "majority of the colored and most of the white people, prefer the present system."[38] This last point had some accuracy. Only a relatively small number of people of color had signed the various petitions over the years, and less than half of the parents and their children, for whatever reason, were boycotting the schools. Divisions within the African American community would continue to plague efforts to end segregation.

The minority report, as expected, was primarily a repetition of the previous year's document. Law and justice supported the integration of Boston's schools, and the report cited Richard Fletcher's opinion on the Salem schools to bolster its argument. It also pointed to other recently desegregated schools as evidence that the children would get along. But it couldn't ignore the split on desegregation among people of African descent and proposed that "such of the colored inhabitants as may prefer sending their children to the separate schools, shall be permitted to do so; and that those who may choose to send their children to the other schools nearest their place of residence shall be entitled to send them, and that it is the duty of the local committee to grant permits in conformity with this rule." Had the school committee been equally divided or had a slight majority leaned toward integration, it still was a fatal concession. As it was, the lack of consensus among Boston people of color simply reinforced the disposition of school committee members to retain segregation. Henry Bowditch tried to gloss over the fifty-nine to sixteen vote passing the majority report. He believed the school committee had treated the issue with "more cordiality" than previously.[39]

No matter whether one looked at the situation of New England people of color as a glass half full or half empty, that glass was only at the halfway mark in the mid-1840s. As of 1845, blacks could not vote in Connecticut, they were not protected by a personal liberty law in Maine, they were in segregated schools in the larger cities of Rhode Island and Connecticut as well as in Boston, they often were restricted to where they might live, they were overwhelmingly poor, they faced a variety of forms of segregation from churches to theaters, their employment opportunities were limited, and they encountered insults, taunts, and humiliation daily. Even so, they were better off than they had been at the beginning of the decade. There no longer were Jim Crow cars on the railroads, black males could vote in every state but Connecticut, every New England state except Maine had enacted personal liberty laws, all of the schools north of Connecticut and Rhode Island with the exception of Boston were integrated, and the prohibition of marriage between people of African descent and people of European descent had been rescinded in Massachusetts—although it still existed in Rhode Island and Maine. Racism and its various expressions remained strong, but something had changed.

White New Englanders had become more sympathetic to African Americans having equal rights. A decade of demands to end slavery and to make people of African descent full citizens had made those ideas less radical and more common. The backlash against abolitionists and advocates of social justice conversely had helped open some people to the possibility of applying the tenets of the Declaration of Independence to all of the region's residents. Some may have been reluctant to advocate ending slavery, but they didn't approve of mobs attempting to curtail free speech. They may not have considered people of color to be their equals, but they didn't condone attacks on black communities. The violence prompted them to give reform a renewed look. Henry I. Bowditch, for example, claimed that witnessing the attack on Garrison in 1835 transformed him. Years later he recalled that the foment had made him question whether "a man cannot speak on slavery within sight of Faneuil Hall and almost at the foot of Bunker Hill? If this is so, it is time for me to become an Abolitionist."[40]

But what tipped the scales, what brought about concrete results, were the efforts of African Americans assisted by their white allies. With only 1.1 percent of the total New England population (ranging from .2 percent in New Hampshire to 3.7 percent in Rhode Island), black New Englanders had to generate significant white support.[41] Sit-ins had dramatized the plight of black New Englanders on the region's railroads and other forms of transportation and had compelled whites to take notice. Boycotts, mass meetings, and petitions economically and politically leveraged corporations and politicians to support reform. A shrewd political deal enfranchised men of color in Rhode Island. African Americans had organized their cause and had been successful, to a point.

Such tactics would not have worked in a white supremacist society. New England certainly had its white supremacists—people such as T. F. Norris—but theirs was a minority view, even in Rhode Island and Connecticut. White supremacists were racists, but racists were not necessarily white supremacists. And while most white New Englanders were racists of some sort, they also were republicans who genuinely extolled a free society, members of families, members of communities, aspirants for a better life, and all the other components that make whole and complex personalities. They could be selfish and altruistic. They could be inconsistent. They could compartmentalize. Had the number and percentage of people of African descent been greater, racist views might have been more prominent in their worldview; but many New Englanders rarely encountered African Americans. Equal rights for people of color often were more an abstraction than an intimate part of life. New Englanders were no more inherently virtuous than any other people, but their history, their demography, their environment shaped different forms of racism in their region than elsewhere in America.

Ralph Waldo Emerson was not a typical New Englander, but his views of African Americans are instructive of the shift of attitude that was occurring. Although just two years older than Garrison, Emerson had lived a much more privileged life—Harvard, a prestigious ministerial post, and by the mid-1830s recognition as an increasingly important public intellectual. His opinions on people of color reflected the views of his class and, to a large extent, the general society. In 1837, the very year he delivered the address "The American Scholar," a year after the publication of his first book, *Nature*, and two years after the attack on Garrison in Boston, he privately divulged in his journal: "I think it cannot be maintained by any candid person that the African race have ever occupied or do promise ever to occupy a very high place in the human family. Their present condition is the strongest proof that they cannot. The Irish cannot; the American Indian cannot; the Chinese cannot. Before the energy of the Caucasian race all the other races have quailed and done obeisance."[42] The statement was neither an endorsement of slavery nor a justification of oppression, but it was a clear expression of a belief in race and the superiority of whites.

By 1845, he would not be so certain. New England was changing, and so was Emerson. He began to question whether the condition of African

Americans was the result of inherent inferiority and to conclude that the degraded state of people of color came from the situation of their lives, not from their native abilities. Late in the year he had to put his newly acquired views to a practical test. Contrary to its previous policy, the New Bedford Lyceum began barring people of color from becoming members and from purchasing tickets to individual lectures. The initial focus had been on the irrepressible David Ruggles who was denied admission, and the Lyceum then had generalized its ruling to apply to all African Americans. The person who reported the surprisingly racist behavior in New Bedford to *The Liberator* recommended that future lecturers—in particular, J. O. Choutes, Charles Sumner, and Ralph Waldo Emerson—refuse to participate. Garrison seconded the suggestion in an adjoining squib. Responding to protest from its own members, the Lyceum met again on November 1 to reconsider its decision to prohibit blacks from attending and reaffirmed its new rule. As a sop to critics, the group voted to admit people of color for free, but only to the North Gallery of the auditorium.[43]

Weeks later, Emerson informed the Lyceum's secretary William Rotch that he had been told that the organization was not admitting African Americans to its lecture series and were that accurate he would decline the invitation to speak there. Being true to his principles cost Emerson about $635 in today's buying power. Later in his journals he would waver on whether people of African descent were inherently inferior, but his public stance—and predominantly his private one—was that all people had equal potential.[44]

PART IV

Mixed Marriages

9

Repealing the Law

SEX, PARTICULARLY BETWEEN lighter-skinned males and darker-skinned females, had long brought people of African descent and people of European descent together, but marriage and deep affection were more rare. From the time of the earliest English settlements, New Englanders had tried to prevent sexual relations outside of marriage. They passed and enforced laws against fornication and homosexuality that applied to everyone. In 1705, Massachusetts lawmakers added an additional dimension when they enacted legislation that provided harsher punishments for black offenders than for whites. More striking, and a precedent for New England, was a provision in the same bill that prohibited marriage of English, Scotch, or people from "any other Christian nation" with any "negro or molatto." Any clergyman (or other person authorized to conduct marriage ceremonies) who oversaw such unions was fined the immense sum of £50.[1] It was in many ways a strange law. It referred to whites but not blacks by nationality and religion, opening the possibility that the legislators were as concerned about cultural integrity as they were about racial purity. And it was a weak law, full of loopholes. Should a couple contract a mixed marriage, the officiator would suffer; but with no provision in the law nullifying the marriage, the contract remained valid. In addition, a couple that married outside the colony and then resided in Massachusetts was legally wed. This was a law that defined caste, but only weakly. No other New England colony followed Massachusetts' example.

When Massachusetts revamped its laws after the Revolution, it enlarged and strengthened its prohibition of mixed marriage. The state added Indians to the subordinate caste, and it declared such marriages that occurred within its borders "shall be absolutely null and void." Marriages that originated elsewhere, however, were still legitimate. Fifty years later in 1836, legislators attempted to repair that gap in the law when they wrote that the marriages of couples who wed outside of the state but who intended to return were invalid. Intent is so difficult to prove that the legislators accomplished little more than to remind constituents of their racist credentials.[2]

Rhode Island in 1798 and Maine in 1820, after separating from Massachusetts and achieving statehood, adopted Massachusetts' 1786 law almost verbatim. Maine soon weakened its law by removing the penalty for officiators and recognizing mixed marriages from out of state.[3] Connecticut, New Hampshire, and Vermont never forbade marriages between people of color and whites. The surprise was Connecticut with its relatively large African American population and its history of racist practices, including being the only New England state to withhold the franchise from black males. Perhaps its legislators believed that caste was so well established that no further law was necessary. Perhaps the state government lacked a small core of true believers who would shepherd a bill to enactment, despite the indifference of most of their colleagues. Or perhaps Connecticut lawmakers believed the likelihood of such marriages was so remote that there was no need for a law. The last possibility, however, would have had to surmount a contradiction. In Connecticut as in all of New England, there was a tension of beliefs. Some whites considered people of color so physically repugnant that they couldn't imagine themselves or other people of European descent forming such unions. And yet they also feared their daughters being swept off their feet by attractive black men. Perhaps we should expect no more consistency in their legislative behavior than in the ambivalence of their attitudes.

Even though the laws of Massachusetts, Maine, and Rhode Island were weak and unenforced—except for the occasional prosecution of an unfortunate clergyman—they still proclaimed a divide between whites and blacks. That was the prime function of the laws, no matter what the motivation of lawmakers. The prohibition of mixed marriages placed people of European descent and people of African descent in distinct castes. The problem for legislators whose commitment to traditional values of equality was stronger than any racist views they might hold was that any attempt to repeal the statute might be perceived as advocacy of marriages between whites and blacks, as support for the dreaded "amalgamation of races." A similar fear silenced many abolitionists and black New Englanders. They were afraid that public demands for removing the prohibition would be so provocative that they would overshadow other and more immediate obstacles to equal rights, such as the desegregation of schools, and would simply reinforce common views that black men lusted after white women and that white abolitionists' long-term goal was a watering down of whiteness and blackness. Some abolitionists and black activists, moreover, disapproved of mixed marriages.[4]

As was so often the case, William Lloyd Garrison went his own way. When he saw injustice, he could not keep quiet. In just the second issue of *The Liberator*, he criticized the Massachusetts governor for neglecting two topics in his address to the legislature: senators and representatives should be urged to attempt to abolish slavery in Washington, DC, and the legislature should repeal the portion of the marriage statute barring intermarriage. He considered the law "an invasion of one of the inalienable rights of every man, namely, 'the pursuit of happiness'—disgraceful to the State—inconsistent with every principle of justice—and utterly absurd and preposterous." And for the next twelve years Garrison's newspaper wouldn't allow readers to ignore the issue. He countered that there was "nothing unnatural in the amalgamation of our species." What

PRACTICAL AMALGAMATION.

FIGURE 9.1 *Practical Amalgamation*, 1839, one of a series by Edward W. Clay. The wooing man on his knee appears to be a caricature of William Lloyd Garrison, while portraits of three abolitionists—seemingly approving the mixed couples— hang on the wall. (The Library Company of Philadelphia).

he considered unnatural was a marriage that united "virtue with vice." Sobriety, for example, should not be wed to drunkenness. "The standard of matrimony is erected by affection and purity, and does not depend upon the height, or bulk, or color, or wealth, or poverty of individuals." On another occasion, Garrison argued that what mattered was a couple's love for each other, not the sanction of the state or of anyone else. Matrimony was a serious undertaking, and "persons cannot be too careful in choosing their partners." He would say no more. But, of course, he did. There was even one episode when his friends thought he had too much played the provocateur. The June 28, 1834, issue of *The Liberator* contained an item from E. K. of West Chester, Pennsylvania, advertising for a wife. "Information would be thankfully received of any young, respectable, and intelligent Colored Woman, (entirely or chiefly of African descent)," the subscriber wrote, "who would be willing to endure the insults and reproaches that would be heaped upon her for being the partner of a white man." Garrison explained to Samuel May that he had carefully weighed the consequences of publishing the ad and was unrepentant, despite "much fluttering among abolitionists generally."[5]

In January 1831, the very month that Garrison started *The Liberator*, state representative John P. Bigelow coincidentally sponsored legislation to repeal the Massachusetts law prohibiting mixed marriages. A Harvard graduate and lawyer, the thirty-three-year-old Bigelow came from Boston's ninth ward—with only eleven African American residents in 1830 (nine of whom lived in households headed by whites), probably the whitest ward in the entire city. He didn't approve of marriages between people of European descent and people of African descent, but he believed the law to be flawed. Because a comprehensive bill on marriage in Massachusetts had been introduced in the House, Bigelow brought up the issue of the prohibition of intermarriage. In particular, he thought that Indians shouldn't be placed alongside other people of color as a separate caste. Bigelow argued that at a time when the Whig-led Massachusetts House opposed Andrew Jackson and Cherokee removal, it was inappropriate to maintain such a distinction. He also contended that the law was unfair to clergymen because it was so difficult to determine who was white and who was of mixed heritage. A clergyman might conduct a marriage ceremony for a couple whom he thought were white, but be fined because one of them was determined to be predominantly a descendant of African forebears. Bigelow concluded his remarks with the assertion that there was no need for a law that applied to so few and that was ineffective besides.[6]

The debate that followed suggested that most of Bigelow's colleagues agreed with him. They reiterated his arguments and added that nullifying mixed marriages made children illegitimate and deprived them of inheritance rights and that "the matter should be left to public opinion." Most qualified their support of repeal by stating that they personally opposed the marriage of blacks and whites. Opposition to Cherokee removal, support for innocent clergy and children, and personal prejudices made public gave the legislators cover to vote for revoking the prohibition of mixed marriages, and the Massachusetts House passed Bigelow's bill. But in Massachusetts, both houses had to pass a bill on three separate occasions and then the governor had to sign it before it became law. In 1831, the House approved the repeal twice but reversed itself on the vote for final passage. John Greenleaf Whittier years later claimed that the repeal clause failed because House members were dissatisfied with other sections of the overall marriage bill, and George Bradburn related that it simply had got crowded out at the end of a busy session.[7] Whittier and Bradburn may have been accurate, but just as likely the politicians were reluctant to be too far in front of where they believed public opinion to be. In any case, the issue was dead for that year.

Boston newspapers—and even newspapers outside the state—attacked Bigelow for not properly representing the wishes of his constituents and for advocating "intermarriages between persons of different colors." He defended himself in a letter to the editor of the sympathetic *Boston Courier*, reviewing his actions and strenuously proclaiming his own aversion to mixed marriages, and his career escaped damage from the backlash.[8] He continually won re-election to the state House, was elected secretary of the Commonwealth, and served as mayor of Boston from 1849 to 1851.

Despite a few futile efforts by petitioners to revive the issue of mixed marriages, the legislature didn't seriously address it again until 1839. In 1832, legislators referred a petition to a select committee that quickly reported back that it was "inexpedient to legislate on the subject." Six years later, Charlotte F. Thompson and fifteen other women of Rehoboth, Massachusetts (soon joined by more than twenty other petitions with more than 2,500 signatures), petitioned the legislature to remove all distinctions of color from the state's laws. At the time, the only such law over which the legislature had authority was the prohibition of marriages between whites and various people of color, a fact the petitions ignored. This would be the approach of petitions in the years to follow. The larger principle of equality before the law would be raised, but mention of its specific application would be avoided. A second characteristic of the petitions was the role of female antislavery societies, whose members would take the lead in pressuring politicians to repeal the law. But as in 1832, the petitions got lost in committee and never came to the full body of the legislature. That was not unexpected when the petitions were compared to the 6,400 Massachusetts citizens who petitioned their government to instruct the state's United States representatives and senators to abolish slavery in Washington, DC, and the 20,000 signatories who called on the legislature to protest the "gag rule" in Congress. Those politicians supporting the marriage law not only made sure repeal never came up for a vote but they also countered the petitions with ridicule, a tactic they would continue to use and prefer rather than debating the principle. One of Boston's representatives, a Mr. Robinson, presented a fraudulent petition—reputedly from Boston's black community—that avowed the memorialists didn't want a change in the law. They supposedly wanted "to preserve the purity of their *race*, and prevent the enormous evils resulting from a mixed *breed*." To the laughter of his assembled colleagues, Robinson introduced the petition with a preamble: "If the ladies, whose petition was the immediate cause of this memorial, were sensible of the estimation in which they are held by the colored gentlemen, it is believed they would despair of success, and submit with as good grace as possible to their fate."[9] As stale as the joke quickly became, opponents to repeal would continually claim that women petitioners simply were trying to enlarge the pool of potential husbands.

Although there were fewer petitions and signatures in 1839—786 women from Lynn, 170 from Brookfield, 211 from Dorchester, and 161 from Plymouth signed brief documents requesting the legislature "to repeal all laws in this State, which make any distinction among its inhabitants, on account of color"—the Massachusetts legislature reluctantly took up the issue. Some Massachusetts newspapers, however, initiated an attack on the female petitioners, even before any discussion on the House floor. The *Boston Post*, for example, took up the previous year's charge that these were lonely women looking to African American men for companionship. Its intent was ridicule and humiliation and its prose not nearly so delicate. It salaciously mused that "perhaps some of these ladies despair of having a white offer, and so are willing to try *de colored race*." The *Dedham Patriot* questioned women's right to petition. It asserted that "those only who have a right to act in political matters are entitled to be heard in petition, address, and remonstrance, on political subjects" and suggested that each memorialist return to "her appropriate sphere where God has placed her."[10] And so it went.

Two other petitions reached legislators before debate began. Samuel Curtis of Lynn and 192 others frivolously called on the legislature to authorize the women petitioners of the town, except for those underage, "a free and full privilege . . . to marry, intermarry, or associate with any Negro, Indian, Hottentot, or any other being in human shape." The other from "Phillis Hathaway and other ladies of color" opposing a repeal of the law later was found to be fraudulent. The intent of both was to discredit those seeking equal rights. Lawmakers gleefully ignored the petitions' purpose and over the objections of some legislators referred both to committee for consideration, joining the Lynn, Brookfield, and Plymouth petitions.[11]

The question was whether the petition from Dorchester also would be referred to committee. On February 9, George Bradburn, an abolitionist and a representative from Nantucket, presented the petition of S. P. Sanford and 210 other women of Dorchester to the chamber. Tall, outspoken, and a Whig, he had little allegiance to his party and frequently went on an independent course, regardless of consequences. He could argue a case eloquently, often insulting opponents along the way, but paid little attention to building coalitions. He was a bold reformer and a mediocre politician. After placing the petition into consideration, Bradburn offered a few remarks explaining why the Dorchester women felt so strongly about the issue. The current law jeopardized the inheritances of children of mixed marriages, was unfair to clergymen, and violated the state's Declaration of Rights. These were familiar themes, and Bradburn spent little time developing them, except for the facetious suggestion that the state should appoint an inspector of skins to help clergymen identify lawful couples. He focused his prime attention on amalgamation, the bugaboo that presented the greatest obstacle to repealing the law. The petitioners didn't ask for amalgamation to be permitted, he emphasized, but only that the marriage restriction be removed. He gave the analogy that a person seeking an end to capital punishment was not encouraging murder. He personally disapproved of amalgamation, as he was certain was the opinion of the petitioners. Besides, the current law did not prevent the creation of mixed children; it only "stigmatizes" them and "robs them of their property."[12]

Supporters of the status quo responded as if they had not listened to anything Bradburn had said. Rather than debate the substance of the prohibition against mixed marriages, they chose to criticize the petitioners and their motives. Benjamin Greenleaf, a representative of Bradford, questioned whether the women really wanted the legislature to pass a law allowing them and other whites to marry blacks and asserted that the petitioners had been deceived and "know not what they ask for." Representative Buckingham of Cambridge challenged the validity of Dorchester's petition and asked what evidence there was that the signatures were genuine. Minot Thayer of Braintree considered the whole proceedings on the subject a waste of time. He sputtered that he was "entirely opposed to all such petitions. And I have no respect for the women who sign them. I don't believe there is a virtuous woman among them." Boston's Representative Gray attempted to halt debate before it became even more vitriolic and moved for an immediate vote. The House then agreed to refer the petition to committee. Behind the scenes a deal had been struck. In an apparent effort to secure sufficient votes, it had created a special committee, to be chaired by Minot Thayer, whose sole purpose was to examine the integrity of the Dorchester petition. Out of 139 petitions (with a total of 17,115 signatures) on a variety of topics submitted to the legislature that session, that was the only petition singled out for examination of authenticity.[13]

The Committee on the Judiciary, chaired by William Lincoln, reported back on February 15. It condescendingly questioned the propriety of women sending petitions, noted that no men had added their names or initiated petitions calling for the repeal of the mixed marriage prohibition, and observed that the petitions from Lynn, Brookfield, Dorchester, and Plymouth all used the same form. Some of the memorialists may have been out of their depth and not understood what they were signing or the context of the document. Others, the legislators claimed, represented themselves as "accomplished politicians in petticoats," learned in the law and political philosophy. But the committee understood that it could not rely only on ridicule and disdain. This time it had to address the arguments. There had been "no inequality of civil rights" in Massachusetts since the days of slavery, it contended. Black men could vote, and they could run for office. The petitioners were wrong to argue that the marriage restriction promoted inequality. Whites could marry whites, and people of color could marry people of color. Neither people of European descent nor people of African descent were declared superior or inferior to the others; all received equal treatment; all were restricted to whom they could marry. So the committee purported. The lawmakers did not deny that children from mixed marriages were at a disadvantage but contended that children of "incestuous marriages" faced the same problems of disinheritance. In their estimation, the legislature had the power to regulate marriages for the common good. It could confirm the form of marriage ceremonies, determine the specific age when people could marry, and establish the "degrees of affinity" between men and women that would ban marriage. Complexion was just another category under its jurisdiction. The restriction was not a frivolous novelty, but an old law created by the founders of the Commonwealth and supported by God and nature. The legislature should not repeal long-held laws, except to remedy "an existing evil." Neither the petitioners nor their families and friends or people of color were claiming they wanted to enter into such marriages. Without those demands, the law should remain intact.[14]

Before offering its report to the Massachusetts House of Representatives, the committee tied up some loose ends. It declared the "Phillis Hathaway" petition (ostensibly from "ladies of color") a fraud and the Samuel Curtis petition "unfit for sober citizens to address to their Legislature." It was skeptical of the Brookfield petition, because all the signatures were "written by the same hand, if not by the same pen," and it chastised several of the petitions for including children's names. Finally, it concluded that "it is inexpedient to legislate on the subject referred to them." A majority of the House happily accepted the recommendation, and the marriage law lived another year.[15]

When the Minot Thayer committee on the Dorchester petition reported to the legislature on April 8, it was anticlimactic. As expected, the committee found discrepancies. Some women—no doubt humiliated by the public attacks in the newspapers and on the floor of the House—claimed that they had been unaware of the petition's intent and asked that their names be removed. Despite the testimony of Sarah Baker, the corresponding secretary of the Dorchester Female Anti-Slavery Society, that she had written several names on the petition with the individual's consent, the committee found these signatures erroneous, others misguided, and were disturbed by the signatures of children. It condemned the petition and its purpose. At that point, with the issue already having been decided for the year, members of the House simply wanted to distance themselves from the subject, and they tabled the report rather than accept it. The heavy-handedness of Thayer and his committee, however, brought a backlash that would live on. Lydia Maria Child individually and the Boston Female Anti-Slavery Society collectively sent new petitions to the legislature before the session expired. The Female Anti-Slavery Societies of Dorchester, Stoneham, and Salem offered resolutions in support of "our sisters of Dorchester and Lynn" and of repeal of the marriage law.[16] The legislature had held off demands for revoking the prohibition for another year, but the political dynamic was changing. The question increasingly appeared to be when the law would be rescinded, not whether.

The next three years established a frustrating pattern. Citizens petitioned the legislature, which set up a special committee. The committee recommended repealing the law, the Senate and House voted in favor of removing the prohibition, *The Liberator* exalted that the law was about to be changed, and the bill failed on final passage. In 1840, there was a huge increase in the number of petitions and signatures—92 petitions and 8,706 signatures—the product of sophisticated grassroots organizing. Most likely in response to the previous year's criticism that there was no male support, 3,674 of the signatures came from men. The Joint Special Committee, to which the petitions had been referred, recommended that the restrictive clause in the marriage law be removed, and both branches of the legislature passed the bill on their first two votes. *The Liberator* over-optimistically informed its readers that the law "will doubtless be enacted to a certainty." The newspaper was half right. The Senate passed the bill repealing the prohibition of mixed marriages, but the House on the vote for final passage rejected it by "a small majority." One representative wrote William Lloyd Garrison that "it was the general opinion of the friends of the Bill that it would not have been finally defeated, had it been introduced at a sufficiently early state of the session."[17] Why that should be true for the House but not the Senate he didn't explain.

The following year began favorably, when George Bradburn was appointed chair of the special committee reporting on the annual petitions calling for the removal of the clause against mixed marriages. Bradburn didn't disappoint, and the committee issued a unanimous recommendation for repeal. Its report called the restrictive law "useless," because mixed couples could easily marry out of state and return without fear of prosecution. In a long list, the report charged that the law encouraged "licentiousness," and was unjust, unequal, of doubtful constitutionality, and a "relic of slavery." Apparently aware of the assessment that the previous year's bill had failed because of a late vote, the committee presented its report to the House on January 19. By the end of the month the House had voted twice to revoke the prohibition of mixed marriages, and *The Liberator* was telling its readers that the bill "will doubtless be enacted in both branches without any serious opposition." Hopes were dashed in the first week of February, when once again a majority of Massachusetts' representatives defeated the bill on the necessary third vote. State senators, however, believed they could convince the House otherwise in March and passed the bill 17 to 13. But the House with a 134 to 127 vote refused to concur.[18]

Each year came closer to success, and 1842 looked promising with the distinguished Charles Francis Adams serving as chair of the special committee. The committee recommended revoking the clause, the Senate passed the bill 24 to 9, but the House barely defeated it on final passage 140 to 136. The tide clearly was turning, and in the House, desperate proponents of the status quo resorted to bald racism. Representative Park of Boston proclaimed: "The whites, as a race, are superior to the blacks. They have a right, and it is their duty to prevent their own race from deteriorating. The mixed blood is depraved, the intellect is inferior, while the animal passions are strengthened." Adams countered by reminding his fellow representatives that the law was ineffective. Maine and New Hampshire without a law prohibiting mixed marriages had very little amalgamation, while Louisiana with such a law had a large mixed population. Mr. Marcy of Greenwich declared that "every parent would rather follow his daughter to the grave, than to see her married to a black man." Representative Thomas, of Charlestown, "observed that every father would rather follow his daughter to the grave than have her married to a drunken man," but that was no reason to have a law prohibiting such unions. Marcy blurted back "that if he were a girl, which he was not, he would not marry a black man."[19]

Marcy's fears were widespread. The previous year on the floor of the House, Representative Lunt of Newburyport had argued that he would rather have any female family member dead than married to "a negro," and similar sentiments had been heard in opposition to the extension of any equal right—from education to transportation—for many years.[20] Seldom were their concerns about their white sons being seduced by black women. At the core of their racism was a deep-seated horror of black male sexuality, but it was more complicated than that. The issue being debated in the Massachusetts legislature was marriage, not fornication. The old fornication laws had evaporated at statehood, and no one was championing their resurrection. People of African descent and of European descent could have sexual relations without prosecution, and mixed offspring—the products of "amalgamation"—might ensue. Sex was not the only concern. At some level, racist whites were afraid that their children, particularly their daughters, might fall in love with a person of color and cement that affection with marriage.

A significant year for equal rights in Massachusetts proved to be 1843. More than 60,000 citizens signed the "Latimer Petition," and the legislature complied with the request. Petitions to desegregate railroads inundated the halls of government; and although only the state Senate passed a bill, the railroads recognized that they must submit to the popular will. Democrats now controlled the House, and they were much more willing to repeal the restrictive clause of the marriage law than the Whigs had been. Petitions calling for an end to the ban on mixed marriages, once again organized by antislavery societies, flooded the House and the Senate. African Americans individually had signed petitions, but as a group they almost always had remained silent. This too changed. In January, more than a third of New Bedford's African American population petitioned to remove the ban, and on February 1 in an open meeting Boston men of color contradicted claims that they disapproved of attempts to overturn the prohibition on intermarriages. They denounced the law as inherently wrong, a violation of the state constitution, a relic of prejudice, and as better belonging "to a slave code than to a free State."[21] The popular tide flowed with proponents of equal rights.

There was little doubt that the Senate would approve revoking the ban on marriages between whites and people of color; but until the House voted favorably on three separate occasions, nothing was certain. It had teased advocates of equal rights too often with early votes and then driven them to despair with last minute reversals. The debate began in earnest on February 8. Representative Gibbens of Boston immediately informed the House that he opposed the bill, and he believed that was true of the state's people of color. In order to substantiate his assertion, he presented a petition purportedly from "colored women of Boston," who charged that "certain colored men" had petitioned the legislature so that they might marry white women. "If the proposed change of the laws take place," they appealed, "we shall be deserted by our natural protectors and supporters, and thrown upon the world friendless and despised, and forced to get our bread by any vile means that may be proposed to us by others, or that despair may teach us to invent." *The Liberator* characterized it as a "worthless hoax" but also, in order to cover the possibility it was genuine, stated that the twenty signatories "are said to be among the lowest and most disreputable of our colored population." Whether the petition—even with hints of the depravity of poverty—was legitimate or not, it apparently influenced few lawmakers. There is little likelihood that Gibbens, with a long history of racist views, was concerned about African American opinions. His initial comment and the petition were debater's points. At the heart of his opposition to the repeal (and to desegregating the railroads, which was before the House at the same time) was that it would undermine caste. He unabashedly feared "levelling and equality."[22]

The repeal's advocates rushed to its defense with the same arguments that had been made year after year. The law violated the state's bill of rights and constitution, it promoted caste and degraded "the colored race," it was ineffective, it undermined opposition to slavery in the South, and it did not encourage amalgamation, because there was a "natural repugnance" to such unions. The bill's opponents also went over familiar ground. God and nature had created distinctions that were fundamental, and repeal of the prohibition would produce decidedly inferior offspring. Despite such objections, the bill passed on the first two votes.[23]

The House scheduled the critical final vote for February 22. Although 1843 seemed to be the year for change, supporters still were apprehensive that they were about to witness a repeat of previous years. In a last ditch effort to waylay the bill, Representative Toppan moved "to postpone the bill indefinitely." There was a brief flurry of words from proponents and opponents, until Representative Church called for the previous question. The moment once again had come. The vote preceded, and the bill passed its last hurdle in the House, 178 to 138. Whether the representatives mirrored their constituents' views is impossible to know, but a majority of representatives from eight counties (including Suffolk—almost exclusively Boston, Essex, and Middlesex) voted for the measure. Three counties were tied, and three counties had a majority of their representatives in opposition. Bristol, the home county of New Bedford with its large African American population, narrowly voted against (15 to 14), as did the Cape Cod county of Barnstable (7 to 5). The only county in significant opposition was Berkshire with its sizable African American population; that westernmost county adjacent to New York voted 16 to 11 against. Governor Marcus Morton signed the bill three days later.[24]

Years of petitions finally had succeeded. One more vestige of caste had been removed. Racism, of course, remained, and probably some of the support for the bill came from representatives who believed that the "natural repugnance" between blacks and whites rendered the bill inconsequential. They voted for repeal of the marriage restriction and against the desegregation of the railroads—an issue with immediate impact. William

Lloyd Garrison, however, could justly celebrate: "Thus has another tremendous blow been given to the monster prejudice." And he recognized that it was more than an abstract victory. "At last, in the Commonwealth of Massachusetts," he wrote Hannah Webb, "human beings who love each other may be united together in 'holy wedlock,' even though the hue of their skin may not perfectly harmonize!"[25]

10

Breaking a Barrier

HAD MASSACHUSETTS LEGISLATORS been aware of how many mixed marriages existed in their state (and in their region, for that matter), they may not have repealed the law. In their own lives they may have encountered or heard of a couple with mixed ancestry, but that would have been rare. Their experience reinforced the idea that people of African descent and people of European descent preferred to live among their "kind." Even if they didn't find each other physically repugnant, they still had no desire to intermarry. But observations and hearsay did not match reality. During the antebellum period there were at least 410 mixed marriages in New England, scattered through no fewer than 209 cities, towns, and villages.

Exactly how many mixed marriages there were is difficult to determine precisely, for there were many couples with conflicting information about their ancestry (see Appendix 4 for an explanation of how I constructed the mixed marriage database). The prominent and light-skinned Congregational minister Amos G. Beman of New Haven, Connecticut, for example, was listed as black in the 1850 census but mixed in the 1860 and 1870 censuses. There was no confusion that his second wife, the English-born Eliza Kennedy, was white. This glitch in the records, however, didn't alter the fact that theirs was a mixed marriage. Nor did the listing of Fred and Jane Little's children as the eldest being white and the two younger being mixed. Multiple records still confirmed that Fred was a New Hampshire farmer with mixed ancestry and that Jane was white.[1]

More complicated was the census depiction of the marriage of Samuel and Marian (sometimes Maria) Clark. In 1850 they lived in Northampton, Massachusetts, where he was a laborer; in 1860 they were in Shutesbury, Massachusetts, where he was a farmer; and in 1870 they had moved to Boston where he was a musician. There was no doubt that Samuel came from European ancestors, but census takers cataloged Marian as black in 1850, mixed in 1860, and white in 1870. Sylvester and Elizabeth R. Winslow Cazneau didn't move as frequently as did the Clarks but still posed a puzzle. They were married July 26, 1841, and lived for at least forty years in South Scituate and Scituate, Massachusetts. Elizabeth came from nearby Hingham, and decade after decade census takers perceived her as black. Sylvester had been born in Spain and worked both as a laborer and a shoemaker but his ancestry was more difficult to categorize. In 1850 he was white; in 1860 he had become mixed; and by 1880 he had somehow transformed himself to black. Edward H. and Mary Jakes—he from Maryland, she born in New Hampshire (though one of five censuses placed her birth in French Canada)—lived their married lives in Claremont, New Hampshire, where they reared three children. Mary was consistently white in all public records, but her husband and children had more chameleon-like characteristics. Edward was a prosperous barber who by 1870 had accumulated $2,500 worth of real estate and $1,000 of personal property. According to census records he came from mixed parents in 1850, was white in 1860 and 1870, mixed again in 1880, and in 1900 had become black. His Civil War registration listed him as black. Their children sometimes were white and sometimes mixed.[2]

Such conflicting information was not rare in the census records. Of the individuals who appeared in my original database, 103 of the 896 (11.5%) had the designation of their "color" changed from one census to another. This may have mirrored the perceptions of the communities in which they lived. The categories were and are arbitrary constructs, and comparing tabulations demonstrates how fluid the idea of race was and is. Instructions to the marshals and assistant marshals in 1850 and 1860 offered no definitions, and directions for later censuses were no more helpful than suggesting various degrees of "black blood" to define "black" and "mulatto." Census takers were supposed to gather their information at "every dwelling house" or "by personal inquiry of the head of every family." What actually took place is impossible to determine. It seems likely that assistant marshals would ask for names, ages, places of birth, perhaps family relations, and whatever else was factually needed. It is less likely that they inquired about gender and color but rather followed their own observations and predilections. It is also possible that some householders may have tried to pass for white, as had occurred in New England from the early eighteenth century. Moving to a new town particularly opened the possibility of establishing a new identity.[3]

Well aware of the possibility of error, I analyzed each potential mixed marriage in the database and tried to determine how likely it was that a marriage consisted of one spouse being of color and the other white. Focusing on the strength of the evidence, I assigned a ranking to each marriage: 1, as certain as a historian can be; 2, highly likely; 3, likely; 4, unlikely; 5, highly unlikely. Most rankings were relatively easy, but the most difficult and most critical threshold was between likely and unlikely. I decided to include only marriages ranked from 1 to 3 for an analysis of the characteristics of mixed marriages. With the preponderance of censuses (two out of three) categorizing Marian Clark as a person of color, her marriage to Samuel Clark received a 3. Sylvester Cazneau presented a tougher choice. Only one of three censuses declared him white, but he was from Spain, presumably with Mediterranean coloring, and might be perceived as a person of color, regardless of his self-perception. So I fudged and gave his marriage to Elizabeth R. (Winslow) Cazneau a 3-4.[4] Essentially I couldn't decide, but anything below a 3 was dropped. The Cazneaus were not a part of the final study. Census records, though abundant, weren't enough to clarify whether Edward H. Jakes and Mary Jakes were a mixed couple. Two censuses found Edward mixed, two white, and one black. But his Civil War registration listed him as black, and he was a barber (almost exclusively an occupation of people of color in the mid-nineteenth century). Ultimately I ranked the Jakes' marriage a 2, highly likely. My revised database now had 19 marriages ranked as all but certain, 101 as highly likely, and 290 as likely. In my estimation there were at least 410 mixed marriages in New England before the Civil War.

Probably there were substantially more. People of color—unless they were slaves—and the poor almost always have been undercounted in the United States Federal Census, sometimes because census takers didn't make sufficient effort, and sometimes because people didn't want to be counted. Assistant marshals for the census might misunderstand the composition of various family groups within a household or might talk to only one family member and assume his spouse and all other family members had the same ancestry, even when that was not the case. Fugitive slaves avoided officials of all types, and people in states where mixed marriages were prohibited had reason to remain hidden, as most likely occurred in Rhode Island.

When comparing the percentage of mixed marriages per state to the percentage of African Americans per state, several phenomena appear. The two southern New England states were less hospitable to mixed marriages than should have been imagined by their populations, while the four other states were more open. From laws to race riots, Connecticut and Rhode Island were the most racist states in the region. Even so, Connecticut still had sixty-one mixed marriages—the second highest for any New England state for the period. Rhode Island, with the third highest number of African Americans, had the fewest marriages found in the database and the most stringent restrictive law. Maine, by contrast, prohibited mixed marriages but didn't enforce the law, and it nearly matched Connecticut in the number of such unions even though its African American population was less than one-fifth the size of the Nutmeg State's. Rhode Island's law undoubtedly had an impact on the number of marriages performed within the state, but it seems highly likely that the actual number of mixed mar- riages was much larger than reported.

Although there were only six towns in Rhode Island with mixed mar- riages, they were scattered throughout five of its six counties. That was typical of all of New England. Fifty-eight of the sixty-seven counties in the region had mixed marriages. Those with none were almost all isolated and meagerly populated, such as Dukes County, Massachusetts (Martha's Vineyard and adjacent islands); Aroostock County, Maine (the north- ernmost county in the state and in all of New England); and Grand Isle County, Vermont (situated in northern Lake Champlain). Among cities, towns, and villages with recorded unions of a person of African descent and a person of European descent, only heavily populated Boston— atypical of the region in so many ways—had more than ten for the entire period before the Civil War, and its fifty-one marriages (12 percent of the total) significantly dwarfed the ten of runner-up New Haven. In some ways Boston mirrored the distribution of marriages in New England; nine of its twelve wards contained mixed marriages, but over half were in the areas of heaviest African American concentration at the base of Beacon Hill in wards 6 and 7 and in ward 2 near the waterfront in the North End.

Mixed couples who lived in Boston and other cities with relatively large African American populations seemingly would have blended in and avoided stares and insults. Unfortunately, that was not necessarily the case. James Congdon reflecting on life in mid-nineteenth century New Bedford—supposedly one of New England's most tolerant towns— wrote: "A respectable negro of our town had a white wife, who was made so utterly miserable by the scoffs and scorn of her neighbors that she did her best to become herself black, exposing her face constantly to the sun,

Table 10.1 Mixed Marriages and African American Population, 1850

States	Mixed Marriage Database		African American Population, 1850	
	#	%	#	%
Connecticut	61	15%	7603	33%
Maine	56	14%	1356	6%
Massachusetts	194	47%	9064	39%
New Hampshire	49	12%	520	2%
Rhode Island	10	2%	3070	13%
Vermont	40	10%	718	3%

The African American population by state comes from the US Bureau of the Census, *Negro Population*, 221. The percentage of mixed marriages per state is from all New England mixed marriages for the period up to the Civil War. The percentage of African Americans by state is in relation to the total African American population of New England in 1850.

until she attained a tolerable color, and might have passed at least for a mestizo."[5]

Mary Achmet of Middletown, Connecticut, behaved similarly. She was the second wife of Hammet Achmet, the only person in the database born in Africa. He had come to Virginia as a slave and apparently George Washington was his master. He may have traveled to New England with Washington in an early stage of the American Revolution, for by 1777 he was a drummer in one of the companies of the First Connecticut Regiment. After the war he moved to Middletown as a free man, married a person of color, raised a family and eked out a living. He milked his role in the Revolution whenever possible—drumming, making and selling drums, and marching about town in uniform. After his first wife died in 1827, he soon married Mary, a white woman. It was an unhappy marriage from the beginning. Hammet was seventy years old, a bit of an eccentric, and perhaps difficult. But townspeople's negative reactions to a mixed marriage contributed to Mary's distress, and she attempted to dye her skin with "a decoction of mahogany chips" and pass for black.[6]

Even one of New England's most respected African Americans, Amos G. Beman, was not immune to the difficulties a mixed marriage could bring. The son of the important reformer and minister of Middletown's African church Jehiel C. Beman, Amos Beman quickly rose to prominence.

Table 10.2 Geographic Distribution of Marriages

States	Towns	5 or more	Counties	With
Connecticut	30	3	8	7
Maine	36	2	16	12
Massachusetts	78	7	14	13
New Hampshire	29	0	10	10
Rhode Island	6	1	5	4
Vermont	30	0	14	12
New England	209	13	67	58

"Towns" are the number of towns with mixed marriages. "5 or more" is the number of towns with five or more marriages. "Counties" is the total number of counties in the state in 1860. "With" is the number of counties with mixed marriages.

At the age of twenty-nine he was ordained as minister of New Haven's Temple Street Congregational ("colored") Church in 1841 and selected as president of the National Convention of Colored Citizens in 1843. He was active in the temperance movement, the struggle for equal rights, and antislavery. By no means wealthy, he accumulated $1,400 worth of real estate by 1850. Then beginning in August 1857, a series of deaths devastated his family. His wife Eunice, two sons, and two daughters—all people of color—contracted typhoid fever. Eunice and eldest son Amos died that month, and one daughter died six months later. Beman addressed his grief by numbing himself with overwork. Within a year of Eunice's death, he married Eliza B. Kennedy. Perhaps Beman believed that his own light skin would inoculate him from recriminations that he had married a white woman, but it appears that his congregation forced him out on account of the marriage. He resigned in January 1858 and flitted from pulpit to pulpit for the remaining sixteen years of his life. After his second wife died he married a woman much darker than himself.[7]

The only reported use of violence against a mixed couple in New England during the antebellum period occurred in Boston. Richard Cooper, a white Englishman, and his black wife and mixed daughter were returning home from church one summer evening in 1846 when an assailant attacked, striking all three of them. The newspaper account gave scant information, other than that the culprit was arrested and held on bail until the municipal court met again. There was no indication of whether the attacker already knew the family or was trying to rob them or whether words had been exchanged beforehand or the violence was a spontaneous act of hate. The key points the *Boston Traveller* attempted to make were that the assailant was a "young colored man" and that the assault reflected the "natural and illegal indignation of . . . people of color" toward "this unnatural, though legal union."[8]

These four anecdotes raise more questions than they answer. The underlying question certainly is, how representative of general New England attitudes and behavior were the episodes? Each took place in a city with a significant African American population in the southern half of the region, where tensions could be high. Urban areas where there was greater anonymity also allowed for the possibility of verbal attacks and more from strangers. It may have been that rural New Englanders felt less threatened or indifferent to the occasional mixed marriage. In Vermont there is even evidence that members of such unions could be participants in community affairs.[9] Or it could be that incidents outside the main population centers were less well reported. We do know there was widespread support, except in Rhode Island, for having no laws prohibiting mixed marriages, but also broad discomfort—if not hostility—among both black and white New Englanders, particularly in urban areas, toward actual marriages. And yet nearly 1,000 people, probably more, defied convention and married across ancestral lines. These four episodes may have been no more than random events with no meaning beyond the local circumstances.

Some of the settlements with unusually large numbers of mixed marriages (at least five) situated themselves outside of town boundaries. The residents were not isolated from people in the main community, but by distancing themselves they would have been able to reduce the possibilities of unpleasant encounters. Nigger-town—later Nigger-town Crossing, and later still sanitized to Atusville—was such a settlement. Its founder was London Atus who first came to Machias, Maine (in New England's far northeast, close to Nova Scotia), as a slave of the village's first minister James Lyon in 1772. Only thirteen years old at the time, he was old enough four years later to participate in the American Revolution as a soldier and as a sailor on a privateer. He gained his freedom after the War and, probably with bounty from his privateering, purchased land outside of town on the site that eventually would become Atusville. By 1789, Eunice (Foss) had joined him. Daughter of one of Machias' founders, she gave birth to a second child before the town fined her for fornication. No one apparently tried to drive the mixed couple apart but rather with the threat of a six shilling fine encouraged them to make themselves and their children legal—and diminished the possibility that the town would be liable for the children's upkeep.[10]

In the course of their long marriage, London and Eunice Atus had twelve children and thus laid the foundation for Atusville as a settlement and as a mixed community. Like his father, John Atus served in an American war, the War of 1812, and received a land bounty and pension. Also like his father, he married a white woman, Fanny (Davis). Together they had seven children. After Fanny died in 1835, John married Alice Berton Sherbin—a member of a prominent Maine African American family, and they had twelve children. Another son of London and Eunice, Nathaniel Atus married a white woman Lydia, and they had at least two children. Susan Atus, a daughter of London and Eunice, first married a man of mixed heritage and upon his death married the white laborer Hiram Scott. She produced one child in her first marriage and six in her second. One of her sons Henry, a fisherman, had a white wife Mary E. (Mariner). At least one other of London and Eunice's daughters, Sophronia—married to the black sailor Peter Henry—continued to live in Atusville. The extended Atus family alone provided enough people for a viable village, but in 1850 at least one other African American family, the Maxwells, lived in the community. There may have been two or three white families as well. Dennis and William Foss (two of Eunice's brothers) headed households, and they were listed immediately after Nathaniel Atus' household in the census. Lemuel Gay and his white household were listed immediately adjacent to John Atus. Almost all of the men were laborers. Some of them held property, but Atusville was a poor, though autonomous, community.[11]

Consisting of a long peninsula and many islands, large and small, Harpswell, Maine, was a perfect location for a mixed settlement. Situated on Casco Bay near Brunswick to the north and across a river from Phippsburg, Harpswell—more water than land—was home to approximately 1500 dispersed residents in the mid-nineteenth century. Not the tourist destination that it now is, the scattered settlements offered a hardscrabble and remote existence for farmers and fishermen. Like Atusville, the mixed community within Harpswell had a single family—the Darlings—at its core. All children of Isaac and Patience Darling—a mixed couple themselves—of Phippsburg, five brothers and sisters and their spouses formed a small fishing hamlet. George Darling, the eldest born in 1803, married twice and both his wives (Mary McIntire, and Joann) were white. Samuel Darling married Sarah (Leavitt), who was white, and her brother Charles Leavitt married Betsey Darling, the middle offspring of the five Harpswell Darlings. Hannah Darling married John Marks, who was white and like the other men was a fisherman. The youngest brother Stephen Darling was born in 1821, and, like his siblings at Harpswell, married a white person, Deborah. Altogether the couples produced twenty-nine children of varying shades. They must have been a census taker's nightmare, for there was frequent "color" confusion in the records. George Darling alone went from white to mixed to white to black in successive censuses. Harriet Beecher Stowe lived only a few miles from Harpswell in 1850 while her husband was a professor at Bowdoin College, but there is no evidence that she was aware of the nearby mixed settlement.[12]

There were many communities on the outskirts of New England towns composed of people of African descent and people of European descent, but Atusville and Harpswell were unusual in having mixed families predominate in their communities. New Guinea outside of Nantucket was in many ways more typical. It was a settlement primarily consisting of African American families with a sprinkling of mixed marriages. One of the few whites to reside there, Thomas Snow was born in Nantucket in 1808, but it is unclear when he first began living in New Guinea. He was a trader and may have sold goods to the local black community. He definitely was living in New Guinea by 1840, for by that census he had entered into a mixed marriage with Lydia (Borden). She died before the 1850 census, and he married Lucretia C. (Tweedy). Both of his wives came from prominent New Guinea families, and both were women of color. His connections and the liquor store he acquired led to prosperity. By 1870, two years before his death, Snow held $1,700 worth of real estate and $3,500 of personal property (most likely including goods for sale). Snow's two marriages, as well as the other three recorded mixed marriages on the island of Nantucket, were housed within an African American pocket, almost certainly where they were most welcome.[13]

In towns with fifty or more people of African descent, that was usually the case. Mixed couples ordinarily lived within an African American cluster or on its fringes. It was more complicated in towns and villages with smaller black populations (163 different towns and 40 percent of all mixed marriages). In 1860, the shoemaking town (and Hosea Easton's hometown) of North Bridgewater, Massachusetts, contained twenty-five people of color in a total population of approximately 6,600 people. The white bootmaker William Reed lived with his mixed wife Elizabeth M. and their two children in the dwelling of Isaac H. Blanchard, a white landlord. There were no other people of color in their neighborhood. The black barber William Jacobs, his mixed wife Mary A., and their two children resided in an altogether different white neighborhood. All of the other people of color lived in two adjacent houses within a third, otherwise white neighborhood. The homeowner of one dwelling was Caleb Easton, a brother of Hosea Easton who had died more than twenty years earlier. Caleb's wife Chloe (Packard), who was white, one adult daughter, and a white boarder completed the family. Also under the same roof was George Washington Easton, one of Caleb and Chloe's sons, his white wife Sarah Jane Powell (born in England), their children, and a sister. Last was Chandler Ross, who was white and—like the other men in the house—a shoemaker. He and his wife Sarah Dunbar Easton, a daughter of Caleb and Chloe, had two children at the time, and two white boarders.

Bootmakers headed families in the house next door. Sylvanus E. Sewell was head of household, or perhaps landlord, for three family units. He lived with his wife Lydia A. and their three children. It was a mixed family to the extent that the census record defined each family member as mixed. Caleb and Chloe Easton's son, Caleb Jr., his mixed wife Eunice A., and their two children formed another family. More complicated was the third unit comprising Parmenas Pierce and Rebecca L. Spooner. They both were thirty-one years of age; he was mixed and she white. Listed with different surnames, they weren't married at the time. Pierce previously had been married to Fanny L. (Wood), and she probably had died by 1860. Parmenas and Rebecca may have cohabited outside of marriage for a short while, but the 1865 Massachusetts census has them married with a four-year-old child and living in Stoughton.[14]

The African American and mixed families may have encountered slights and insults in North Bridgewater, but there is no record of such antagonisms. Six family groups connected by family and occupation lived in close proximity to one another, but two others—one mixed, one African American—lived quite separate from other families of color. This appears to have been a matter of choice rather than of fear or of comradery of color. Such variety of housing arrangements was typical, though not universal, for New England towns with small African American populations and few mixed marriages.

A majority of New Englanders in a mixed marriage were born in the same state where they later resided with their spouse, and the figure increases to nearly two-thirds when adding those born in another of the New England states (see Appendix 5). Almost 10 percent were born in the

Mid-Atlantic states, nearly 5 percent were born in the South, and roughly 20 percent were foreign-born. Those statistics apply to the entire time period up to the Civil War. But there were changes over time and differences between New England states. During the 1850s, there was a sharp decline in the percentage of those who were born in the same state where they later dwelled, and a comparable marked increase in the number of foreign-born. To a certain extent these shifts show the volatility of small numbers, but nevertheless they also mirror the general history of the region.

These statistics are more meaningful when connected to specific people. Francis Green began life in Colrain, Massachusetts, close to the Vermont border. His uncle taught him the trade of blacksmithing, and he also worked for a few years as a teamster. Nearing the age of twenty in 1835, he moved to Brattleboro, Vermont, where Andrew Bradshaw, the town's only barber, introduced him to the craft. Once he was confident in his skills, Green departed for Massachusetts where he practiced barbering in Greenfield. By 1855, Bradshaw had died and his family—for a while the only people of color in Brattleboro—had left. "Barber Green" (as he was called most of his adult life), by then a widower and with a small son in tow, returned to Brattleboro and set up shop. Two years later he married Madelia (Pierce), a white woman native to Vermont. They had one child who died in infancy. Their marriage lasted until 1880 when Madelia died of tuberculosis. By then, Green was sixty-five years old, and he soon retired from barbering. He may have been weary of cutting hair and shaving whiskers, but three other barbers—all white—were then providing competition. He was the last barber of color in Brattleboro that century. Green may have moved frequently early in life, but even so he stayed in a small territory of northern Massachusetts and southern Vermont. Madelia never left her home state.[15]

Mont Vernon was a small upland town in southern New Hampshire, particularly suited to the production of apples and blueberries. During the nineteenth century its population never reached 1,000 inhabitants. Yet four mixed couples—all of whom spent their entire lives within the state—made Mont Vernon their home. Cesar Parker, a black laborer, and his white wife Margaret (Spear), were the first on record. They lived for at least twenty years in the town. When they both died in the mid-1850s within a year of each other (she eighty-one and he ninety), three other mixed families had joined the community. All of the men were laborers, and they moved regularly between towns in central Hillsborough County.

In 1860, they were in Mont Vernon. Two of the families were related. Daniel Douglas, who was white, and Mehitable (Johonnot), who was mixed, had three children, one of whom, James, lived with them. Another son Peter resided close by with his white wife Nancy. From September 1862 until June 1865, he served in Company B of the New Hampshire 13th Infantry Regiment. The third couple, Joseph and Sarah Haskel (he mixed, she white), lived in a separate part of town with their four children. Every person of color in mid-century Mont Vernon was a spouse in a mixed marriage.[16]

Although the 1880 census stated that his father was Swedish, each census from 1860 to 1880 declared Frederick Allen to be black. Born in Pennsylvania in 1812, he worked his way up the maritime trade, eventually becoming a sea captain. He owned real estate worth $1,000, and his personal property was nearly as valuable. His time on land was productive as well. He and his white wife Climinia settled in Eden, Maine (her home state), and reared twelve children. Frederick Allen and his children were the only people of color in the entire town.[17]

Eight of the twenty-nine people originally from the South came to New England already in a mixed marriage. The two couples from Virginia—David and Betsey Burow who settled in Orange, Connecticut, and George and Sarah Thompson in Cambridge, Massachusetts—fled from a state where mixed marriages were illegal. But the two couples from South Carolina—P. J. and Charlotte Besslow who moved to New Bedford, Massachusetts, and D. S. and Martha Hayward to Cambridge, Massachusetts—had broken no laws by their marriages. In both Virginia marriages the husbands were black while the wives in the South Carolina marriages were of African descent. There is no indication whether any of them had been slaves.[18]

Three-quarters of those in mixed marriages who migrated from outside the United States came from Ireland, England, or Canada. Others trickled in from western Europe, South America, Mexico, the Caribbean, Africa, and islands off Africa. Most of the men who came from England (the second most represented country) arrived as laborers or with no particular skills. John Barnes was different. He was a spinner who brought his craft to the cotton mills of Fall River, Rhode Island. There he met and married Louise E. Barnes, herself an immigrant from the West Indies (one record has her coming from South Carolina). His early training paid off, and by 1870 at the age of thirty-five he already had accumulated $2,000 worth of real estate and personal property valued at $400.[19]

By far the most numerous people from outside the United States who married African Americans were the Irish, most of whom had fled famine in their home country. There were fifty-four mixed marriages with an Irish spouse, spread through every New England state and in thirty-three different towns. More than a quarter were in greater Boston (Boston, 9; Chelsea, 3; Charlestown, 2; Cambridge, 1). Most of these households—like the general population—were located near the ocean or a navigable river. But a few were as remote as Rutland, Vermont, and Williamstown, Massachusetts. Of all states and countries where people in mixed marriages were born, Ireland's 54 were the fourth most numerous, trailing Massachusetts with its 142, Connecticut with 69, and Maine with 61. Most Irish came to New England poor and lived in neighborhoods with other impoverished people, including many African Americans. Although there were antagonisms, there should be no surprise that there also were marriages. Boston's sixth ward had more people of color and more marriages with Irish spouses than any other ward, and as elsewhere in the city, all of the Irish spouses were female. Boston's experience was just a slight exaggeration of the rest of the region. For all of New England, forty-six Irish spouses (85 percent) were female; only eight were male (15 percent). All of the men were laborers, except William Greawnay of Falmouth, Maine, who was a fisherman, and Patrick Gleason of Stewartstown, New Hampshire, who was a farmer with real estate worth $1,000.[20]

The Irish pattern of husbands of color married to white wives proved to be the general norm. Nearly four out of five of the 410 mixed marriages had a husband who public records listed as black or mixed and a white wife. There were slight variations from state to state, but—except in Rhode Island with only ten marriages—the pattern was constant. White marriage partners, moreover, generally preferred mixed to black spouses. In 1850 and 1860 according to the dubious distinctions of census takers, 57 percent of white wives had mixed rather than black husbands (126 to 97), and 70 percent of white husbands had mixed rather than black wives (51 to 22). This tendency probably reflects reality, but considering that such a prominent person as Amos G. Beman was at times designated as mixed and at others as black we shouldn't exaggerate its value.

At least half of the people in mixed marriages were poor, as is demonstrated by the occupations of the men and their real estate holdings (see appendices 6 and 7). A majority of them were unskilled laborers, fishermen, sailors, and small farmers. Only one-quarter of the men in mixed marriages held real estate, and many of those holdings were meager, valued at only $300 or less. Even so, there were a surprising number of families who were solidly middle class or slightly better off. Farmers and skilled laborers, despite the fluctuations of weather and employment opportunities, had the security of land and expertise, and people engaged in service (such as barbers and porters), shopkeepers, and professionals were sometimes able to accumulate substantial wealth.[21]

Less than 20 percent of unskilled laborers owned real property, and those who did possessed low-valued land. Two exceptions were the Irishman John Doyle who with his mixed wife Elizabeth lived in Calais, Maine, and Isaac B. Anthony who with his Irish wife Bridget resided in Uxbridge, Massachusetts. Each of those men held $1,000 worth of real estate in a census where Doyle was described as a day laborer and Anthony as a farmworker. No other unskilled laborer owned more than $500 worth of property, and most possessed $300 worth or less. Machelon Freeman (listed as black in the census) of Gardner, Massachusetts, was more typical in several ways. In 1850 and 1860, roughly half of all black males in mixed marriages were unskilled laborers while the percentage of mixed males and white males was no more than 41 percent, generally lower. Married to Mary Freeman (listed as white), Freeman worked as a general laborer and as a stone layer. Somehow the Massachusetts native acquired $400 worth of property by 1860, though it was downgraded to $200 by 1870. He and his wife supported six children.[22]

Five of the eleven fishermen in mixed marriages owned real estate. Four of them lived in Maine (Stephen Darling, Charles Leavitt, and John Marks in Harpswell, and William Greawnay in Falmouth) and the fifth, Thomas Howland with his white wife Dorcas (Ellis), resided on Cape Cod at Brewster. Both born in the area, the Howlands were a young couple when they married—he twenty years of age and she but seventeen. Thomas, a jack-of-all-trades, made the most of what employment opportunities there were. He fished, he shipped out as a sailor, and he worked for others on their farms. Together they had four children, but as he was so frequently at sea, Dorcas must have been the more attentive parent. They eventually acquired $400 worth of real estate, second highest among the fishermen.[23]

Although records show that approximately 20 percent of mariners in the database owned real property, that figure is inflated because it includes master mariners and one sea captain. More revealing is the fact that thirty-two of the forty-one mariners—these certainly common sailors—didn't own land. Stephen Snow was one of the more fortunate. He met Susannah

M. (Foster) in his hometown of Rochester, Massachusetts, near the coast east of New Bedford. She was from Georgia and a person of color. They married just months after the Massachusetts legislature repealed the mixed marriage law and stayed together through their long lives. By 1850, he had earned enough from his sea voyages, supplemented by income from working as a shipwright, to attain $900 worth of real estate. One of their children died as a toddler but two others lived to adulthood. Shortly after the conclusion of the Civil War they moved to Florida, where he became an orange grower and she became white.[24]

Farmers, of course, were the group that overwhelmingly owned real estate. Thirty-one of the thirty-seven in mixed marriages owned property ranging in worth from $100 to $8,000. Sloppy census taking or tenant farming explains the six who may not have owned the land on which they worked. The extremes in property values are deceptive, for most lived in a comfortable middle range. Only seven farmers owned land worth less than $400 and only three held property valued above $2,000. Benjamin Capron (listed as white) was born in Massachusetts shortly after the Revolution as was his wife Elizabeth (Haynes), daughter of the distinguished African American minister Lemuel Haynes and Elizabeth (Babbit). They must have met in Rutland, Vermont, where Lemuel Haynes led the Congregational church. As the Caprons grew older (by nineteenth-century standards), they built one of the most valuable farms in the area, worth $8,000. Perhaps part of their success can be attributed to cheap labor. In 1850 they still had four adult children living with them as well as a younger daughter and five other people ranging in age from eleven to twenty-two. Census records listed the three adult sons as laborers. The oldest son Nelson was forty-one and listed as "idiotic." Another son was a farmer on adjacent land. More typical in value of his land, if not in other characteristics, was Thomas Sharp who by 1860 had developed a farm worth $1,200 in Windsor, Connecticut. Sharp, quite likely, was a fugitive slave from New York who had done well. He married Wealthy (Griswold) Stevens (listed as white) in 1833, and they had three children. He lived to be seventy-eight and she to be at least seventy-two.[25]

One-third of the skilled workers in mixed marriages (18 of 53) owned real estate that generally indicated comfortable lives; only three of them held property worth less than $600. None of them—with the highest value of their real estate $2,000—came close to the wealth of farmer Benjamin Capron, but their economic status would have placed them as solid citizens in their communities. There was a wide variety of skills

represented among them—carpenters, coopers, masons, blacksmiths, a
surprising diversity considering the employment restrictions on people
of color. The most common occupation among the skilled workers was
shoemaker, and Emory Cobb's $1,400 worth of property was middling for
that trade. His heritage was both African and European, and his second
wife Catherine (Parmeter) had only European ancestors. They both were
born in Massachusetts and lived in Natick. Although over fifty years old, he
enlisted in the 23rd United States Colored Infantry in May 1864 but died
from an unnamed disease in Boston five months later. The white carpenter Marcellus Martin Parker, the son of a physician, also served in the Civil
War but returned home safely to Rockland, Maine. He had an extra incen-
tive in fighting for the Union, for his wife Jesse Acker was a former slave
from Florida. Her mother had been a slave, and her father was white, presumably her owner. How she relocated in Maine is unknown, but she and
her husband had five children and acquired real estate valued at $700.[26]

The most striking characteristic of those who provided service was
that they all were people of color, with those listed as mixed more numerous than those listed as black. People in mid-nineteenth-century New
England viewed service occupations—waiters, porters, stewards, barbers,
and others—as African American work, both an advantage and a stigma
for those so engaged. This was a small window of opportunity for men
of African descent. Barbering was the most common occupation among
those in mixed marriages who owned real estate. Nine of the twelve
men in service fields cut hair for a living, and they were relatively prosperous. Only Albert Alexander of Calais, Maine, held property valued at
less than $1,000. The others, including Francis Green and Edward Jakes,
had real estate worth between $1,000 and $2,500. Edward Cassell (listed
both as black and mixed) began as a porter but did even better when he
became a caterer, amassing by 1870 real estate worth $6,000 and per-
sonal property valued at $8,000. He and his Irish wife Margaret lived in
Salem, Massachusetts, and had no children of record. Bostonian William
H. Lewis found serving as a steward, a waiter, and a cook relatively lucrative. He was one of only two Bostonians (both people of color) in mixed
marriages who had acquired real property, and his was worth $4,500. It
was a second marriage for his white wife Emeline Cutter (Leathers), who
had been born in Danville, Vermont. They lived in Boston's sixth ward on
Southac Street in the heart of the African American community.[27]

Nearly all shopkeepers in mixed marriages (five of seven) held real
property, and all but one of them was a person of color—the exception

being the saloonkeeper Thomas Snow. Of the five, the two grocers had middling properties valued at $700 and $800, the two saloon keepers possessed real estate worth $1,700 and $3,000, and, wealthiest of all, a clothing retailer held real estate worth a whopping $9,500. Samuel Copeland (listed as black, from Virginia, and thirty-seven years old), his Irish wife Alice, seven children, and a servant lived in Chelsea outside of Boston in 1860. His income from selling clothing not only provided a substantial home, but it also supported the large household and left him personal property (most likely in part inventory) worth $3,500.[28]

None of the nine professionals—clergymen and physicians—was white. Five of the group held landed property that, with the exception of the real estate of the physician Miles Williams of Norridgewock, Maine, that was worth only $150, was quite valuable. Late in his life, New Haven clergyman Amos G. Beman held property valued at $5,000, but two physicians—James M. Solomon of Attleborough, Massachusetts, and Samuel Birmingham who moved from Pelham, New Hampshire, to New Bedford, Massachusetts—owned real estate worth $10,000 each. More moderate were the $1,500 holdings of John N. Mars. Mars overcame his modest beginnings as the son of former slaves in Norwalk, Connecticut. As a young man he converted to Christianity and eventually was ordained as a Methodist minister. He served congregations in New York and New Jersey before settling in Athol, Massachusetts, where his first wife Silvia (Gordon) died in 1838. Eight years later he traveled to Salem where he married his second wife Elizabeth J. (Holt) who was white, seven years his junior, and a native of nearby Beverly, Massachusetts. Mars was an abolitionist, and during the Civil War he became an advocate of African American military service. At the age of fifty-eight he was commissioned an officer and became the chaplain of the 35th US Colored Infantry Regiment. But he was too old for the rigors of military life and received an honorable discharge in November 1863. He returned to the ministry in New England and a decade later retired to Athol where he and Elizabeth died.[29]

Mixed marriages exemplified a breakdown in the caste system, but it is unlikely that many people entered such unions as a political act. There were easier, though not necessarily painless, ways to advocate equal rights. Part of the attraction for some spouses may have been flaunting convention, enjoying a foray into subversion. Perhaps status mattered to some. Whiteness, regardless of class, generally offered higher status than darkness. The opposite side of the equation would be a white person attracted to a wealthier—or less poor—person of color. Equivalency could be a factor in any marriage, not just mixed marriages. Real estate might be balanced by movable property, or higher social standing by ready cash. A prosperous black barber, for example, might even the scale with a poor white woman. There are many possibilities to explain why a couple might marry, but we can analyze too far. Human beings don't always make deliberate choices. Other sparks may fly that attract two people together. Love like racism comes in many forms.

PART V

Hitting the Wall

11

Fugitives

FOR THOSE IN the struggle for equal rights, complacency was never an option. An advance could always be reversed. African American men had been eligible to vote in all the New England states at the beginning of the nineteenth century, for example, but by 1820 both Rhode Island and Connecticut had withdrawn that basic right. The town of Nantucket had desegregated its schools one year, re-established segregation the next, and ultimately opened its schools to all children by the mid-1840s. By 1850 there seemed to have been progress in New England. Although the region's brand of racism still was prevalent, there were few remaining laws that promoted caste. But New England was not an island impervious to outside authority. The central government could interject policies protecting the interests of the southern, slaveholding elite—as well as of other special interests. Vigilance was essential.

The threat that the slaveholding states would leave the Union produced political remedies in the nation's capital that challenged the advances of people of color in New England. Led by old warhorses Henry Clay and Daniel Webster, who were joined by younger politicians with leadership ambitions, the central government passed a series of laws designed to retain southern loyalties while still offering tidbits tasty enough to attract necessary northern votes. The so-called Compromise of 1850 pleased few, angered many, but postponed disunion. One of its components, the Fugitive Slave Law, placed the freedom of all African Americans in jeopardy—a price that southern slaveholders demanded and enough others in Congress were willing to pay.[1]

Ostensibly the purpose of the Fugitive Slave Law was to give slaveholders the means to retrieve escaped slaves outside the jurisdiction of the owner's home state, particularly those areas hostile to slavery and with

personal liberty laws. The law required United States marshals and deputies to assist slaveowners in capturing people of color, supposedly their
escaped slaves. Marshals in turn were authorized to deputize anyone in
the vicinity to lend help. Refusal to participate or obstruction of the process subjected the marshal or civilian to a steep fine or criminal prosecution. The law instructed the captors to take the alleged fugitive slave
before a federal commissioner where the owner or his representative had
to demonstrate ownership—either through a slave-state affidavit or a witness' testimony. The commissioner received a $5.00 fee if he denied the
owner's claim and $10.00 if he declared the person of color a fugitive slave
and subject to the slaver's will—all paid, as were all other expenses, by the
federal treasury. The alleged slave had no right to habeas corpus, to testify
on his own behalf, or to have a jury trial. The flimsiest evidence potentially
could send any African American into slavery, should the commissioner
agree. Although the Fugitive Slave Law may have had the limited goal of
returning escaped slaves to slavery, its neglect of real protection for the
accused opened the possibility that anyone with dark skin could be made
a slave.[2] This was a calculated slap in the face of northern abolitionists and
a genuine threat to all free African Americans.

The reaction of people of color was immediate and often they panicked.
Within Boston alone, forty people fled for Canada in the first three days
after the law's passage. With as many as one-fifth of all black Bostonians
fugitives from bondage, the fear of capture or even the kidnapping of
long-time residents was palpable. By early October, at least 200 African
Americans had left the city, the "cradle of liberty" known for its Massacre,
Tea Party, and nearby Bunker Hill. Membership in black churches plummeted. The African Methodist Church quickly declined by eighty-five congregants, the Twelfth Baptist Church by sixty, and on it went. Nearly all
of the frightened migrants were fugitive slaves, but some were relatives
of those in greatest danger and a few were freeborn people of color who
feared for their own safety and despaired of justice.[3]

Almost immediately after President Millard Fillmore signed the
Fugitive Slave Act into law, people of African descent began to organize
for their mutual defense from slave catchers. Black citizens of Portland,
Maine, resolved that in the absence of constitutional guarantees they
would "protect our own right to freedom, at whatever cost or risk." People
of color in Springfield, Massachusetts, proclaimed that under the circumstances they would use "every means which the god of love has placed in
our power to sustain our liberty," and they created a Vigilance Association

to guard any fugitive from capture and to identify oppressors. African American Bostonians met as a political body at the end of September, and they repeated the need for self-protection. Aware that all in their community were in jeopardy and that heavy penalties forestalled their usual allies, they—like their compatriots in Portland and Springfield—referred to laws higher than those made by humans. "As we prefer liberty to life," they declared, "we mutually pledge to defend ourselves and each other in resisting this god-defying and inhuman law, at any and every sacrifice, invoking Heaven's defence of the right." At a meeting the following week they prepared to create a "League of Freedom, composed of all those who are ready to resist the law."[4] These were words that David Walker would have applauded.

Walker even would have been encouraged by the response of most white New Englanders. There were a few, such as the textile entrepreneur Amos A. Lawrence, who actively supported the Fugitive Slave Law. Lawrence went so far as to offer help "in any capacity" to a marshal. Others with economic connections to the slave states—manufacturers and workers alike—were happy that the Union had been preserved but disappointed that the political package had included such a drastic measure. The vast majority of white New Englanders, however, believed the Law to be a travesty of justice and a blight on the region's Revolutionary ideals. Understanding public sentiment, New England politicians holding office in Washington stayed clear of the Fugitive Slave Bill. Not a single senator voted for it, although four—Hamlin of Maine, Hale of New Hampshire, Clarke of Rhode Island, and Phelps of Vermont—absented themselves. Daniel Webster had left the Senate to become secretary of state in the Fillmore administration. Only one New England representative, Samuel A. Eliot of Boston, voted for its passage. Those who opposed the law proved prescient, for Free Soilers joined by "conscience Whigs" and Democrats swept the ensuing fall elections in New England, a clear rebuke to the law and its supporters.[5]

Sparked both by the injustice of the law and by the flight of black residents, many New England towns held meetings. Some were little more than a slight expansion of the local antislavery society, but many drew in a broad spectrum of townspeople of both African and European descent. They sought to express their opposition to the Fugitive Slave Law, their concern for the safety of people of color, and their wish that those who had fled would return. Lowell, Worcester, and Milford in quick succession passed resolutions not only proclaiming their outrage at the unconstitutionality of the law but also creating specific means of repelling attempts to capture any person of color. Worcester citizens pledged "our lives, our fortunes, and our sacred honor" that they would not allow "a fugitive from labor" to be apprehended. They established a Vigilance Committee, which among its duties was to ring the town bells "to alarm the whole population" whenever a US Marshal or anyone else came to town to capture a fugitive.[6]

Boston's African American community requested that all the city's residents meet in protest, and the response demonstrated how times were changing. Three hundred of the city's prominent and well-established citizens signed an invitation calling for the people of Boston to meet at venerable Faneuil Hall to consider the impact of the Fugitive Slave Law and what could be done. The former mayor of Boston, Josiah Quincy, who had led raids on black neighborhoods in 1823, headed the list of signatories. The son and grandson of American presidents, Charles Francis Adams, added his name. Even as unlikely a prospect as William Lincoln, who had led the fight in the state legislature a decade before to preserve the prohibition on mixed marriages, signed on. Abolitionists' names sprinkled the list, and almost without exception they came from high status professions—the ministers Theodore Parker and Samuel May, the lawyers Richard H. Dana Jr. and Charles Sumner, and the physician Henry I. Bowditch. Although he had attended the earlier African American meetings, William Lloyd Garrison's name was missing. Lewis Hayden, who would play a leading role in opposition to the Fugitive Slave Law, was the token person of color on the list. More outspoken members of the community such as William C. Nell and Robert Morris, although they would attend the meeting, were omitted. The signatories—though missing the textile entrepreneurs of the city—represented much of Boston's elite and middle class, and their presence assured other residents that active opposition to the Fugitive Slave Law was mainstream and not the work of the fringe.[7]

The tactic worked, and on October 14, Boston citizens filled the hall. Most of the seats in the gallery were reserved for women, and men sat and stood everywhere else. There were no areas prohibited to people of color, who constituted a "considerable number." According to *The Liberator* the assemblage consisted of "the bone and muscle, the earnest and true, the moral and religious, the reliable and invincible portions of the community." After an opening prayer, Charles Francis Adams, the presiding officer, addressed his fellow townspeople. The "spirit of caste," Adams explained, had led Congress to pass a law that placed one segment of the population in jeopardy of losing its freedom and threatened with prosecution anyone else who attempted to intervene. Only the accident of birth determined who was oppressor and who was victim. Adams called on the audience to imagine a reversal of circumstances where they were persecuted by the "most absolute government in Europe." He then referred to "the higher law of God" that prevailed over the law of tyrants but hesitated from advising any "measures of violence or excess." Adams refrained from advocating violation of the law, but just barely. "Words . . . are of little avail in this struggle," he exhorted the responsive crowd. "We must act." What those actions should be included working to overturn the law, but there was a hint that he believed even more should be done to stop injustice.[8]

Frederick Douglass was less discreet. Still fatigued from his journey to Boston from his home in Rochester, New York, he took the podium as the authorized spokesman for the city's black community. Along the route he had witnessed and heard the despair and fear of a "suffering and horror-stricken people." Many were leaving for Canada "without the means to live" and those who remain "imploringly ask you what you will do to protect them from the pursuing bloodhounds." Bringing cheers from the crowd, Douglass declared that fugitives were entitled to their freedom. "Fortitude, determination, and downright heroism" had brought them to the North, and slaveowners primarily wanted to capture them as examples to those still in bondage. He described several instances of the perils of escaping slavery and asked whether those assembled in Faneuil Hall "would consent that these fugitives should be taken back." The crowd resoundingly shouted "No!" He then described the torture of a woman who had been recaptured and asked whether the audience "would let the slave-hunters carry that woman back." Again "No!" thundered from throughout the hall. At the conclusion of a skillful address, Douglass reminded those present that people of color were too few to defend themselves from the will of 18 million whites. If Bostonians did nothing, their streets would flow with the "innocent blood" of those resisting re-enslavement.[9]

To assure anyone still not moved by Douglass or Adams that the meeting was in the tradition of their forebears, Richard Henry Dana Jr. read a letter from Josiah Quincy—too old and infirm to attend—recalling that Massachusetts had opposed the capture of fugitive slaves on its soil for all the years of its statehood and would continue to do so for another sixty years, despite the Fugitive Slave Law. Dana then presented a series of resolutions condemning the law as contradictory to the Declaration of Independence and the Constitution, refusing to assist in "returning a fugitive," and calling for the law's repeal. The most radical resolution stated that "we individually pledge to our colored fellow-citizens who may be endangered by this law, all the aid, co-operation, and relief, which the obligations of each of us to the supreme law of God and right impose upon us" and entreated all who had fled to return. The last resolution created a committee of fifty to serve as a Vigilance Committee. After speeches by various antislavery luminaries, including Wendell Phillips, Theodore Parker, and Charles Lenox Remond, the hall passed the resolutions unanimously. The Reverend Mr. Culver was the last speaker, and to the delight of the crowd he commented that the resolutions didn't go far enough. He proposed that an additional resolution: that "Constitution or no Constitution, Law or no Law, we will not allow a fugitive slave to be taken from Massachusetts." Amidst "great and prolonged applause," it too passed.[10]

Until this point the Fugitive Slave Law was only an abstract threat to the people of New England, but that soon would change. No later than October 22—only slightly more than a month after the enactment of the Law—two slave catchers from Macon, Georgia, arrived in Boston intent on capturing William and Ellen Craft. The Crafts had been in the city for nearly two years, and in abolitionist circles the story of their escape was renowned for how they had outwitted their masters and authorities. They both were native to Georgia. She was the daughter of her first master and a slave mother and was "almost white," so white that she was "frequently mistaken for a child of the family." Her mistress was so embarrassed and annoyed by the confusion of visitors that she gave the eleven-year-old Ellen to her daughter as a wedding present. As a maid to her new owners, she became a family favorite and had her own small room. William, who was tall with European features but skin dark enough to stamp him as a slave, had been trained as a cabinetmaker. After meeting as young adults, they fell in love, but Ellen was reluctant to marry, not wanting to raise children in slavery. They married despite her reservations, and in December 1848, devised a plan to run away.[11]

With roughly a thousand miles across the slave states between Macon, Georgia, and Philadelphia, it was no simple matter to gain freedom, but their strategy was ingenious. Because Ellen could pass for white, William suggested that they travel as master and slave. It would be unthinkable for a female mistress to be accompanied by her male slave; so Ellen would have to be disguised as a man. Reluctant at first to attempt the impersonation, Ellen soon agreed to take the risk if William would purchase her attire. That was the next obstacle, for in Georgia it was illegal for anyone to sell goods to a slave without the master's consent. William, however, was

ELLEN CRAFT.   WILLIAM CRAFT.

FIGURE II.I *Ellen and William Craft*, from Still, *The Underground Railroad*, plate following 368.

aware that just about anything was available for a price, and he discreetly bought separate items from different sellers. Ellen made a pair of pants to complete the ensemble. To avoid immediate detection of their departure, they took advantage of the Christmas custom among "some of the best slaveholders" to give passes to their favorite slaves for a few days' holiday. As the day of their escape approached, Ellen realized that they would have to register their names at hotels along the way and at the Charleston cus-tomhouse. Their problem was that neither of them could read or write and that they would have to persuade someone to sign for them. Ellen hit on the plan of binding her right hand in a poultice and a sling and "with propriety ask the officers to register my name for me." To offset her smooth chin, she decided to make a second poultice to be wrapped in a handkerchief covering her lower face and tied at the top of her head. Last, William bought her green spectacles. He required no special costume, but he purchased a white beaver hat that would cover his hair and forehead.[12]

Early in the morning on December 21 after William cut Ellen's hair "square at the back," they set out for freedom. They took separate routes to the railroad station where Ellen as a young gentleman purchased tick-ets for herself and her slave. William sat in the "negro car" while Ellen had her first experience of sitting in a regular railroad car as an equal to the other passengers. Just before the train left on its 200-mile journey to Savannah, a gentleman sat down beside Ellen. She nearly panicked, for she recognized Mr. Cray, a friend of her master and a frequent visitor to their home. He had dined with the family on the previous day. Cray

on occasion had spoken with Ellen, and she now feared he would rec-
ognize her voice. When he attempted to strike up a conversation, Ellen
feigned deafness. Fortunately, he respected her "disability," and she
and William arrived in Savannah that evening without further incident.
Upon reaching the steamboat for Charleston, Ellen bolted for her cabin
and William explained that his master had severe rheumatism. And so it
went. At Charleston they learned that the steamer for Philadelphia didn't
operate during the winter, but they were able to take a different ship to
Wilmington, North Carolina. Forced to improvise a new route, they took
a train to Richmond, Virginia, and another to just beyond Fredericksburg
where they traveled on a steamer for Washington, DC, before boarding
another train for Baltimore. By then, three and a half stressful days had
passed, since they had fled Macon. It was now Christmas Eve. All that
separated them from freedom was one last railroad ride to Philadelphia.[13]

Initially all went well. William saw "his master" onto her car; but as he
was about to enter his, an officer on the platform stopped him. Because
so many fugitives went through Baltimore for Pennsylvania—the first free
state north, there were special regulations and surveillance. The officer
asked William where he was headed. When William respectfully answered
"Philadelphia" and with his master, the officer informed him that he was
going no farther unless his master "can satisfy them in the office that he
has a right to take him along." William notified Ellen of their predicament,
and together they fearfully walked to the office with no plan in mind. To
make matters worse, the train was soon to depart. Any delay increased the
possibility that they would be caught and punished. Ellen summoned all
the courage she had and boldly asked what was the problem. The person
in charge reiterated what the officer on the platform had told William.
That attracted the attention "of the large number of bustling passengers"
who sympathized with an "invalid" young slaveholder. Encouraged by the
crowd around her, Ellen insisted that she had purchased tickets for herself
and her slave in Charleston for Philadelphia and should not be impeded.
The officer held his ground and repeated that the master and his slave
could go no farther without proper identification. As the bell rang for the
train's departure, the officer ran his fingers through his hair not sure what
to do and then, somehow softening, told the conductor to let them board.
Early Christmas morning they arrived safely in Philadelphia.[14]

The Crafts were fortunate to meet local abolitionists who recommended
that they go to Boston where it would be safer. After a three-week sojourn
with a Quaker family they traveled north without incident. William set

up a shop as a cabinetmaker and Ellen contributed to the family income as a seamstress. By 1850, they lived in the heart of the Boston African American community in the sixth ward and under the roof of Lewis Hayden, a prominent member of the Vigilance Committee. In October 1850, the slave catchers Hughes and Knight, representing the Crafts' former owners, appeared in town, threatening their growing prosperity and, most important, their freedom. The agents quickly acquired a warrant for the Crafts' capture from Judge Levi Woodbury and presented it to a United States Marshal. Not waiting for the marshal to take the Crafts into custody, Knight wrote a letter to William Craft attempting to entice him and Ellen to his hotel. William had been warned and saw through the ruse. The abolitionist Henry I. Bowditch transported Ellen to the home of Ellis Gray Loring in Brookline, but William was determined to stay and defend his freedom. When Bowditch met Craft in his shop, the cabinetmaker had a "horse pistol" on his bench along with his tools.[15]

After a week the marshal still had not served the warrant, and the slave catchers were experiencing duress. The Vigilance Committee, now boosted to more than 100 members with thirty to forty of them members of the bar, immediately began a campaign of harassing Hughes and Knight. Defenders posted placards describing the two men throughout Boston, and authorities arrested Hughes and Knight for slandering William Craft. Only after posting bail of $10,000 did they escape jail, but they were arrested twice more during the first week for conspiring to abduct William Craft. Each time they posted bail of $10,000, by then totaling $30,000. Simultaneously, members of the Vigilance Committee repeatedly called on the slave catchers and advised them to leave town. Boston's African American community, including those on the Vigilance Committee, met at Belknap Church and resolved "to resist unto death any attempt upon our liberties." Nearly two weeks after arriving in Boston, Hughes and Knight, frustrated by the unwillingness of local authorities to fulfill requirements of the Fugitive Slave Law and intimidated by implied threats, scurried from the city. The situation, nonetheless, remained perilous for fugitive slaves, and the Crafts decided to leave the country. Needing to be less conspicuous than attempting to leave from an American port, they soon sailed from Halifax, Nova Scotia, to England where they lived until the end of the Civil War. Their former masters sent word to President Millard Fillmore of the resistance in Boston, and an infuriated Fillmore vowed to make sure the Fugitive Slave Law was enforced in the future.[16]

Although few Bostonians publicly supported slavery or the Fugitive Slave Law, a substantial number were shocked that an October meeting in Faneuil Hall resolved to resist a law—particularly one designed to preserve the Union by appeasing the South—and that the Crafts and their allies (including officials who never executed the warrant) had put the resolution into action. In typical Boston fashion, they called for their own meeting in Faneuil Hall. On a Tuesday afternoon in late November 1850, they packed the hall and passed resolutions lauding the Constitution, the "Compromise," and law and order. Without naming the Crafts or anyone else directly, they condemned those who would defy the "supreme law of the land." This "Union" meeting like others in the North that fall intended to assure southern slaveholders that northerners would keep their part of the congressional deal.[17]

The next fugitive for whom a warrant was issued in Boston, Frederick Minkins (his slave name was Shadrach), would not avoid capture as easily. Minkins had fled from John DeBree, a purser in the United States Navy stationed at Norfolk, Virginia, on May 3, 1850. By February 1851, he was working as a waiter at Taft's Cornhill Coffee House, just a block from the Boston courthouse. Somehow DeBree learned where Minkins was, and he sent John Caphart with documents and the power to represent his interests. It was rumored in the Boston press that DeBree wanted to test whether the city would enforce the Fugitive Slave Law. Caphart arrived on February 12, soon received a warrant from Commissioner George T. Curtis, and gave it to a marshal under the command of Deputy Marshal Patrick Riley. United States Marshall Charles Devens was away in Washington, DC, and Riley as principal marshal was in charge.[18]

Riley planned to apprehend Minkins early in the morning of February 15, but none of the marshals were familiar with the alleged fugitive's appearance. He eventually arranged to have deputies stationed nearby the Coffee House and for a witness who could identify Minkins to meet them there. When Riley arrived around 11 o'clock, the identifier had not appeared. Riley and another marshal, Frederick Warren, entered the Coffee House and to avoid suspicion sat down and ordered coffee. Their waiter fit the description of DeBree's slave Shadrach. He had a "dark copper complexion, about five feet eight inches high, rather stout built." But still the witness who could confirm the fugitive's identity hadn't shown up. Riley and Warren paid the waiter and rose to leave. The waiter, who indeed was Minkins, went to the barroom to deposit the money, and there two deputy marshals grabbed him and whisked him the short distance to the courtroom. Riley

rushed to inform the City Marshal that they might need crowd control outside the courthouse and to alert the mayor of the situation. By 11:30 he was
in the courtroom with the prisoner, deputies, and Commissioner Curtis.[19]

Seth J. Thomas appeared as the attorney for DeBree, and Curtis asked
Minkins if he wanted counsel. Minkins did. During the delay until the
defendant's lawyers arrived, the courtroom filled with spectators—black
and white, men and women. Minkins' legal team (Samuel E. Sewall,
Ellis Gray Loring, Charles List, Richard H. Dana Jr., Charles G. Davis,
and Robert H. Morris) were all members of the Vigilance Committee.
After talking with Minkins, they asked to see the documents supporting
DeBree's claim that his runaway slave Shadrach and Frederick Minkins
were the same man. They also requested a postponement of the hearing
so that they could prepare a defense. Thomas objected, but Curtis set the
hearing for Tuesday morning, three days later. During the time Minkins'
lawyers were examining the documents, Riley realized he had a problem. As a result of the Latimer Law, no city jail could be used to confine
an alleged fugitive slave. He sent a deputy marshal to ask Commodore
Downes whether there was a place at the Navy Yard where Minkins could
be detained until Tuesday. Downes turned down the request. The courtroom would have to serve as the prisoner's cell. Curtis then ordered the
courtroom to be cleared. Minutes later, by then about 2 o'clock in the
afternoon, all who remained were Minkins; one of his lawyers Charles
G. Davis; Elizur Wright, the editor of the *Commonwealth*; Riley; and about
six other deputy marshals. The area outside the courthouse and the hallways inside quickly filled with African Americans. Riley commanded
Wright and Minkins' lawyer to leave. As they opened the door, between
ten and fifteen black men (some reports stated as many as 100) burst into
the room and helped Minkins escape. He had been held for three hours.
Within days, he was safely in Canada.[20]

Repercussions followed. President Fillmore issued another proclamation. He deplored the breaking of the law and emphasized that the principal lawbreakers were persons of color. He also called for all officers in the
vicinity to assist in enforcing the law and for the prosecution of all who
assisted in the escape. Riley was embarrassed by the marshals' incompe-
tence and attempted to place blame on the city marshal and mayor. Many
Boston newspapers chastised the perpetrators for not allowing the process to run its course and bringing dishonor on the city's residents. The
Boston Daily Atlas in an editorial, for example, claimed the rescue was not
only unlawful but unnecessary, for several Boston citizens would have

"purchased his freedom if the law had decided against him." For the most part, these reactions were no more than political spin. More serious were the charges of aiding and abetting Minkins' jail break filed against ten men, seven of whom were indicted by a grand jury and scheduled for trial. Elizur Wright of the *Commonwealth* and Joseph K. Hayes, superintendant of Tremont Temple, were white. The lawyer Robert Morris and four cloth- ing dealers (Lewis Hayden, James Scott, J. P. Colburn, and Thomas Paul Smith) were African American. Years later Hayden, a fugitive slave himself who became a prominent figure in the struggle for equal rights, acknowl- edged that he had led the break. At the time, there was a real possibility that seven men would go to prison so that Minkins could be free. Scott was the first to go to trial, but the jury—apparently evenly divided—was unable to reach a verdict. Hayden was next, and his jury also was hung, though closer to conviction with nine of the twelve finding him guilty. The prosecution began the trial of Morris but abandoned it after a few days, most likely recognizing the futility of their efforts. Even though these Massachusetts jurors swore that they would uphold the Fugitive Slave Law, some of them were unable to find Scott or Hayden guilty beyond a rea- sonable doubt and that pattern probably would have held with all seven defendants.[21]

Thomas Sims could not have picked a worse time to arrive in Boston after escaping slavery. Twenty-three-years-old (some accounts state he was younger), he had been a bricklayer in Savannah, Georgia. His master, the rice planter James Potter, lived in Chatham, ten or twelve miles away. Sims, like many urban slaves, was relatively autonomous, paying wages of around ten dollars each month to Potter but otherwise keeping the remainder of whatever money he earned and living on his own. He had a wife and several children. On February 22, 1851—just a week after the rescue of Frederick Minkins—he inquired whether the *M. & J. C. Gilmore*, which was about to sail for Boston, was hiring a cook. After being told his services were not needed, he stowed away. Two weeks later, as the brig entered Boston harbor, the ship's mate found him. The captain locked him in a cabin, but Sims used a pocket knife to force the lock open and on one of the *Gilmore's* small boats rowed to the apparent safety of the city where he soon lodged in a seamen's boardinghouse. Hoping to arrange for his family to join him, he wired home for funds and inadvertently divulged his location.[22]

It was a short respite from the toils of slavery. Less than a month later, he was in a Boston courtroom, charged with being Potter's fugitive slave. Only a few days before, seven men had been indicted for assisting Minkins' escape. Authorities at all levels were determined to show that they could enforce the Fugitive Slave Law in Boston. Skeptical and angry southerners waited to be convinced. Sims, through no fault of his own, became a pawn on a larger national stage. Mid-evening of April 3, Sims left the company of friends, and two marshals grabbed him; after a short skirmish they placed him in a carriage and took him to the courthouse. The grand jury room, considered property of the central government, became his cell. The next morning he appeared before Commissioner George T. Curtis. Seth J. Thomas, as in the Minkins' case, served as counsel for the claimant. Former United States senator and recently elected congressman Robert Rantoul Jr. along with Charles G. Loring and Samuel E. Sewall were attorneys for the defendant. Since these proceedings were more like a hearing for an extradition than a trial, the defense faced huge obstacles. Thomas presented documents from Georgia stating that a Thomas Sims had escaped from his owner and then questioned witnesses who claimed that the fugitive slave was the defendant. That was all that needed to be established to send Sims back to Georgia. Loring for the defense asked for a delay so that they could prepare their case, and Curtis adjourned the hearing until the next morning.[23]

Officials took every precaution to prevent another jailbreak. They filled Court Square outside the courthouse and the hallways inside with police, special police from the Watch Department, and marshals. The New England Guards, the Boston Light Guard, the Pulaski Guards, the Massachusetts Volunteers, and the Roxbury Light Infantry were stationed nearby at various times and were on alert. Authorities went so far as to gird the entire building with chains and only allowed lawyers, those who had official business, and journalists to go in the building. Even judges had to duck under the chains to enter. Saturday morning a "posse of police officers" escorted Sims and United States Marshal Sawin from the jury room to the courtroom to begin the day's deliberations. Rantoul cross-examined the previous day's witnesses, and Thomas presented three men from the *Gilmore* to testify that Sims had been a stowaway on the voyage from Savannah to Boston. After cross-examining the ship's officers, Rantoul began the argument for the defense. His strategy, as it had to be, was scattershot. He attempted to have Sims transferred to another court under the charge that he had resisted arrest and injured one of the marshals; he presented an affidavit from Sims stating that he was born free in St. Augustine, Florida, and that his freedom papers had been given to a Morris Potter of Savannah; and he outlined an argument he wanted to develop that denied the constitutional authority of commissioners in fugitive slave cases and of the law itself. But he needed time, and he requested a five-day delay to Thursday. Curtis granted him only until Monday and adjourned the court for the day.[24]

By then, most must have realized that there was little likelihood that Sims would regain his freedom, but the Vigilance Committee—now swollen to more than 200 members—and the defense lawyers worked feverishly nonetheless. People came to Court Square each day to observe and to protest the proceedings, but with the overwhelming number of police and marshals there was no opportunity for a rescue. Many of the leaders among African Americans were missing for fear of being arrested for the Minkins rescue. There was no violence and few demonstrations, just frustration and sorrow. An exception was the rally on Boston Common—Faneuil Hall having been denied—where Wendell Phillips likened the situation to the period of British military occupation that culminated in the Boston Massacre. A mass meeting in Tremont Temple followed, but few in power were listening. The speeches and cheers of solidarity proved to be little more than verbal defiance that rallied reformers together but had no influence on the proceedings.[25]

During the days preceding Commissioner Curtis' decision, Sims' legal team—expanded with the addition of Richard Henry Dana Jr. and Charles Sumner—seemed to be everywhere. They argued before the state Supreme Court several times and before the United States District Court requesting a writ of habeas corpus. The lawyers and the Vigilance Committee attempted to engage the Massachusetts legislature. They offered a petition from Sims asking for a special law that would give him a writ of habeas corpus, and they prompted committee hearings on the charge that city assistance was violating state law. None of this was successful. On Friday, April 11, Curtis in a long and complicated decision found that Sims was a fugitive slave and that he must return to Georgia.[26]

When Henry I. Bowditch arrived at Court Square about 3:00 A. M. the next morning, the illumination of a single gaslight revealed 100 policemen with double-edged swords and roughly the same number of armed volunteers, all in preparation for the stealthy rendition of Thomas Sims. He quietly acknowledged the presence of others, including Theodore Parker and William F. Channing, who were there to witness the sad event. At 4:15 the police formed a closely locked, double file between the door of the courthouse and Court Square. Members of the city watch formed a second double file and the "volunteers with closed platoons arranged themselves in a long line leading into Court Street." Soon the courthouse door opened, and Sims, unshackled but tightly escorted by marshals, was led out. When he was well in the midst of the "armed men," the order was given to march and the assembled force guarded Sims through the square and Court Street into State Street down to the wharf and the waiting ship. Along the way spectators shouted "Shame" and "Infamy" and hissed their sense of disgrace. By 5:01 a tugboat began pulling the *Acorn* out of the harbor, and Sims returned to slavery.[27] Southern slaveholders, appeased by Massachusetts officials and cotton merchants and manufacturers, had won a grim victory.

Not until three years later was there another fugitive slave case in New England, and it, like the Sims case, had a context that elevated its importance. The Missouri Compromise that had prohibited slavery in territory north of 36° 30' latitude had stood for thirty-four years when Stephen A. Douglas, a senator from Illinois, proposed its repeal in 1854. Douglas wanted to organize the Nebraska Territory so that a railroad could connect Chicago to San Francisco, but he couldn't gain enough votes in the Senate without capitulating to southern demands. It was a calculated risk and a violation of the hard-earned accord the two major sections of the country had made in 1820. He knew it would produce a firestorm in the North, but he believed the damage would be short-lived. The Kansas-Nebraska Act became law on May 22, 1854. New Englanders who had supported the Compromise of 1850 including the Fugitive Slave Law felt betrayed and began to defect, despite the possibility that it would harm their relations with southern customers. They renewed their allegiance to their region and expressed their distaste for the Slave Power.[28]

Two days after the passage of the Kansas-Nebraska Act, marshals apprehended fugitive slave Anthony Burns in Boston. Tall, stout, literate, mid-twenties, with a scar on his face and a bone protruding from one hand (it had not been set properly after an accident), Burns had a modest demeanor. In some ways his situation was similar to Thomas Sims'. He had lived and worked at a number of skilled positions in Richmond, Virginia, while his owner Charles Suttle resided in Alexandria. William Brent, a Richmond merchant, had leased Burns for several years previously and often had acted as Suttle's agent in leasing Burns to others for a year at a time. Burns had much more autonomy than his plantation counterparts. In March 1854, he was working as a stevedore when he stowed away on a ship sailing to Boston. Two months later he was employed in a clothing store, when federal marshals captured him on his way home in the evening.[29]

Authorities fabricated the initial charge for his detention—robbing a jewelry store—so that news of a fugitive slave being held in the

FIGURE 11.2 *Anthony Burns*, 1855, an engraving by John Andrews based on a drawing by Barry from a daguerreotype by Whipple & Black. Scenes from Burns' life surround the portrait. (Library of Congress).

courthouse could be hidden from the general population. Charles Suttle and William Brent, however, were well aware of Burns' capture and met with him that night. Burns greeted the two with polite hellos: "How do you do, Master Charles?", "How do you do, Master William?" His deference, civility, and familiarity ultimately proved his undoing. For his part, Suttle attempted to intimidate his runaway, implying that he would be severely punished if he resisted rendition. When the two Virginians left, marshals manacled Burns and held him in the jury room—his cell for the duration. As Richard Henry Dana Jr. was strolling to his office near the courthouse the next morning, he learned of Burns' situation. Rushing inside he offered his services to the captive, who initially rejected them for fear of future mistreatment. Dana, nonetheless, attended the hearing. After Brent's testimony identifying Burns as Suttle's fugitive slave, Dana asked for a postponement. He explained that Burns had not retained him and suggested that after his initial shock of being in custody he might change his mind. Commissioner Edward G. Loring granted a two-day delay.[30]

The Vigilance Committee in Boston hadn't met as a group for three years, and their meetings beginning Thursday, May 25, were chaotic. Everyone had an opinion, but no one was able to take a lead. The only concrete agreement was to have a public protest at Faneuil Hall on Friday night. Committee members sent invitations to sympathizers outside of Boston to strengthen their collective voice. Among the recipients was the Reverend Thomas Wentworth Higginson. The thirty-year-old, son of a Boston merchant, Higginson was the Unitarian minister in Worcester. Three years earlier, then a minister at conservative Newburyport, he had participated in discussions with the Vigilance Committee and had been frustrated that no one supported a jailbreak of Thomas Sims. This time he was not willing to settle for words only or to rush outside and point "the finger of scorn" at Suttle and Brent as they passed by (as many of his colleagues did). A smaller group of the Vigilance Committee discussed actions they might take, but no plan emerged. Discouraged, Higginson left for the train station to meet Martin Stowell, one of many Worcester men he had asked to join him. As they walked from the station, Stowell outlined a plan of rescue. At the height of the Faneuil Hall meeting that night—when marshals would least expect anything unusual—a core group of men would force their way into the courthouse and free Burns. Higginson wanted to solicit the approval of the executive committee, but he had to settle for individual conversations as each man appeared at

Faneuil Hall. There was no clear agreement, but Higginson was under the impression that Theodore Parker "hastily approved."[31]

Parker, Wendell Phillips, and others led a rousing rally in Faneuil Hall condemning the "Nebraska bill" and the detention of Burns and provocatively calling for deeds, not just words. In the meantime, Higginson, Stowell, Lewis Hayden, and a small group of their friends and followers singly walked to Court Square. Fortune appeared to be with them. The Massachusetts Supreme Court was holding a late session and "ordinary visitors could pass freely." Higginson planted himself near a door that was partially opened and waited for the signal that would be shouted at Faneuil Hall for a massive attempt to free Burns. Inside the hall a man in the audience bellowed: "Mr. Chairman, I am just informed that a mob of negroes is in Court Square, attempting to rescue Burns." That was the alert. Pandemonium broke out. Higginson had hoped that members of the Vigilance Committee would lead the way, perhaps giving dignity and authority to the assault. Instead, those who first burst upon Court Square were, to Higginson's thinking, "the froth and scum of the meeting, the fringe of idlers on its edge." As the roar of the angry and excited crowd grew louder, some began to throw bricks and other objects at the building. Inside the courthouse marshals and forty to fifty special policemen stationed themselves to prevent entry. Some of the Worcester men found a beam that they along with Hayden and his colleagues used to batter the east door. Higginson and a "stout negro" headed the team; and when the door began to give, the two of them (and only those two) gained entry. Six to eight special policemen battled them with swords and fists and quickly thrust them back out onto Court Square. Higginson acquired a "severe cut" on his chin, but otherwise he and his fellow would-be rescuer suffered only minor bruises. Unbeknown to Higginson, one of the special policemen James Batchelder (a Charlestown truckman who had volunteered) had been mortally wounded. At first Higginson and others believed that a pistol shot had killed Batchelder, and he feared that the perpetrator was Stowell or Hayden, both of whom fired shots that night. The medical examiner's report later concluded that Batchelder had been stabbed, possibly through a broken panel in the door he had been defending. Higginson bitterly realized that a policeman had died and yet Burns remained in custody.[32]

Authorities immediately arrested suspects (including Higginson who had not been armed), and brought in troops: two artillery companies with one cannon positioned in Court Square, US Marines from nearby

Fort Independence, the Independent Corps of Cadets, the Boston Light Infantry, and the Boston Light Dragoons. For a short period, crowds were cleared from Court Square and ropes installed to prevent the populace from entering the area. Those actions should have offered no surprise. What had changed were the attitudes of the cotton Whigs and their adherents. Unlike the Shadrach episode, Boston newspapers and prominent men did not chastise the thwarted rescuers—even with the death of Batchelder—nor did they side with law officials or even the Pierce administration. Instead they joined the cause to liberate Anthony Burns. The textile magnate Amos A. Lawrence previous to the courthouse riot had offered Richard Henry Dana Jr. a blank check to pay attorneys for Burns, and after the incident he and other wealthy individuals raised the funds to purchase the fugitive slave's freedom. Unfortunately, ambitions of local politicians, District Attorney Benjamin Hallett in particular, and national political maneuverings killed the deal shortly before the Reverend Leonard Grimes—who had brokered the arrangement—was about to pay Suttle $1,200.[33]

Burns' last hope was the commissioner's hearing. Seth Thomas, the attorney for the claimant, was not as skillful as he had been in other rendition proceedings, and Richard Henry Dana Jr. leaped on every weakness. Thomas' chief witness William Brent stated he had last seen Burns in Richmond on March 24. Dana produced nine witnesses who testified that they had been with Burns in Boston two to three weeks earlier. Brent gave a general description of the alleged fugitive slave with few details except for mentioning two scars, one on his face and the other on his hand. Dana established that there was not a scar on his hand but rather a quite noticeable protuberance of a bone. The law required that the claimant must have legal right to the slave, but Dana contended that since Suttle had leased Burns for a year only, the lessee could initiate a rendition. When Dana concluded his closing argument, he left Commissioner Loring with ample possibilities to find for the defendant. But Loring would disappoint. On Friday morning June 2, Loring ordered Anthony Burns back to slavery. He acknowledged the flaws in identifying Burns as Suttle's slave who had fled from Richmond, Virginia. Instead he based his decision on the greeting that Burns had given Suttle and Brent on the evening of his capture.[34]

Authorities had prepared for the moment so that Burns would be on a ship headed for Virginia before nightfall. In the early afternoon, troops and city police emptied Court Square of all but those who had business inside the courthouse. They then cleared the streets to the wharf where the steamer awaited. Police and militia (more than 1,500 men had been called up for the occasion) lined the streets and intersections as a barrier to spectators and would-be rescuers. Cavalry, marines, artillery companies, marshals, police, and special officers readied themselves to escort Burns to the wharf where the steamer *John Taylor* awaited. Shortly after 3:00 in the afternoon Burns left the courthouse. National Lancers on their horses, a corps of United States artillery, and a corps of United States Marines led the way. About 120 special officers formed a "hollow square," and Burns with marshals nearby was placed in the center. Behind the captive were a corps of Marines, a "field piece, drawn by a span of horses and manned by a detachment of six of the members of the Fourth Regiment United States artillery," and another corps of Marines. It was a massive show of military force, all to return a single slave to Virginia. Had Burns noticed as he was marched to the ship, he would have seen mourning cloths hanging from office windows and would have heard the tolling of church bells and groans, hisses, and cries of "Shame" from 50,000 sympathetic spectators straining to get a glimpse of him. Rescue was impossible, and he soon boarded the *John Taylor*. At precisely 3:20 the steamer left the wharf.[35]

Despite immediate efforts to purchase him, Anthony Burns would remain a slave for two more years before supporters were able to buy his release. None of the men arrested or indicted for the attempted rescue was convicted, though the legal process dragged on for nearly a year. Massachusetts, Rhode Island, Connecticut, and Maine passed personal liberty laws far more protective of the rights of alleged fugitive slaves than they had enacted a decade earlier. Never again would a fugitive slave be returned to slavery from New England, although several attempts would be made. The Anthony Burns episode combined with the Kansas-Nebraska Act brought about a sea change in New England sentiments. Even those who initially had grudgingly supported the Fugitive Slave Law changed their minds. The antislavery movement became socially acceptable, and there was an increased willingness among white New Englanders to accept the equal rights of African Americans.[36] But racism hadn't died. What was different were attitudes about New England and about the slave South. People wanted to distinguish their region from the South and the Slave Power. They identified themselves as much by who they weren't as by who they were. In the short term, black New Englanders benefited, but there were limits to progress.

12

Inching Ahead

WHILE BOSTONIANS WERE resisting the rendition of the Crafts, Minkins, Sims, and Burns, their schools remained segregated. Nowhere else in New England north of Connecticut and Rhode Island were African American children barred from attending school with children of European descent. Being an exception within the region had been a hallmark of Boston since its creation. As the population, economic, political, and cultural center of New England, it had the most of nearly everything and everyone—churches, brothels, theaters, newspapers, people of color, Irish, poor, wealthy, abolitionists, racists. It was full of, indeed a magnet for, contradictions and contrarians. It was the heart of revolution and the home of conservatives.

Despite the ruling of the School Committee in 1846 that preserved segregated schools, many black Bostonians continued their struggle for equality by boycotting the Smith School (located in the First African Baptish Church) that housed both the primary school and the grammar school restricted to African Americans. To the extent that enrollment continued to drop (roughly a 50 percent decline from pre-boycott levels in 1844 to an enrollment of fifty-three in 1849), the tactic was a success. But without an educational alternative that poor parents could afford, the tactic was a disaster. Even families with middling incomes might be hard-pressed to send their children to a tuition-charging school. In 1847, Benjamin Franklin Roberts took action into his own hands and attempted to place his five-year-old daughter Sarah in the Otis School—a public primary school open only to white students. The Otis School was less than half the distance from their home as the Smith School. More important, Sarah's admission would be a blow to the caste system of education. The thirty-two-year-old Roberts was a nephew of Hosea Easton, and both the Roberts and Easton families had long been active in antislavery and in working to attain equal rights for people of color. Both bright and mercurial, Roberts was an activist in all of its meanings, seeking concrete accomplishments more than rhetorical gestures. Failure angered him. He had been trained as a printer and in 1837 had attempted to establish his own newspaper the *Anti-Slavery Herald*. It not only would be a voice of African Americans; it also would train young men of color. His hopes were quickly dashed. The country was in a depression, another African American newspaper— though based in New York—had recently launched, and *The Liberator* already was well established with loyal subscribers of African descent. The newspaper folded within a month, and he blamed white abolitionists who, he believed, wanted "to muzzle, exterminate and put down the efforts of certain colored individuals effecting the welfare of the colored brethren." Roberts withdrew from reform efforts for the next decade.[1]

Why Roberts chose 1847 to challenge Boston's segregated school system is unclear. Sarah was not the Roberts' oldest child. She had a brother Benjamin Franklin Roberts Jr. who was five years older. Perhaps he had been attending Smith School all along, and his father only recognized the injustice when Sarah became eligible for public education. Whatever the reason, once Roberts was moved to act, he was unrelenting. When the School Committee repeatedly denied Sarah admission to any school but Smith School because of her color, Roberts sued the city under a statute that required remuneration to any child barred from city schools. It was a long shot, since the School Committee had directed Sarah to a specific school rather than prohibiting her from attending any, but Roberts enlisted attorney Robert Morris to show the illegality and injustice of Boston's segregated schools. After the Suffolk County Court of Common Pleas ruled against Sarah, Roberts and Morris appealed to the state Supreme Court to overrule the judgment.[2]

Roberts didn't limit himself to Sarah's case but joined with other black Bostonians to end the caste system of education. At a "meeting of colored citizens" on July 31, 1848, he was one of a small committee that offered resolutions to be considered. The underlying principle was "that as we all belong to one common family, having one common cause, it is our belief that *separate schools* for the education of children are injurious in their effects upon society and ought to be abolished." Their specific target was Smith School, which they wanted abolished, and they pledged to offer no assistance in choosing instructors or in any way "to better the condition of the school." The issue of *The Liberator* that described the meeting

FIGURE 12.1 *First African Baptist Church* (Boston), photograph taken after 1933 by Arthur C. Haskell. Known also as African Meeting House, it served multiple purposes for the African American community, including as a school. (Historic American Buildings Survey, Library of Congress).

stated that the resolutions were "unanimously adopted." Not only was that description untrue but it also masked a deep split in the African American community. The leaders of the July 31 meeting, sometimes called "integrationists," wanted all vestiges of caste removed and all schools opened to all children. Their opponents, sometimes called "segregationists" by the integrationists, were composed of some who believed that in a racist society their children would be better served in separate schools and of others who feared their children would receive no schooling at all were Smith closed.

They wanted all Boston schools to be available to all children while still keeping the Smith School for children of color. Among their chief advocates was Thomas Paul Smith who served as secretary of the meeting.[3]

Smith, like Roberts, came from a prominent New England black family. His grandfather Thomas Paul was the founding minister of Boston's first African American church, the Belknap Street Church, and an ardent abolitionist and reformer. His zeal for social change may have been too advanced for his congregation and the reason it forced him out after a quarter century of service. One of Smith's aunts Susan Paul was an active member of the Boston Female Anti-Slavery Society and a teacher at Smith School before her untimely death in 1841. An uncle, Thomas Paul, the son of the minister and a brother of Susan, had attended Smith School, was one of the students at the short-lived Noyes Academy, and had graduated from Dartmouth College. Thomas Paul Smith also had been a student at Smith School, and when prevented from matriculating at a Boston high school he had attended the prestigious Phillips Academy in Andover, Massachusetts, for two semesters. His experience at Phillips may have been unpleasant and may have contributed to his opposition to abolishing the Smith School. He was secretary at the July 31 meeting when only twenty-one years old, a clear indication of the strength of his family connections.[4]

Animosities simmered between the two groups until the following summer when they came to a boil. The integrationists petitioned the mayor and aldermen to abolish the Smith School and to open all of the other city schools to all of the city's children. Thomas Paul Smith petitioned the School Committee to appoint Thomas Paul as the principal of Smith School. Both groups petitioned the School Committee to support their respective positions. The face-off took place before the School Committee on August 8, 1849. Benjamin Roberts and others spoke for the integrationists, but their chief representative was Robert Morris who argued the case for integration for three hours. He talked of the inconvenience as well as the expense for African Americans from all parts of the city having to send their children to a single location, but he primarily focused on the injustice and illegality of segregated schools "in a Commonwealth whose constitution expressly declares, that all classes of inhabitants are entitled to equal privileges and immunities." Morris concluded his remarks by stressing that the petitioners were not asking for special favors but rather were contending for an "inalienable right." Smith, who to one reporter looked "scarcely out of his teens," required far less time. His was a nuanced argument. He agreed with Morris that children of color should have the same rights as all other children and that they should be allowed to enter white schools should they have the "moral courage." But Smith expected that white students would jeer and sneer at black students and that therefore African American children would be better off in separate schools "where they could retreat and obtain some education." He believed that most black parents agreed with him and that if given the choice of a separate school with a "competent teacher to their liking," they would choose it. Needlessly, he added that the controversy had been provoked "for selfish and party motives, by those who had no real interest in the education of the children." The conflict of philosophies and solutions of how to benefit children of color divided neighbors and families, as was exemplified by John H. Roberts, a nephew of Hosea Easton and a younger brother of Benjamin Roberts, who along with Robert Wood seconded Smith.[5] Such antagonisms between people with similar causes is not unusual, then or now, but it can produce anger between natural allies as great as toward those who are diametrically opposed to them. That unfortunately was the situation in Boston.

Two days before the School Committee was to give its decision, Boston's African American community held "a very large and enthusiastic" meeting. William Cooper Nell, who long had fought for the integration of Boston schools and who was a calming and reasoned influence, took the lead. Speaking for a small committee, he presented a series of resolutions that essentially repeated the arguments against an "exclusive" school and for the inclusion of children of color in the white schools. There was a mild rebuke to those in their midst who had opposed their cause, but no one was named—a small olive branch. Both Thomas Paul Smith and John H. Roberts delivered remarks in opposition, and in the process Smith acknowledged that he was in the minority. The formidable John T. Hilton cuttingly interjected that he was "mistaken in representing himself in the minority, for John C. Calhoun, Henry Clay, the American Colonization Society, and the entire pro-slavery community, were with him." With no more acrimony the meeting adopted the resolutions and adjourned.[6]

On August 29, the School Committee delivered its judgment. The Reverend Dr. Bigelow, representing the special committee that had examined the issues, reported that a majority recommended the status quo—keeping the Smith School open and the rest of Boston schools closed to African American children. As a sop to the black community, the majority also advised that "preference should be given to competent colored applicants in election to the office of Master" of the Smith School. The special committee's reasoning was that with Boston's blacks divided, the Roberts case still pending before the Supreme Court, and the possibility of discord between students in desegregated schools, any change to the current system was premature. Charles T. Russell in his minority report agreed that the Smith School should "be continued but advocated that all other schools should be integrated. The School Committee accepted the majority report and approved searching for a "colored Master" to fill the vacancy at the Smith School.[7]

The integrationists were furious with the School Committee and especially with Thomas Paul Smith and his allies. In their meeting on September 3, they could barely contain their frustration and anger. Again Nell tried to reduce the tensions within the community but even he was impatient for success and exasperated by those who would impede destroying the caste system. He reviewed the decision, condemning the clergymen who dominated the committee for their "illiberality" and their reasoning for rejecting change as well as Smith for the role he played. Nell then proposed resolutions that called for their equal rights, "severely censured" Smith, protested the selection of Thomas Paul as teacher at Smith School, and praised Charles T. Russell for his minority report. The last was both surprising and contradictory, for the minority report was identical to Smith's position. But these were impassioned times. The resolutions weren't punitive enough for Henry Weeden. He protested that "it was now necessary to draw the lines between the friends of equal rights among us, and those few individuals, who had continually opposed us," and he proposed an additional resolution to muzzle those opponents unless the meeting voted to hear them. That was too divisive for Nell, Morris, Hilton, and others who were able to quash Weeden's resolution and have their own passed. Even so, according to John H. Robert's account, when Smith had risen in opposition to the resolutions, he had not been allowed to speak.[8]

Matters grew worse. The opening of Smith School with Paul as its principal and teacher posed a new threat to the boycott. Paul was a respected educator and a son of the community. Parents, despite the principle of equal rights, would be tempted to place their children under his tutelage. When the school year began, supporters of the boycott attempted to block, intimidate, and persuade students from entering the building. The arrival of a policeman scattered the boycotters, but only twenty-three children registered that day. Retaliation came in the evening. Integrationists held

a meeting in the Belknap Street Church and in the building first minis-
tered by Thomas Paul Sr. declared his son "unworthy their confidence or
respect." While deliberations continued, supporters of the Smith School
and Thomas Paul Jr. stood inside the door and tried to disrupt the meeting with "hisses and various other demonstrations." Leaders cautioned
the audience to pay the dissidents no attention, but some individuals in
the assemblage decided to force the intruders outside. A melee transpired
when the routed protesters began throwing stones and other objects at the
windows. It required policemen to restore order. The meeting would have
been a disaster had not the boycotters inside agreed to raise funds so that
parents could afford to send their children to "temporary schools."[9]

After the fiasco of September 17, all sides tried to tamp down emotions
and reestablish some dignity to their efforts. When the integrationists
next met on September 24, there were no disturbances or interruptions;
and they passed a resolution calling for law and order and no violence.
Speakers informed the audience that the struggle for equal school rights
might drag on for some time and solicited contributions to support
"Independent Schools." The good news was that two clergyman, Stockman
of Boston and Foster of Danvers, had offered to teach. Only Foster ever
taught in the single school they were able to create, but that one school
was enough to sustain the boycott for the short term. Smith School in
the 1849–1850 school year had the lowest student enrollment—averaging
twenty-five students—since the boycott began, even with the guidance of
Thomas Paul. But in the long run, parents had to weigh the goal of desegregated schools against the immediate educational opportunities of their
children.[10]

Smith wasn't present at the meeting, but he requested William
Lloyd Garrison to allow him to state his position in *The Liberator*. In his
"Vindication," he began in a conciliatory manner by claiming that the
differences between his side and others were "very trifling." Mountains
had been made from molehills, "a wide and boisterous river" from a "nar-
row and easily crossed" brook. He unequivocally stated that he was "in
favor of the privilege of common ward schools being given to all." But
he supported black institutions, including Smith School, and denied that
they were exclusive. Whites had never been denied admission to a black
church, society, or school. It was whites who maintained exclusive institutions, and that was where the attention of the African American community should be focused. To Smith, it made no sense to close an African
American school because whites didn't admit people of color to theirs.

He had been born and reared in black Boston, since the age of fourteen had worked for "our common elevation," and these consistently had been his views. Smith didn't reveal that he was much more of a segregationist than the "Vindication" article implied. Privately he had made clear that he believed people of color were best served in African American institutions led and conducted by black people. He believed white attitudes and conduct were too pernicious for people of African descent to trust integration. Had Smith concluded with peace-making remarks, he might have narrowed the chasm between the disputants. But he couldn't resist setting the record straight—and then some—about certain charges made against him. His chief target was Robert Morris. He bristled at Morris' suggestion that he had nominated Thomas Paul for Smith School because doing so benefited him. He categorically denied the charge and countered that his efforts had been "wholly gratuitous and voluntary, without remuneration and without reward." Morris as a lawyer was the one who "scours the country, gets men in scrapes and gets them out," all in the pursuit of "that very gold."[11] Smith may have purged his own venom, but he unnecessarily poisoned relations with many who might have been his natural allies in the greater cause. He and other hotheads throughout this fray were younger men, ranging in age from Smith in his early twenties to Benjamin Roberts in his mid-thirties. More than principle was at stake.

Supporters of equal rights met most Monday nights at the Belknap Street Church. In many ways these were stopgap affairs keeping people connected until the Massachusetts Supreme Court heard and decided upon the case of *Sarah C. Roberts v. the City of Boston*. William C. Nell described them more as "free and easy *reunions*" rather than as gatherings devoted to speeches and resolutions. To be sure, there were resolutions primarily praising friends and castigating opponents and speeches telling of successes in open schools outside of Boston, updating the audience on the "temporary school" and the need for contributions, reminding people that "a man's a man, or black or white," and generally attempting to keep spirits high.[12] The boycott continued, but mostly they waited.

Finally, on December 3—more than a year after Robert Morris had filed an appeal—the case came before the state Supreme Court. Charles Sumner, who in two years would become a United States senator, addressed the court for Sarah Roberts and equal rights for all. It was a powerful effort. He framed his remarks with two basic questions: "Can any discrimination, on account of color or race, be made, under the Constitution and Laws of Massachusetts among the children entitled to the benefit of our public schools?" and does the School Committee of Boston have the power to exclude "colored children" from its public schools except those restricted to black students? The bulk of his comments attempted to substantiate why "no" was the proper and legal response to both. A central principle of the Commonwealth of Massachusetts, Sumner stated, was that "all men, without distinction of color or race, are equal before the law." The state constitution made no distinctions between people. When the state legislature crafted laws for the creation and regulation of public schools, it made no distinctions between children. State laws had established only one kind of school, "the general Public School, free to all the inhabitants." The courts of Massachusetts, moreover, "have never recognized any discrimination founded on color or race, in the administration of the public schools, but have recognized the rights of all the inhabitants." Excluding children of color from the public schools, he concluded, was an "inconvenience" of time and money not applied to white children and therefore was "a violation of equality" and "in the nature of Caste."

Sumner devoted much of the remainder of his argument to denying that the Boston School Committee had the authority under the Massachusetts constitution and laws to discriminate "on account of color or race," a phrase he hammered on repeatedly. He acknowledged that the committee had the power "to determine the number and qualifications of students." The sticking point was the meaning of "qualifications." Sumner contended that qualifications were limited to "age, sex, and moral and intellectual fitness." It was the weakest part of his argument, a mere assertion and a questionable one considering the gender of Sarah Roberts. The logic of his claim that separate schools were not equivalents was stronger. If there was no legal ground for the existence of segregated schools (in short, no law establishing such entities), then they could not be legal equivalents. Schools for blacks only were not equal to white schools, because they did not legally exist. And even if the separate schools were equivalent, black children have "an equal right with white children to the general public schools." Anticipating a "separate but equal" argument or ruling, Sumner had attempted to neutralize it before it was presented. At the closing of his presentation he introduced what was then a novel notion. Separate schools harm white children by teaching them to be racists. Caste education leads to whites viewing people of color "as a separate and degraded class." Everyone benefited by "mutual acquaintance." The Massachusetts Supreme Court had banished slavery in the Commonwealth, Sumner reminded the jurists; now was the time for the Court to "obliterate the last of its footprints."[13]

City Solicitor Peleg W. Chandler represented Boston and immediately took the offensive. The Roberts suit, he began, sought compensation, on the assumption that Sarah Roberts had been "unlawfully deprived of public school instruction." That simply was not the case, he contended. Sarah Roberts had been admitted to a public school. The objections to Smith School were that it wasn't the closest to her home and that it was a school designated for children of color. Chandler stated that Boston children— white and black—were not always admitted to the nearest school; and the second objection was no more valid, for white children had to attend white schools. The central question, in Chandler's estimation, was whether the School Committee had the power to continue a policy that had been in effect for half a century and had been initiated by people of color. He reasoned that the city charter, which was constitutional, had given the School Committee the power to administer Boston's schools and that the committee "were the exclusive judges of the best manner of executing the power given them." The School Committee "acted on the ground that the colored and white citizens were a different race; and that it would be better for both to remain separate." Chandler found himself in the same murky area that had weakened Sumner's argument: by what authority did the School Committee have the right to segregate schools? Both had had to stray from a strictly legal position and had taken a subjective and even arbitrary path of determining the validity of the committee's judgment. Chandler had the one advantage that segregated education had been established in response to a request from Boston's African American community and that "perhaps a majority" still favored it. Chandler closed with respectful words for those "who were sincerely desirous of elevating their condition by an honest application of the means in their power" and with a scolding of parents who were boycotting.[14]

Four months later on April 8, 1850, the Massachusetts Supreme Court gave its unanimous decision, written by Chief Justice Lemuel Shaw. The court rather briefly dismissed the question of "whether the plaintiff had been unlawfully excluded from public school instruction." It decided that the Boston School Committee had given Sarah Roberts a ticket of admission to one of its primary schools—"in all respects as well fitted to advance education of children under seven years of age, as the other primary schools"—but that she had chosen not to attend. The remaining and key question was whether the School Committee had the power to create segregated schools. Shaw and his colleagues then began a tortured and tortuous explanation of why Boston's committee and all school committees had such authority, an account that had little legal logic but a great deal of verbiage validating the prejudices and opinions of the justices. They began this section of the ruling by agreeing with Sumner that the Massachusetts constitution and laws provided that "all persons, without distinction of age, or sex, birth, or color, origin, or condition, were equal before the law." But then they contended that while the general principle was "perfectly sound," it didn't necessarily apply to individual cases. Men may have different rights than women, adults than children, and people of European descent than people of African descent. An individual's rights depended upon "laws adapted to their respective relations and conditions." The jurists made no attempt to show legal precedent or any other evidence to substantiate their opinion. It just was because they said so. The Massachusetts legislature, they continued, directed towns to provide education and to elect school committees to administer the schools. There were no instructions on how the schools should be organized or on qualifications for admission. That had been left up to each school committee. The Boston School Committee, using its best judgment for the welfare of both "classes" of people, had the power to segregate schools because the legislature had not denied it. The court found for the city of Boston. The decision was bad enough when confined to one city, but for the next century it was cited as a precedent by other states' courts and by the United States Supreme Court in *Plessy v. Ferguson* for similar "separate but equal" rulings.[15]

The decision was a heavy blow to those who had worked long and hard to integrate Boston's schools, but rather than admitting defeat they decided to continue the boycott and devised new plans for ending educational segregation. Having failed with Boston's School Committee and Massachusetts courts, they now focused on the state legislature. They enlisted the help of the New England Anti-Slavery Society for a petition drive. To show that they weren't pawns of white abolitionists and that they truly wanted school integration—despite apparent splits among people of color—they chose to have separate petition drives for black signatures and for white signatures. Perhaps "segregated petitions" was a necessary tactic, but nonetheless it was a peculiar one considering the cause behind them. In gratitude to Benjamin Roberts the meeting organized a festival in his honor. By late June, Roberts was traveling the state collecting signatures. When he reported on the success of his efforts in August, he already had moved his family across the Charles River to Cambridge where the schools were integrated.[16]

The petitions reached the legislature in February 1851, a day before Frederick Minkins' escape and at a time when enrollment at Smith School had climbed to sixty-five students. Supporters of integrated schools selected Roberts as one of the men to present their case to the legislative committees. Thomas Paul Smith all the while was winning his way back into favor among Boston's African Americans. He was one of the participants in Minkins' rescue and along with Lewis Hayden among the men indicted for aiding and abetting. A month later he reported for the Committee of Resolutions at an anti-colonization meeting and in company with Robert Morris, William J. Watkins, and others gave a speech. There still may have been lingering resentment for his role in keeping Smith School open (particularly after he testified before a state house committee), but he clearly was a partner in the movement for equal rights.[17]

Spring moderated winter's cold, but it brought no joy for people of color in Boston. Authorities returned Thomas Sims to slavery, and on May 6 the state senate tabled the committee report on integrating schools. The state house of representatives tried to reconsider the bill on May 22, but a close vote of 130 to 122 defeated it. It was a bitter pill for all integrationists, but it was particularly hard for Benjamin Roberts. He couldn't forget Thomas Paul Smith's opposition—treasonous behavior in his opinion—and he orchestrated an assault in retaliation. His brother John might have been targeted as well, but probably familial connection or his being at sea spared him. On the evening of May 7—the day after the senate tabled the report on school desegregation—as Smith strolled home from his used clothing shop, a gang of black men grabbed him, beat him, and covered his mouth with a plaster of "tar and other substances." They sought to punish, frighten, and silence him, literally and symbolically. The attack was not the public ritual of humiliation reminiscent of eighteenth-century tarring and feathering. It was a personal act of thugs. Smith somehow managed to escape, and he identified Julian B. McCrea, William J. Watkins, and Benjamin Roberts (all proponents of integration and equal rights) as three of his assailants. The following evening, Robert A. Shephard lured Smith from his shop by suggesting that another shopkeeper Coffin Pitts wanted to repay him some money. It was all a ruse, and attackers beat Smith for a second time. Sources disagree, but either on the morning of the first attack or the morning after both attacks, Smith's brother Elijah struck back. Crying, "You are the damned villain who attempted to kill my brother," and brandishing a hatchet he charged Roberts who easily countered the attack. Authorities arrested six men—including Elijah Smith, Benjamin Roberts, Julian B. McCrea, and William J. Watkins—but only Roberts and McCrea were found guilty of the assaults.[18]

The boycott sputtered on, and it wasn't until 1853 with the case of Edward Pindall that the movement to integrate Boston schools re-energized itself. William Pindall in August applied for his five-year-old son Edward to attend the primary school closest to their home, and Edward had been admitted. The boy made "fine progress in his studies" for the first two weeks, until his teacher Sarah A. Turner "nosed the fact out" that he had African ancestry. It had been difficult to detect, for both father and son appeared to be white. She asked the trustees to have him removed from her class, although there had been no objections from his classmates or their parents, and school authorities transferred Edward to Smith School. William Pindall objected and with Robert Morris' legal counsel brought suit against the city. A year later the case was tried in the Court of Common Pleas before a judge and jury. The central issue was "whether the boy was sufficiently 'colored' to come within the rule of the Supreme Court, that the city of Boston has a right to provide separate schools for colored children." Evidence showed that both of William Pindall's parents were white and that his wife—though "light-colored"—had mixed ancestry. Two doctors examined Edward and testified that he was "one-sixth or one-eighth African blood, but were not positive that he was not of Spanish blood." The all-white jury agreed with the city, barring Edward from the public white schools in Boston.[19] Why Morris never raised the Massachusetts legal precedent that a person with more than 50 percent European ancestry was white is unknown.

The Pindall case was not without consequence, however; earlier in the year the suit had prompted Boston's mayor and city council to examine the issue of segregated schools. The city's Committee on Public Instruction—composed of the mayor, two aldermen, and the president and four members of the common council—wrote a report that entreated the School Committee to give integration a "fair trial." It noted that the entire state had integrated its schools except for Boston and that their city had "no rule or regulation excluding colored children from our schools." Elsewhere schools were operating with "harmony, pleasantness and success," and those children would "grow up without that unchristian prejudice against color." The report also indicated the committee's concern that religious sects increasingly were demanding separate schools. Desegregating Boston schools would send an appropriate message to the entire community. The city council on June 22, 1854, ordered that the report be sent to the School Committee with its approval. A week later two council members had second thoughts and asked for reconsideration so that the report would be transmitted without recommendation. In a twenty-one to fourteen vote the council agreed to remove their approval. The weakened report did not convince the School Committee to eliminate segregation, but it demonstrated that Boston was undergoing a transformation of opinion.[20]

Encouraged by the report, William C. Nell and Lewis Hayden began a new petition drive for the legislature. When the Massachusetts legislature began its session in January 1855, power had shifted. Voters had become alienated from the Whig Party with its Fugitive Slave Law and from the Democratic Party with its Kansas-Nebraska Act and elected a Know-Nothing governor as well as a predominantly Know-Nothing legislature. The re-aligned state government became more sympathetic to antislavery and to the rights of African Americans but more wary of the growing Irish and Catholic population. The abolitionist Charles W. Slack chaired the Committee on Education that reviewed the petitions demanding an end to segregated schools. Separately he and two other representatives of the Know-Nothings met with Boston's African American leaders and learned that their top priority was integrating the schools. What Lewis Hayden, Leonard Grimes, and others offered in exchange was left unspoken.[21]

The Committee on Education with Slack at its head began its deliberations already determined to recommend a bill prohibiting segregated schools, and there were no surprises. It found no basis in the state constitution or in state laws giving anyone authority to exclude children from schools on account of "color, race, or religious opinion." It applauded Sumner's argument in the Roberts case and noticed that Chief Justice Shaw and his colleagues had left an opening when they judged that the Boston School Committee had the power to segregate as long as there was no "special legislation" forbidding the practice. After reviewing reports from school systems throughout the state, the Committee on Education concluded that "colored children make less progress in a separate school" and that "no practical inconvenience need follow the abolition." For all those reasons it offered a bill that disallowed segregation in any of the state's schools because of "race, color, or religious opinions." With minimal debate the House and Senate passed the bill, and the governor soon signed it.[22]

With the law now in place, William C. Nell worked indefatigably to ensure that students of color were prepared for integrated schools. He met with school officials, teachers, and parents during the summer to smooth the transition. To overcome parental concerns about how their children would be treated and how well they would do, a week and a half before school began he published an article in *The Liberator* bulging with success stories of African American students in integrated schools throughout the state. His efforts and modified white attitudes toward people of color paid off. The school year began almost without incident. Whites craned through windows, "probably in anticipation of trouble" as the *Boston Evening Telegraph* phrased it, to see children—black and white—walking to school. At Phillips School a few white boys made "a little merry sport at the colored pupils," but the principal quickly admonished them to be polite; and at Bowdoin School some white girls "indulged in a little obloquy," but soon stopped. Otherwise it was a peaceful day, and so were those that followed. As a concession to Thomas Paul Smith and his allies, school authorities had left Smith School exclusively for children of color, but only seven children arrived for classes. With so little support for a separate school, the School Committee closed Smith School a week later.[23] After fifteen years of meetings, boycotts, petitions, and lawsuits, school segregation had ended in Massachusetts.

The protests for school integration had been essential. Without them there would have been little public understanding of the injustice of caste education and almost certainly no legislative action. Local movements throughout Massachusetts, except Boston, had integrated their schools. But there were limits to their effectiveness in Boston with its relatively large African American population—not so large as to determine its own path but large enough to scare racists—and its conservative white elite. The boycotts in particular may have produced as much harm as good. They had bonded participating parents to each other and to reform, but they had deprived children whose parents were too poor to pay for private schools of education; and there is no evidence that they changed the minds of people who had the power to desegregate. Inadvertently, the bullying tactics of the South had made the difference. The Fugitive Slave Law, dramatized by the renditions of Thomas Sims and especially Anthony Burns in 1854, in close connection to the Kansas-Nebraska Act, convinced many New Englanders that there was a Slave Power subverting their values and even their way of life. The integration of Boston schools was one way to distinguish themselves from southerners.[24]

Massachusetts' success, however, didn't translate well to the larger cities in Connecticut and Rhode Island. There, racism nourished by plan-
tation slavery had deeper roots. But the Bay State did inspire African
Americans in southern New England to work for integration, particularly
in Providence, Rhode Island, where the transplanted New Yorker George
T. Downing had taken the lead. By 1855 Downing was one of the wealthiest
African Americans in New England. He had moved to Newport, Rhode
Island, in 1846 to open a summer branch of his father's New York res-
taurant. It had proved lucrative, and he had begun a catering business in
Providence in 1850, where he then lived. His entrepreneurial ambitions
culminated in 1855 with the construction of a luxury hotel in Newport. But
he meant to do more with his life than make money. Downing contacted
Charles Sumner, William Howe of Boston city schools, and others to initiate a movement in Providence similar to Boston's. In 1857, he, other black
reformers, and some whites petitioned their city school board and later
the Rhode Island legislature to integrate the Providence schools but were
repelled. Arguments on both sides were familiar—schools for children of
color had a "high reputation" and there was no need for change that would
ultimately harm blacks and whites alike; our "colored citizens" are entitled
to equal rights and benefits, and integration is working well elsewhere—
and the votes were close, but for the time being the status quo prevailed.[25]
The desegregation of schools would not come to Bristol, Newport, and
Providence, Rhode Island, until after the Civil War.

13

The Wall

IN LATE SEPTEMBER 1854, delegates to the Colored Men's State Convention spent most of two days summing up the situation for African Americans in Connecticut. They were responding to state representative Olmsted who three years previously had conveyed to the legislature that "the colored men in this State were dying out, their hopes crushed, their manhood gone." The delegates offered no explanation of why they had waited so long to reply, but their memories were long and their retorts vigorous. Rather than dwelling on the problems they faced, they lauded the progress that had been made during the previous quarter century. Contrasting New Haven then with twenty years before, clergyman and reformer Amos G. Beman told of remarkable advancement. Its people of color had gone from owning no property to the current "two hundred thousand dollars worth of real estate." There had been neither church nor school that welcomed black people; now there were four schools, seven churches, and a "Literary Society with a Circulating Library." Ebenezer D. Bassett added that the "colored citizens of New Haven who cannot read and write are as few as were those who could, thirty years ago." Although he unhappily depicted the town's segregated schools as a "necessary evil," he was proud that the African American schoolhouses were "commodious," the teachers appropriately paid, and the enrollment increased from 80 to 190 students.[1]

Not to be outdone, delegates from other cities related how well their African American residents were doing. In Hartford, Peter Davis stated, its 700 people of color owned $70,000 worth of real estate. Like Beman, he didn't discuss how broadly the property was distributed, but it certainly is possible that at least one-quarter of the people lived in homes possessed by a family member. Only four people (presumably adults) were illiterate, and there were two schools with a total of 90 to 100 students. Middletown's 137

African Americans, according to Leverett C. Beman, held $26,000 worth of property, had two churches, and only three residents who could neither read nor write. He boasted that there were "no colored schools, for the reason that they are not needed, the white schools being open to 'all classes and colors.'" Bridgeport also had integrated schools with sixty-three children of African descent attending. Its 400 black residents owned $51,597 worth of real estate and had established two churches and one hotel. Two of their number in that seaport town were sea captains.[2]

Separate from the Connecticut convention in his hometown of Boston, William C. Nell, always a booster, provided a list of recent African American accomplishments in an 1855 issue of *The Liberator*. Edward Garrison Draper had just graduated from Dartmouth College, William Simpson had been winning praise as a crayon artist, and Lewis Hayden had enlarged his new store. And employment opportunities were expanding. A large business firm had hired a "colored book-keeper," several stores employed black clerks, the city had licensed an African American auctioneer, and one "colored boy" had told him that he had just been accepted as an apprentice to a white machinist. Nell believed these anecdotes should help dispel white doubts of the abilities of people of color and should stimulate black individuals to "a higher ambition."[3]

No one could deny that the world of Amos G. Beman and William C. Nell was vastly superior for people of African descent than had been the world of Hosea Easton and David Walker. African American men, except in Connecticut, could vote and hold office. Schools, except in the largest cities of Connecticut and Rhode Island, were integrated. Railroads, stagecoaches, hotels, and cultural venues (with occasional aberrations) were free from discrimination. People of African descent and of European descent could marry one another and live peaceably, even in Maine and Rhode Island where such marriages were legally prohibited. Riots no longer were directed at people of color. Fugitive slaves were safer in New England than in any other section of the United States. There was an emerging, if still small, black middle class. All of this was cause for celebration.[4]

But the overall improvement had not eliminated caste or produced full equality. For the most part, official discrimination had ended. There were few laws in New England that defined an African American's rights as different from anyone else's. The most significant exception was the franchise in Connecticut. The state constitution specified that only "white males" could vote. State legislators, nonetheless, made regular attempts to strike the word "white" (and occasionally, as in 1858, to eliminate the word "males" as well). By 1855, substantial majorities of the legislature favored extending the franchise to black males, but they lacked the two-thirds required to amend the state constitution. Joseph Maddox, the representative of Killingworth and an unrepentant racist, led the seventy-nine members (37 percent of the total) who defeated the amendment. Maddox ("better known as Doctor Maddox") claimed that there was a natural "aversion to the colored race" and denied that whites had in any way injured them. When he asserted that "their condition had been ameliorated by bringing them from Africa here" and that God "had designed that they should be sent here into slavery," the legislature exploded with derisive laughter. Maddox defensively sputtered: "Gentlemen might laugh, but their laughter did not controvert the facts."[5]

Maddox provided an easy target, and Amos G. Beman took aim. Days after Maddox and like-minded representatives killed the amendment, Beman challenged the Doctor to a public debate on the question of whether "white" should be removed from the state constitution as a qualification for voting. He proposed they meet at a time and place selected by three representatives—one chosen by Maddox, one by Beman, and a third determined by the other two. The House of Representatives caught the spirit of the occasion, offered their hall for the debate, and recommended three men to umpire. Maddox had nothing to win and much to lose, and he managed to duck what well might have been a humiliating night. Beman addressed the House by himself. But no effort could gain the support of two-thirds of the legislature, even though it was substantially in advance of the general citizenry. In 1857, 19,148 Connecticut voters opposed a referendum to expand the franchise to all men compared to 5,553 who supported it. Only with the Fifteenth Amendment to the United States Constitution in 1870 did African American men in Connecticut receive the right to vote.[6]

Restrictions of militias to whites only were more complicated to overturn. New England had a long tradition of autonomous town militias where almost all men in a community—clergymen, the disabled, and the aged were exempt—formed a unit and chose their own officers. The United States Constitution altered the colonial arrangement by transferring power to organize, arm, and discipline militias to Congress, and Congress had passed laws stipulating that militias might only be composed of white, male citizens. Black New Englanders pressured their state legislatures to override what they considered unconstitutional laws and to let them join militias or create their own. It wasn't so much that African American men wanted to become soldiers or to participate in military affairs—though such motives shouldn't be ignored—but rather that they aspired to be equal members of society, not an outlying caste. As Bostonian William J. Watkins put it: they sought "to be placed in a position in which we shall be able to show ourselves as men, and honorable men, and thereby give the lie to the American doctrine of our innate inferiority."[7]

In Massachusetts in 1852, the same people who were endeavoring to protect fugitive slaves and integrate Boston schools started petitioning— the legislature repeatedly and in 1853 the Constitutional Convention of Massachusetts—for the inclusion of men of African descent in the national militia. Their petition to the Constitutional Convention was typical of these appeals for equality. Robert Morris, William C. Nell, and other signatories argued that the state constitution and its bill of rights defended the rights of all its citizens without distinction. The same was true of the United States Constitution, particularly where it stated that the "citizens of each State shall be entitled to all the privileges and immunities of citizens in the several States." The problem came from Congress when it stipulated that only "white male citizens" could serve in the militia. That law, the petition contended, "making this unnatural distinction" violated both the national and the state constitution and "therefore ought to exert no controlling force over the legislation of any of the States." But such logic did not convince those governmental bodies.[8]

After their petitions were rejected, a group of Boston African American men formed their own military company. The Massasoit Guards, as they called themselves, enrolled eighty men at its inception in 1855. John P. Coburn led the company as its captain, and Robert Morris was one of its four lieutenants. They applied to the state's commander-in-chief, Governor Henry J. Gardiner, for a loan of arms. In their application they pointed out that the governor of Rhode Island had honored a similar request from "a colored company in Providence." Massachusetts Attorney General John H. Clifford advised Governor Gardiner not to comply. He held that the United States Constitution had made the militia a national institution and had prohibited states from keeping troops without the consent of Congress. Because Congress had restricted the militia to whites, Massachusetts could not enlist people of color nor arm the Massasoit Guards without breaking national law. Although Gardiner sheepishly acknowledged the "colored heroes of the Revolution," he informed Morris that he would not provide arms. Morris, as usual, quickly recovered from the setback, and in a public letter informed readers that the Massasoit Guards would raise its own funds for arms. Recognizing the contradiction of a segregated military company, he assured people that "its ranks are open to all citizens of good moral character." He also asserted second amendment rights "to keep and bear arms" and that no one should challenge the unit's right to drill and parade.⁹

By the end of the decade the Massachusetts legislature had passed several bills opening the militia to people of African descent, but each time Governor Nathaniel Banks vetoed them. Not until the creation of the Fifty-fourth Regiment during the Civil War were Massachusetts African Americans allowed to serve.¹⁰

Efforts in New Hampshire were more successful, though conducted in a somewhat bizarre environment. In the 1857 session of the New Hampshire legislature, Representative Clark proposed an amendment to the bill that would revamp the militia system of the state. It removed the word "white" from the qualifications for service. Representative Stevens, amid laughter, suggested that the exemption of clergymen and physicians should be eliminated as well if Clark believed "it such a great privilege to be obliged to do military duty." Representative Robinson (who was a physician) flippantly commented that he "shall protest against being put in the same category with negroes," and laughter filled the chamber once again. Somehow the amendment passed "amid great merriment on all sides."¹¹

What many of the New Hampshire legislators didn't understand was how demeaning and hurtful such distinctions were. By the mid-1850s, most African American New Englanders were little affected by racist laws— though the removal of any vestiges of caste was welcome. More common were the slights, the insults, the subtle discrimination that could happen at any moment, the sneer from a stranger that reminded people of color that they were perceived as different. These were all barriers to true equality.

Although most New England churches had stopped the practice of perching people of color on upper balconies, the practice had not entirely died away, particularly in Boston, Connecticut, and Rhode Island. There were at least four churches with segregated congregations in Boston alone. Charles Lowell had been minister of the Unitarian West Church for more than twenty years when in 1854 he suggested that for the convenience of older black worshippers a pew be designated for them on the ground floor near the entrance; but his white flock even rejected that modest proposal. The *Hartford Republican* reported a similar resistance to integrated seating at a Congregational church in its state. An old couple of African descent long had trudged up the stairs to the gallery where they were allowed to sit.

When the wife had died, her feeble husband began sitting below. Christian charity prevailed for two months, but then he was told that he could only attend services in the gallery. Unable to climb the stairs, he stayed home. There were several attempts by individual church members to provide him a "slip" on the ground floor and there was even a vote in his favor (soon overturned), but he was in effect banished from the church. The newspaper editorialized that it had thought the days of "Jim Crow cars" and "negro pews" had passed. It found much to its surprise that "soulless" corporations had overcome their "colorphobia" but that some Christian churches had not. The *Hartford Republican* concluded that "the railroads are ahead of the churches in decency—the steam-engines in advance of the deacons."[12]

Theaters and other cultural institutions usually were free from racist practices, but on occasion a person of color might be barred from a particular production or required to sit in a section designated for "coloreds." For an African American venturing out for an evening of entertainment or enrichment, it became a variation of Russian roulette. No matter how respectable the persons of color, no matter that they were appropriately dressed for the occasion, no matter that they already possessed tickets, there was always the possibility of rejection and embarrassment. One of those occasions was on May 6, 1853, at the Howard Athanæum in Boston. Sarah Parker Remond and Caroline E. Putnam, sisters of Charles Lenox Remond and residents of Salem, along with William C. Nell had purchased tickets for a performance of the opera *Don Pasquale*. At the theater, they climbed the steps to the "family circle" on the second tier. As they were about to take their seats, Henry Palmer (an agent for the opera company) stopped them, asked to see their tickets, told them that they couldn't sit in that section, and directed them to the gallery among the reporters. They asked if they might stand where they were and just listen. Palmer refused the request but offered them their money back. As they stood there, Charles P. Philbrick, a policeman, and the Athanæum manager Mr. Willard arrived. Philbrick began to force them down the steps, in the process tearing Remond's dress and injuring her shoulder. Sarah Remond pressed charges, and Palmer and Philbrick were taken to a Police Court where the judge rebuked them and the theater—primarily for not warning ticketholders in advance of seating restrictions—and issued a small fine. The two sisters also filed a civil suit but withdrew it when they were given similar tickets for the opera.[13]

John Stephenson, like the Remond sisters, had reached a point in his life where he could reasonably expect to receive some respect. By 1856 he had risen to be chief clerk for the Boston firm of Morey, Ober & Co. and, along with several other African Americans including the seemingly ubiquitous William C. Nell, was a member of the Mercantile Library Association. It was a prestigious cultural institution that sponsored an annual lecture series, published a small journal of articles by members, and of course served as a library. As the city of Boston prepared to honor its native son Benjamin Franklin, the association raised funds for a statue that was to be placed in City Hall Square. On September 17, the day of the dedication and celebration, it was one of many organizations that walked the seven miles of the procession, its members joining an estimated 200,000 to 300,000 people participating.[14]

Stephenson and other members who chose to march assembled at the association rooms and received their badges. Four abreast they progressed

FIGURE 13.1 *Sarah P. Remond,* by an unknown photographer. (Collection of the Massachusetts Historical Society).

to the Common where they waited until all organizations were assembled for the parade to City Hall Square. Stephenson walked with a "companion" who also was of African descent and a friend. At the Common, James A. Woolson, the chief marshall of the association, approached his companion and asked him to "withdraw from the Procession, stating that, on account of his being a colored man, the Association did not like to have him there." The man protested but left without incident. Apparently no one, including Stephenson, came to his defense. Half an hour later Ira Chase Jr., president of the Mercantile Library Association, accompanied by Woolson and a trustee, drew Stephenson aside and, according to Stephenson, made the following request: "Will you not do us the kindness to leave the procession and go to the rear, and there remain between our Association and the next, and keep away the boys? We have,' said he, 'in the procession, some Southern boys, and you know how it is respecting you and them.'" Stephenson couldn't believe what he had heard; but with "no fellow of the Society taking up my cause, or befriending me, while some jeered and others laughed," he departed and on October 3 in a public letter withdrew from the association.[15]

Many members had been unaware of the incident. When the association met on October 10, Stephenson's account of the incident was their only topic. William C. Nell offered a resolution to create an investigating committee, and the body of members appointed a nominating committee for the purpose. That committee quickly returned with a majority and a minority report. The majority report recommended that the matter be dropped, but the association membership voted it down. Before there was greater chaos, Chase gave his version of the episode. His description differed little from Stephenson's. The chief difference was that Chase claimed that he merely "expressed a desire that he [Stephenson] would oblige the officers by taking a lower position" but that the decision was entirely up to him. Rather than debate the issue, Chase proposed that the association "meet the subject at once, and settle the whole business." So the affair ended.[16] The association had embarrassed itself and sought to mend its ways. Whether Stephenson reactivated his membership is unknown.

Robert Morris' life story in many ways reads like a "rags to riches" tale, but no matter how successful Morris became he was not protected from the prejudices and humiliations that all New England people of color might experience. Born in Salem in 1823 to York Morris, a waiter, and Nancy Morris, he attended public schools until the age of fifteen, when he was sent to Boston as a servant to Ellis Gray Loring, a lawyer and abolitionist.

Loring soon recognized Morris' extraordinary abilities and taught him the law. In 1847, Morris became the second African American in the United States certified as a lawyer, and his practice immediately thrived, highlighted by a series of equal rights cases and his appointment as a justice of the peace. By 1850 he, his wife Catharine, and their children Catharine and Robert Jr. were living in the Boston suburb of Chelsea. It was a small, overwhelmingly white town of 6,701 residents, of whom thirty-seven were people of African descent. The eight African American households were scattered throughout the town. Morris and his family resided in a white, lower-middle-class neighborhood composed primarily of traders and artisans. Chelsea grew rapidly in the 1850s. By 1860, the overall population doubled while the number of African Americans quadrupled. Black families (now including Benjamin Roberts and his family) continued to reside in most parts of town, but a small enclave of six contiguous households with thirty-five people had developed as well.[17]

In 1858, Morris, who was becoming increasingly prosperous, decided to move to a more affluent part of Chelsea that the Cary Improvement Company was developing. Enoch Bartlett had built "a fine mansion with about 10,000 feet of land" in the Cary domain that caught Morris' attention. Before beginning negotiations, Morris told Bartlett that there might be objections to his buying a house there. In particular, he had learned that Simeon B. Ray, a corn broker, and Joseph H. Sandford, a bookkeeper, feared that his presence would depreciate the value of their property. Bartlett assured Morris that he was in the business to make money and that Morris' money was "as good as any other man's." He also had talked with John Low, an agent of the Cary Company, and mentioned that if they prevented the sale he no longer would build houses on their land. The lawyer and the builder shook hands, and Morris apparently had bought a house.[18]

Unfortunately, the saga didn't end there. Ray and Sandford threatened to sell their houses or to move and lease to "Irish tenants." Both Low and Bartlett developed second thoughts. The next day Bartlett discussed his dilemma with Morris. When Morris learned the names of those opposing him, he countered that the two most prominent men in the vicinity, John Taylor and Nehemiah Boynton, supported his becoming their neighbor. Bartlett was somewhat reassured, but he made it clear that he would not complete the deal without the approval of the Cary Improvement Company. Morris then approached Low and was informed that the directors of the company would refuse the sale if there were persons who didn't want him for a neighbor. Reluctantly, Morris informed a "mortified" Bartlett of the conversation and that under the circumstances he was "obliged to give it up." Morris in fact was not a man who gave up, and days later he had his account of the affair published in the *Chelsea Telegraph & Pioneer*. Although there is no more information about what transpired, the 1860 census shows Morris and his family living in a $10,000 house in the neighborhood of Simeon B. Ray, Joseph H. Sandford, John Taylor, and Nehemiah Boynton.[19] He had won but—knowing that there would have been no difficulty had he been white—not without cost.

Despite being born into a Philadelphia family of wealth and influence, Charlotte Forten continually thought of herself as an outsider. Her mother Mary Virginia Forten died a month before she turned three in 1840, and her father Robert Bridges Forten often was distant and didn't provide the affection she craved. Her grandparents, parents, aunts, and uncles were leading abolitionists and reformers, and their quest for justice and equality contributed to her acute awareness of being "an outcast from the rest of mankind." She longed for a place, especially her imagined England, where she would not be judged by her dark skin. In 1853 when she was sixteen, her father sent her to Higginson Grammar School in Salem. She first lived with the family of Charles Lenox Remond and found him as removed as her father but loved the Remond women. Higginson Grammar School and Salem Normal School, where she matriculated two years later to prepare for being a teacher, were mixed blessings. The teachers recognized and encouraged her academic talents, and Mary Shepard, the principal and a teacher at Higginson, was caring and sympathetic. She found few friends among the students, however. They might be kind and cordial to her at school; but if she encountered them on the streets they would ignore her or give her only the slightest sign of recognition. She commented in her journal that "I, of course, acknowledge no such recognition, and they soon cease entirely." She found it nearly impossible "to love and trust hardly any one whose skin is white, however lovable, attractive and congenial in seeming." One of her few friends, Lizzie Church (who was white as were all the girls at Higginson) "gently reproved" her for not returning a hug at the end of the school year. Charlotte thought that she wasn't a cold person; it just wasn't in her nature to be expressive of her feelings. And this was the problem of being Charlotte Forten and being a person of color in a world dominated by people of European descent who might be uncaring or outright racist. She could delight in walking on Boston Common or attending the theater or viewing the Horticultural Exhibition, but she was always waiting for the other shoe to drop.[20] She may have been predisposed to be wary, but she also lived in a society where a cruel act could occur at any moment.

These were serious problems that primarily affected middle-class and elite people of African descent. They were barriers to full equality and sources of unease and tension, but for the most part they could be surmounted. Sarah Remond and Carolyn Putnam eventually saw the opera, John Stephenson was vindicated by an abashed Mercantile Library Association, Robert Morris gained his mansion, and Charlotte Forten Grimké lived a rich and rewarding life, though no doubt marred by the reasonable expectation of racism. A substantial portion of New England African Americans (well more than half), however, faced a wall with few chinks—the double whammy of racism and disdain for the poor. White (and some black) Americans and many people in other parts of the world viewed poverty as a badge of dishonor. In early America, the common attitude was that God had intended for some to be rich, some poor, some high in power, some oppressed. The so-called American Dream that displaced the theological, hierarchical worldview was no more sympathetic to those in poverty. In a land of opportunity, only the lazy and unambitious were poor. Or so proponents thought. Social and economic mobility for all hard-working and conscientious citizens proved to be more an ideal than a reality, despite anecdotes to the contrary.

Poverty was a wall holding back people of all ethnicities, and it was much more difficult to surmount than barriers separating working class from lower middle class or middle class from upper middle class. Poor people by definition ate less well, dressed less well, were housed less well than other people. Adults typically had less education than other people, and their children might attend school less frequently than other children because of the necessity of supplementing family incomes. Their connections were primarily with other poor people who were struggling with similar desperate lives. Their aspirations could be as bleak as their conditions.

For African Americans, the wall was reinforced by racism. It's difficult to know with certainty how many people of color in New England were impoverished. We can exclude professionals (clergy, doctors, dentists, and lawyers); sea captains; shopkeepers, traders, and merchants; manufacturers such as sail makers; service providers (barbers, waiters, porters, and stewards); skilled labor; farmers who owned their land; and fishermen who owned their boats and gear. Among men of African descent in mixed marriages, by way of comparison, not quite half were in occupations that would place them above poverty (see Appendix 7). And the number of occupations gives a false sense of economic opportunity. African American professionals and shopkeepers primarily served other people of color. Whites rarely patronized them. That limited those fields almost entirely to larger cities and to the size of the black population within them. In addition, shopkeepers needed some capital to buy or lease the space for their stores and to stock their shelves. That helps explain why so many of them were in the used clothing business—a venture with merchandise that required fewer funds to establish and was affordable to low-income customers. Many skilled trades ostracized people of African descent or made it very difficult for them to apprentice, and even then, people of European descent might not purchase their goods or employ them. A slight majority of African American men in mixed marriages were unskilled laborers, common sailors, tenant farmers, or client fishermen, and almost all of them were poor. That still doesn't account for the 22 percent of men in mixed marriages for whom the census records list no occupation. There may have been clerical errors of some sort that left the category blank, but the vast majority of that group almost certainly were unemployed, partially employed, or seasonally employed. In short, they too were poor. It is highly likely that black men in mixed marriages were more prosperous than the general population of African Americans. If the 57 percent of men of African descent in New Haven for whom the 1850 census listed no occupation was typical, then a figure placing at least 75 percent of black New Englanders in poverty seems probable. To make matters worse—although employment opportunities may have been slightly improving in the 1850s for middle-class African Americans—the rapid increase of immigrants, particularly the Irish, and of competition for unskilled work as well as changes in seafaring occupations made escaping poverty for most people of color all the harder.[21]

As long as poverty was so extensive, equal rights would remain unfulfilled. At some level, those who had struggled so long for African American equality recognized the necessity to address economic inequality. Certainly that goal was behind the attempt to create a manual labor college in the 1830s, as were the continual efforts to provide high-quality education for children of color. By the 1850s, almost all schools in New England had been integrated, assuring that black children had access to as good an education as white children. But the problems of poverty required more. William C. Nell, Amos G. Beman, and others continued to promote uplift, particularly by publicizing accounts of African American success.

They must have believed that such stories would inspire people of African descent to work hard and to raise their aspirations and would convince people of European descent to hire black New Englanders and to purchase their goods and services. Nell also wanted to demonstrate that people of color had long been integral to New England society. In 1855, his book *The Colored Patriots of the American Revolution* appeared, and a few years later he initiated Crispus Attucks Day—more important as a public celebration of African Americans' place in the American narrative than as an accurate depiction of Attucks' role in the Boston Massacre.[22]

When people entered Faneuil Hall on the evening of March 5, 1858, it had been seventy-five years since Boston last had commemorated its Massacre and the first time that the memory of Crispus Attucks was the focal point. Nell presided over the event, and he had enlisted an electrifying group of speakers—Theodore Parker, Wendell Phillips, William Lloyd Garrison, Charles Lenox Remond, and John Rock. Rock spoke first, and he stole the show. Just thirty-two years old and a resident of Boston for only five years, he had quickly gained prominence. Despite a modest background as the son of John and Maria Rock in Salem, New Jersey, he had taught school for four years, studied both medicine and dentistry in Philadelphia, and practiced both professions in Philadelphia, then Boston. Rock was the second African American to become a member of the Massachusetts Medical Society. But long hours had contributed to ill health.[23]

Rock was not feeling well as he addressed the audience (he soon would leave for Paris to receive medical care), but then his passion returned. He used the occasion to counter the charge that people of African descent were cowards for having allowed themselves to be enslaved. He asserted that only "superior force keeps us down" and that other peoples have behaved similarly. African Americans had fought in the Revolutionary War. "They fought for liberty," he asserted, "but they got slavery." Despite adversity, he was proud to be a person of color, and he would not "turn my back upon my race. With it I will sink or swim." Without using the words "black is beautiful," he proclaimed: "When I contrast the fine tough muscular system, the beautiful, rich color, the full broad features, and the gracefully frizzled hair of the negro, with the delicate physical organization, wan color, sharp features and lank hair of the Caucasian, I am inclined to believe that when the white man was created, nature was pretty well exhausted—but determined to keep up appearances, she pinched up his features, and did the best she could under the circumstances." There was a tinge of racism—even defiance—in those remarks, but generally, Rock was

JOHN H. ROCK, COLORED COUNSELOR.—(Photographed by Richards, Philadelphia.)

FIGURE 13.2 *John Rock*, from an illustration in *Harper's Weekly*, February 25, 1865. (Library of Congress).

turning the conventional aesthetic on its head and showing how arbitrary such distinctions were. The audience responded with "great laughter."[24]

The final section of Rock's speech turned to poverty, racism, and the eradication of both. In words reminiscent of Hosea Easton and David Walker, he exhorted that "whenever the colored man is elevated, it will be by his own exertion" and that people of color needed to forsake the "grog shop" and gambling and to raise their aspirations. Here Rock straddled the fence between boosters who optimistically believed in the possibility of a society where blacks and whites were equal partners and separatists who pessimistically despaired of whites ever overcoming their racism. He believed that whites must not only stop oppressing people of color but also encourage "their trades and business," and he envisioned a world without racism or poverty. "When the avenues to wealth are opened to us," he proclaimed, "we will then become educated and wealthy, and then the roughest looking colored man that you ever saw, or ever will see, will be pleasanter than the harmonies of Orpheus, and black will be a very pretty color."[25]

Rock's analysis of the present was credible, and his vision of a better world was stirring. But he did not satisfactorily explain how to get from one to the other. How do we break the connection between the racism that creates and preserves poverty and the impoverished circumstances that promote the racist contention that people of color are inferior? How do we shatter the cycle of poverty? Rock, like Americans more than 150 years later, didn't have the answers. A portion of black New Englanders would do well, despite occasional taunts and barriers. Robert Morris would gain his "mansion," Lewis Hayden was elected state senator, and John Rock joined the small fraternity of lawyers who argued cases before the United States Supreme Court. But most people of African descent in New England at best would barely scrape by.

PART VI

Epilogue

14

Miles to Go

RUMORS HAD BEEN floating for months when in the March 24, 1865, issue of *The Liberator* William Lloyd Garrison confirmed that he would discontinue the newspaper at the end of the year. Ignoring the mission he had stated in the first issue, thirty-five years before, that the newspaper's twin goals were to end slavery and to establish equal rights for people of color, he claimed that he had founded the *Liberator* "for the express purpose of effecting the extinction of slavery." With the anticipated passage of the Thirteenth Amendment, it was "historically fitting" to terminate the newspaper. He assured readers that he was not retiring from promoting reform; he simply would approach those ideals in other ways. Garrison was almost sixty years old, and he admitted that "something of repose and seclusion is coveted by us, in order to recuperate both mind and body."[1] The formal end of slavery provided him a graceful excuse to exit the frontline of battle.

Garrison made the same assessment a month and a half later at the American Anti-Slavery Society annual meeting. He argued that there was no need for an antislavery organization after slavery had been eliminated and proposed a resolution calling for the society to disband. There still was work to be done, but individuals mingling "with the masses" could accomplish it. Abolitionists no longer were outsiders but rather one with the country. But here he was not the sole proprietor able to make a unilateral decision. Others disagreed. Charles Remond countered that the society from its beginning had had a larger purpose than only ending slavery and that its structure still was necessary for bringing equal rights to people of color. Wendell Phillips, as usual, was more blunt. It was premature to declare slavery dead or to terminate the society. Frederick Douglass elaborated on Phillips's theme by stating: "Slavery is not abolished until the black man has the ballot." The vote on Garrison's resolution wasn't close. Only forty-eight members voted with the society's president while 118 opposed his motion. Hoping to proceed as if there had been no resolution, the society nominated Garrison to continue as its president, but he declined. Wendell Phillips then became president of a society that would limp on for another five years until the Fifteenth Amendment extended the franchise to black males. Garrison, however, was too important to the American Anti-Slavery Society's members for them to close their meeting without acknowledging his contributions, and they passed a resolution regretting Garrison's decision but praising him as "the real Liberator of the American Slave." Fittingly, members cast their votes unanimously by rising in honor of their departing president.[2]

Garrison's announcement and the American Anti-Slavery Society meeting were portents of changing priorities. Reform-minded New Englanders dispersed in various directions. Some focused on the newly liberated freedmen to the south and on reconstructing that region. Others concentrated on such causes as women's rights, temperance, and labor. No one denied that forms of racism still persisted in New England, but many shared Garrison's belief that the basic work for equal rights had been accomplished or soon would be and welcomed the opportunity to invest in their own lives. And some died far too soon—John Rock in 1866, only forty-one years old; sixty-three-year-old Charles Lenox Remond in 1873; William Cooper Nell, the heart of the movement throughout the antebellum period, in 1874 at age fifty-seven.

To a certain extent the optimists were correct. There was a reform wake following the Civil War, just as there had been at the conclusion of the Revolutionary War. The Massachusetts legislature passed a law in 1865 prohibiting any "distinction, discrimination, or restriction on account of color or race ... in any licensed inn, in any public place of amusement, public conveyance, or public meeting," and in 1866 the Rhode Island legislature desegregated the state's schools. But then substantive measures at the state level essentially ceased. With a single exception there would only be tweaks on equal rights in New England for the remainder of the century. Six years after the passage of the Fifteenth Amendment, Connecticut brought its constitution into line by striking the word "white" from the qualifications to vote. From time to time Massachusetts added new venues that could not discriminate, such as skating rinks in 1885, and both Massachusetts and Connecticut passed laws preventing insurance companies from discriminating in the issuing of policies. Rhode Island in

1881 and Maine in 1883 overturned their laws—long unenforced—against mixed marriage. The most important legislation came from Rhode Island in 1884 when it enacted a law prohibiting discrimination in public places, on public conveyances, and on jury service.[3] No matter these advances, the bulk of black New Englanders continued to be blocked by the wall of poverty and racism. They couldn't afford to attend theaters, ride first-class on trains, or purchase life insurance. They needed education for their children—a dual responsibility of parents and the state—and a fair shot at employment of all types.

Even with its significant limitations, New England at the brink of the Civil War was ahead of the rest of the nation in providing equal rights. The forms of racism there had different proportions and different expressions than elsewhere. Paternalistic racism and even the absence of racism, as in mixed marriages, overwhelmingly outweighed the more virulent strains of exclusion, white supremacy, and violence. There were assaults and mob actions to be sure—as frequently directed at white abolitionists as at black residents and activists—but there were no lynchings, no reign of terror. It was possible for local, African American–led movements to form and be joined by white allies. New England by 1860 had achieved nearly all of the desegregationist goals set out by Hosea Easton and David Walker thirty years earlier, but the rest of the country in different degrees lagged far behind. The nation, as it readied for a war between sections, was a cultural patchwork, as it still is today.

New Englanders were no more inherently virtuous than any other people, but they had had different historical experiences. Their land and climate, except for pockets in Rhode Island and Connecticut, didn't suit large-scale agricultural slavery. During the colonial period, large families and neighbors provided a sufficient labor force for small farms and small enterprises. Slavery never became a central institution, and the number of enslaved people of African descent remained a small part of the total population. Emancipation didn't produce the same fears of retaliation and upheaval of established ways that it would elsewhere. White New Englanders didn't need to build ideologies, hierarchies, and institutions to control people of color whether enslaved or free, and those they did create were easier to topple. They behaved with greater empathy because their circumstances—their parameters of choice—were different.

Nothing is permanent. Forms of racism, like a disease, can recede and resurge. Whether prejudice or discrimination based on false constructions of difference can ever be eradicated completely remains an open question.

More than 150 years since the advent of the Civil War, the United States as a whole—often kicking, screaming, or killing—has caught up with the New England of 1860, but widespread poverty continues to disproportionately plague people of color. The racist wall shows signs of deterioration, but it has not yet been pulled down. The aspirations of Hosea Easton, David Walker, and William Cooper Nell have yet to be fulfilled.

Acknowledgments

I CAN'T IMAGINE a book of history being written in splendid isolation. By necessity and choice, historians work collaboratively, and it makes the process all the more fun. Although this book bears my name only, the number of contributors is nearly endless.

Two longtime friends head the list. Both Gary Nash and Norm Rosenberg read the manuscript, offered insightful and sometimes provocative suggestions, and were always encouraging. Librarians are among my favorite people, and John Wade of the California Institute of Technology and Leslie Jobski of the Huntington Library were especially helpful. As I was investigating mixed marriages, I contacted 134 historical societies and 68 creators of family trees, and their responses were informative, gracious, and generous of time and materials. I particularly want to thank Eve Anderson (Thomaston Historical Society), Ben Baker (Manchester Historical Association), Mary Louis Beardsley, Lee Blake (New Bedford Historical Society), Celia Briggs (Friendship Public Library), Joyce Ball, John Carnahan (Brattleboro Historical Society), Pat Casey (New Hartford Historical Society), Rosario Castronova, Sue Cifaldi, Delores Costa, Mary Ann Devins (Hartford Historical Society), Ann Frey (Pejepscot Historical Society), Ted Groom (Totoket Historical Society), Paul Hart (Barkhamsted Historical Society), Judy Haynes (Boylston Historical Society), Holly V. Izard (Worcester Historical Society), Frances Karttunen (Nantucket Historical Association), Sandra Kent (Mont Vernon Historical Society), Marilyn Labbe (Killingly Historical & Genealogical Society), Inga Larson (North Andover Historical Society), Dawn Littleton, Marty Lund, Martha Mayo (Center for Lowell History), Cliff McCarthy (Springfield Museums), Betty Miessner (Scituate Historical Society), Wendy Pirsig

(Old Berwick Historical Society), Dale Plummer (City Historian of Norwich, Connecticut), Ginny Reinhard (Orange Historical Society), Tyler Resch (Bennington Museum), Barbara Rimkunas (Essex Historical Society), Maureen Rukstalis (Yarmouth Historical Society), Allan Rumrill (Historical Society of Cheshire County), Ed Saleski (Stoddard Historical Society), Diana Overlock Sewell (Warren Historical Society), Deborah Shapiro (Middlesex County Historical Society), Mary Sheldon (Nobleboro Historical Society), Antonia Stephens (Sturgis Library), Carrol Moore Sweeney, Suzanne Teixeira (Totoket Historical Society), Betsy Tyler (Nantucket Historical Association), Christina Vida (Windsor Historical Society), Judy Warner (Harvard Historical Society), Connie Wiberg (Deer Isle Historical Society), Jenn Williams (Lawrence Historical Society), Allen Wilson, Christine Hilliard Wilson, Amelia Woodworth (Old Newbury Historical Society), and Carl Zellner (Charlestown Historical Society).

Friends and family may not have offered professional advice (though some did), but they were always supportive and frequently asked questions that helped me clarify unclear ideas and, let's face it, I simply enjoy their company. I especially want to thank Don Archer, Steve, Patricia, and Rose Archer, Julie, Steve, Derek, and Jason Mayo, Barbara and Terry Douglass, Lori Slater, Richard Blackwood, Bruce and Mary Campbell, Bill and Janice Geiger, Les Howard, Anne Kiley, Alan Lamson, Dave and Beth Macleod, Ron Munro, Phil O'Brien and Ann Topjon, Dick and Jan Potter, Emily Rosenberg, and Dennis Thavenet. And most of all thanks to my main collaborator and best friend, Ginny.

APPENDIX I

1830 New England Cities with 100 or More African Americans

1. Boston, Mass.—1,876
2. Providence, R.I.—1,205
3. New Haven, Conn.—530
4. Newport, R.I.—439
5. New Bedford, Mass.—383
6. Hartford, Conn.—338
6. South Kingston, R.I.—338
8. Portland, Maine—312
9. Nantucket, Mass.—277
10. Salem, Mass.—267
11. Norwich, Conn.—262
12. Stonington, Conn.—258
13. Greenwich, Conn.—257
14. Warwick, R.I.—218
15. Middletown, Conn.—211
16. Sheffield, Mass.—180
17. Bristol, R.I.—171
18. New London, Conn.—170
19. North Stonington, Conn.—169
20. Pittsfield, Mass.—166
21. Fairfield, Conn.—162
22. New Milford, Conn.—157
23. West Hartford, Conn.—153
24. Colchester, Conn.—146
25. Groton, Conn.—143

26. Litchfield, Conn.—142
27. Lebanon, Conn.—141
28. Sharon, Conn.—135
29. Norwalk, Conn.—133
30. Dartmouth, Mass.—131
31. Griswold, Conn.—130
32. New Shoreham, R.I.—129
33. North Kingston, R.I.—121
34. Newtown, Conn.—116
35. Bridgeport, Conn.—108
36. East Haddam, Conn.—104
37. Williamstown, Mass.—102
38. Pomfret, Conn.—100
38. Charlestown, R.I.—100

Total = 10,480; 49% of all African Americans in New England
Towns with 300 or more = 5,421; 25% of all African Americans in New England

APPENDIX 2

1830 New England Cities with 5% or More African Americans

1. New Shoreham, R.I.—10.7 (129 of 1,205)
2. South Kingston, R.I.—9.2 (338 of 3,663)
3. Charlestown, R.I.—7.8 (100 of 1,284)
4. Sheffield, Mass.—7.6 (180 of 2,382)
4. Stonington, Conn.—7.6 (258 of 3,397)
6. Ervings Grant, Mass.—7.5 (34 of 454)
7. Providence, R.I.—7.3 (1,205 of 16,507)
8. Colchester, Conn.—7.0 (146 of 2,073)
8. Lisbon, Conn.—7.0 (81 of 1,161)
10. Greenwich, Conn.—6.8 (257 of 3,804)
11. Lenox, Mass.—6.3 (82 of 1,299)
12. North Stonington, Conn.—6.0 (169 of 2,840)
13. Griswold, Conn.—5.9 (130 of 2,212)
14. Huntington, Conn.—5.8 (79 of 1,371)
15. Boxborough, Mass.—5.6 (27 of 479)
15. Bristol, R.I.—5.6 (171 of 3,034)
15. West Hartford, Conn.—5.6 (153 of 2,716)
18. Lebanon, Conn.—5.5 (141 of 2,555)
18. New Haven, Conn.—5.5 (530 of 9,615)
18. Newport, R.I.—5.5 (439 of 8,010)
21. Sharon, Conn.—5.2 (135 of 2,615)
22. Norwich, Conn.—5.1 (262 of 5,161)
23. Brunswick, Vt.—5.0 (8 of 160)
23. New Bedford, Mass.—5.0 (383 of 7,592)
23. Pomfret, Conn.—5.0 (100 of 1,981)

1830 Towns Residential Distribution

Towns with 100 or More African Americans

Towns	Family		Black Household		White Household		Alone	
	#	%	#	%	#	%	#	%
Boston, Mass.	1,002	53.4	551	29.4	297	15.8	26	1.4
Providence, R.I.	437	36.3	295	24.5	449	37.3	24	2.0
New Haven, Conn.	216	40.8	109	20.6	196	37.0	9	1.7
Newport, R.I.	86	19.6	181	41.2	163	37.1	9	2.1
New Bedford, Mass.	212	55.4	102	26.6	63	16.4	6	1.6
Hartford, Conn.	171	50.6	42	12.4	125	37.0	0	0.0
S. Kingston, R.I.	144	42.6	107	32.0	86	25.4	1	0.3
Portland, Maine	218	70.0	59	18.9	29	9.3	6	1.9
Nantucket, Mass.	128	46.2	108	39.0	40	14.4	1	0.4
Salem, Mass.	108	40.4	103	38.6	47	17.6	9	3.3
Norwich, Conn.	126	48.0	38	14.5	94	35.9	4	1.5

Towns	Family		Black Household		White Household		Alone	
	#	%	#	%	#	%	#	%
Stonington, Conn.	98	38.0	91	35.3	69	26.7	0	0.0
Greenwich, Conn.	155	60.3	2	0.8	99	38.5	1	0.4
Warwick, R.I.	82	37.6	78	35.8	56	25.7	2	0.9
Middletown, Conn.	126	59.7	22	10.4	61	28.9	2	0.9
Sheffield, Mass.	126	70.0	20	11.1	34	18.9	0	0.0
Bristol, R.I.	100	58.5	30	17.5	41	24.0	0	0.0
New London, Conn.	26	15.3	78	45.9	66	38.8	0	0.0
N. Stonington, Conn.	104	61.5	20	11.8	44	26.0	1	0.6
Pittsfield, Mass.	70	42.2	35	21.1	60	36.1	1	0.1
Fairfield, Conn.	94	58.0	6	3.7	59	36.4	3	1.9
New Milford, Conn.	89	56.7	14	8.9	53	33.8	1	0.6
West Hartford, Conn.	115	75.2	7	4.6	31	20.3	0	0.0
Colchester, Conn.	58	39.7	27	18.5	60	41.1	1	0.7
Groton, Conn.	76	53.1	42	29.4	24	16.8	1	0.7
Litchfield, Conn.	88	62.0	10	7.0	36	25.4	8	5.6
Lebanon, Conn.	69	48.9	20	14.2	52	36.9	0	0.0
Sharon, Conn.	96	71.1	4	3.0	33	24.4	2	1.5
Norwalk, Conn.	61	45.9	8	6.0	62	45.9	3	2.3
Dartmouth, Mass.	76	58.0	32	24.4	17	13.0	6	4.6
Griswold, Conn.	79	60.8	24	18.5	27	20.8	0	0.0
New Shoreham, R.I.	58	45.0	46	35.7	25	19.4	0	0.0

Towns	Family		Black Household		White Household		Alone	
	#	%	#	%	#	%	#	%
North Kingston, R.I.	46	38.0	48	40.7	27	22.3	0	0.0
Newtown, Conn.	73	62.9	10	8.6	32	27.6	1	0.9
Bridgeport, Conn.	61	56.4	4	3.7	42	38.9	1	0.9
East Haddam, Conn.	83	79.8	9	8.7	12	11.5	0	0.0
Williamstown, Mass.	70	68.6	5	4.9	27	26.5	0	0.0
Pomfret, Conn.	70	70.0	2	2.0	28	28.0	0	0.0
Charlestown, R.I.	21	21.0	60	60.0	19	19.0	0	0.0

Towns with Fewer Than 100 African Americans and Densities of 5.0% or More

	Family		Black Household		White Household		Alone	
Ervings Grant, Mass.	0	0.0	0	0.0	34	100.0	0	0.0
Lisbon, Conn.	46	56.8	12	14.8	22	27.2	1	1.2
Lenox, Mass.	48	58.5	1	1.2	33	40.2	0	0.0
Huntington, Conn.	54	68.4	2	2.5	22	27.8	1	1.3
Boxborough, Mass.	12	44.4	15	55.6	0	0.0	0	0.0
Brunswick, Vt.	0	0.0	8	100.0	0	0.0	0	0.0

Constructing the Mixed Marriage Database

Uncovering so many mixed marriages was a surprise. Like many historians, I was aware of a few isolated instances of mixed marriage and of an occasional pocket—in particular in Boston—where such marriages existed, but I was unprepared for the breadth and frequency that occurred in antebellum New England.[1] Analyzing the 1830 federal census first alerted me to the phenomenon. It's a primitive census—as were all prior to 1850—fulfilling the requirements of the Constitution for representation and taxation, and little more. Organized by town within a county and a state, it names only the head of household and indicates the gender, age (within a range rather than a specific number), and ethnicity ("white" or "colored") of all members of the household as well as whether a person of African descent were free or a slave. There is no identification of the relationship of people within the household. Even so, as I was compiling a database of all African Americans in 1830 New England, I began to notice some unusual arrangements. There were groupings with only one man and one woman of similar age but where one was "white" and the other "colored." Often there were children as well (typically listed as "colored") who fell into age categories that could make them the offspring of the couple. But were they a couple? Without additional information, a person could reasonably imagine other relationships. Perhaps they were unmarried or one of them was a servant or a boarder. Perhaps the census taker had erred, and both adults should have been placed in the same ethnic category. The census also revealed other types of households with three or more adults of mixed ancestry and children. Some clearly were boarding houses or public institutions, such as almshouses, but there was the possibility that they contained mixed marriages as well as extended families.

Intrigued by the possibility of finding many marriages between people of European descent and people of African descent, I went through the census for the New England states a second time—looking only for mixed marriages—and began compiling a database of those unions. I was cautious of which couples I would include. Almost all households with only one adult man and one adult woman of similar age but different reported ethnicities were tentatively placed in the database. Households with multiple adults of different ancestry and children were more complicated. In cases where there were four or more adults nearly equally divided by gender, age, and ethnicity, there might be two mixed marriages or one "white" marriage and one "colored" marriage. Those I left out. Where there were households of differing ages—for example, two black adults over fifty-five, a black man between thirty-six and fifty-five, a black man between twenty-four and thirty-six, a white woman between twenty and thirty, and three black children between birth and ten—I assumed there might be a mixed marriage. But which of the two men was the husband? I almost always selected the man closest in age to the woman and placed the couple and their presumed three children in the database for further investigation. Households with three adults, one much older than the other two, probably consisted of a husband, wife, and elderly parent, and I generally entered them in the database as well.

This was a start, but the 1830 census by itself was inadequate. I then analyzed every federal census from 1790 to 1840. For the most part, the eyestrain wasn't worth the results. Nothing relevant appeared until the 1820 census, and it showed only nine possible marriages that also existed in the 1830 census or the 1840 census. The 1840 census was better, with sixteen marriages that also had appeared in 1830 as well as more than fifty new marriages. The 1850 census proved to be the breakthrough. There were 51 marriages that matched earlier records, and an explosion of roughly 150 new marriages. The first census after the Massachusetts legislature repealed the prohibition on mixed marriages was in 1850, and it appeared that there might be a connection between that legislative action and the burst of recorded marriages. Massachusetts had a gain of 320 percent from 1840 to 1850, but as it turned out, its percentage increase was in the middle of widely varying states—from 0 percent in Rhode Island (with its enforced law against mixed marriages) to a 540 percent gain in Connecticut. Massachusetts had the largest raw number for both 1840 and 1850, but its rate of growth was roughly the norm for the region.[2] The repeal of the law apparently had little influence on whether a mixed couple would marry. What had changed was the census form.

Most important for identifying marriages of any type, the 1850 census named every person and organized them—where appropriate—by couples or families within households. In male-headed households, the husband appeared first, followed by his wife and children in order of age. Although there was no category to specify relationships, the nature of the grouping was clearly implied. Specific ages for each person rather than an age range and surnames also helped establish family connections. If the household held more than a single family, other people or other families were grouped. Elderly parents, other relations, boarders, and servants, for example, were listed after the children. In addition to age and name, the census

Table A4.1 Numbers of New Mixed Marriages

States	1840	1850	Gain
Connecticut	5	27	540%
Maine	9	17	189%
Massachusetts	19	61	320%
New Hampshire	11	13	118%
Rhode Island	0	0	0%
Vermont	4	13	325%
New England	48	131	273%

attempted to identify gender, color ("white," "black," or "mulatto"), occupation, value of real estate, place of birth, school attendance, literacy, and disabilities.

The 1860 census added an additional category (worth of personal property) but otherwise was identical to the 1850 census and equally valuable. It allowed me to augment the database with around 185 new, potential mixed marriages. With roughly 450 marriages for the period preceding the Civil War, I then shifted from adding new couples to authenticating what I had. I followed, where possible, each person in every census through 1920. Deaths and disappearances ended the search for most people much earlier than the twentieth century. I combed birth records, marriage records, death records, and Civil War registrations and service. I contacted 134 historical societies and 68 creators of family trees in ancestry.com. to acquire further confirmation of marital status, but my greatest hope was to find personal documents, such as letters and diaries. Here I was disappointed. Despite the response of most of the correspondents (many of whom were enormously helpful), I never found that hidden cache of papers.

Place of Birth of People in Mixed Marriages

Before 1850—77 persons

    Native state—49 (64%)

    Other state—19 (25%)

        New England—15 (19%)

        Mid-Atlantic—4 (5%)

        South—0 (0%)

        Midwest—0 (0%)

    Other country—9 (12%)

        Ireland—3 (4%)

        England—2 (3%)

        4 other countries—4 (5%)

1850—222 persons

    Native state—136 (61%)

    Other state—52 (23%)

        New England—30 (14%)

        Mid-Atlantic—16 (7%)

        South—5 (2%)

        Midwest—1 (0%)

    Other country—34 (15%)

        Ireland—10 (5%)

        England—6 (3%)

        Canada—8 (4%)

        7 other countries—10 (5%)

1860—371 persons

    Native state—168 (45%)

    Other state—107 (29%)

        New England—44 (12%)

Overall—670 persons

    Native state—353 (53%)

    Other state—178 (27%)

        New England—89 (13%)

Mid-Atlantic—39 (11%)	Mid-Atlantic—59 (9%)
South—24 (6%)	South—29 (4%)
Midwest—0 (0%)	Midwest—1 (0%)
Other country—96 (26%)	Other country—139 (21%)
Ireland—41 (11%)	Ireland—54 (8%)
England—19 (5%)	England—27 (4%)
Canada—16 (4%)	Canada—24 (4%)
9 other countries—20 (5%)	Other countries—34 (5%)

"Before 1850," "1850," and "1860" refer to the first time a marriage appeared in the records, not to the date of birth. The Mid-Atlantic is the area from New York to Maryland. The South is from Virginia southward.

APPENDIX 6

Occupations of Males in Mixed Marriages

Occupations, pre-1850—Black Males	Occupations, pre-1850—White Males
unskilled laborer—— 9 (27%)	unskilled laborer—— 4 (57%)
fisherman———— 3 (9%)	fisherman————0 (0%)
mariner————0 (0%)	mariner————0 (0%)
farmer————9 (27%)	farmer————2 (29%)
skilled laborer—— 6 (18%)	skilled laborer————0 (0%)
service———— 2 (6%)	service————0 (0%)
shopkeeper————0 (0%)	shopkeeper———— 1 (14%)
professional———— 4 (12%)	professional————0 (0%)

Occupations, 1850—All Males	Occupations, 1850—Black Males
unskilled laborer——48 (43%)	unskilled laborer— 18 (53%)
fisherman———— 6 (5%)	fisherman————0 (0%)
mariner————13 (12%)	mariner————4 (12%)
farmer————18 (16%)	farmer————4 (12%)
skilled laborer———— 12 (11%)	skilled laborer——1 (3%)
service———— 11 (10%)	service———— 5 (15%)
shopkeeper———— 1 (1%)	shopkeeper————1 (3%)
professional———— 2 (2%)	professional———— 1 (3%)

Occupations, 1850—Mixed Males	Occupations, 1850—White Males
unskilled laborer — 20 (41%)	unskilled laborer — 10 (36%)
fisherman ———— 3 (6%)	fisherman ———— 3 (11%)
mariner ————— 3 (6%)	mariner ————— 6 (21%)
farmer ————— 7 (14%)	farmer ————— 7 (25%)
skilled laborer —— 9 (18%)	skilled laborer —— 2 (7%)
service ———— 6 (12%)	service ————— 0 (0%)
shopkeeper ——— 0 (0%)	shopkeeper ——— 0 (0%)
professional ——— 1 (2%)	professional ——— 0 (0%)

Occupations, 1860—All Males	Occupations, 1860—Black Males
unskilled laborer — 55 (34%)	unskilled laborer —26 (47%)
fisherman ———— 2 (1%)	fisherman ———— 0 (0%)
mariner ————— 28 (17%)	mariner ————— 5 (9%)
farmer ————— 8 (5%)	farmer ————— 1 (2%)
skilled laborer ——35 (21%)	skilled laborer ——11 (20%)
service ———— 27 (17%)	service————— 8 (15%)
shopkeeper ——— 5 (3%)	shopkeeper ——— 4 (7%)
professional ——— 3 (2%)	professional ——— 0 (0%)

Occupations, 1860—Mixed Males	Occupations, 1860—White Males
unskilled laborer— 17 (22%)	unskilled laborer— 12 (38%)
fisherman————— 1 (1%)	fisherman————— 1 (3%)
mariner————— 18 (24%)	mariner————— 5 (16%)
farmer————— 3 (4%)	farmer————— 4 (13%)
skilled laborer——— 14 (18%)	skilled laborer——— 10 (31%)
service————— 19 (25%)	service————— 0 (0%)
shopkeeper——— 1 (1%)	shopkeeper ——— 0 (0%)
professional——— 3 (4%)	professional——— 0 (0%)

"Mariner" includes master mariners as well as common sailors; "service" includes barbers, waiters, porters, stewards; "shopkeeper" includes traders as well as shopkeepers; "professional" includes clergymen and physicians. "Farmer" is more complex. Some people were listed in a census as farmers but without any value placed under real estate. That could mean the person was a tenant farmer or that he didn't give a value for property he owned. In either case, I placed the person as a farmer. The percentages refer only to the category, such as "Occupations, 1860—Black Males," in which they appear.

APPENDIX 7

Occupations and Value of Real Estate of Males in Mixed Marriages

Unskilled Larorer—18	Skilled Laborer—18
$350 average	$1056 Average
$300 median	$900–$1000 median
$100–$1000 range	$200–$2000 range
Fisherman—5	Service—12
$380 average	$2363 average
$200 median	$1000–$1800 median
$100–$1000 range	$200–$6000 range
Mariner—9	Shopkeeper—5
$789 average	$3140 average
$900 median	$1700 median
$100–$3000 range	$700–$9500 range
Farmer—31	Professional—5
$1121 average	$5330 average
$800 median	$5000 median
$100–$8000 range	$150–$10000 range

Notes

1. Price and Stewart, "Introduction," in Price and Stewart, eds., *To Heal the Scourge of Prejudice*, 1–16; for more on Easton and his remarkable family, see Price and Stewart, "The Roberts Case," 88–115.
2. Easton, "An Address Delivered before the Coloured Population of Providence, Rhode Island, on Thanksgiving Day, Nov. 27, 1828," in Price and Stewart, *To Heal the Scourge of Prejudice*, 51–52.
3. Easton, "An Address," 53–59.
4. Easton, "An Address," 59–62.
5. Goodman, *Of One Blood*, 26–27; Finkenbine, "Boston's Black Churches," in Jacobs, ed., *Courage and Conscience*, 170–171, 174; Hinks, *To Awaken My Afflicted Brothers*, 95–96; Horton and Horton, *Black Bostonians*, 52; Levesque, "Inherent Reformers—Inherited Orthodoxy," 506.
6. Hinks, *To Awaken My Afflicted Brothers*, passim, but particularly 66, 69–70; Goodman, *Of One Blood*, 28; Horton and Horton, *In Hope of Liberty*, 172; Jacobs, "David Walker and William Lloyd Garrison," in Jacobs, *Courage and Conscience*, 9; Quarles, *Black Abolitionists*, 16; Stuckey, *Slave Culture*, 118; Wilentz, "Introduction: The Mysteries of David Walker," in Wilentz, ed., *David Walker's Appeal*, xii.
7. *David Walker's Appeal*, passim; Hinks, *To Awaken My Afflicted Brothers*, 204–205; Jacobs, "David Walker," 98–99.
8. *David Walker's Appeal*, passim; Hinks, *To Awaken My Afflicted Brothers*, 108, 198–199, 249–250; Wilentz, "Introduction," xv-xvii.
9. Wilentz, "Introduction," xviii-xix.
10. Stuckey, *Slave Culture*, 118; Moss, "Tarring and Feathering of Thomas Paul Smith," 223; Adams, "Disfranchisement of Negroes in New England," 545; Horton and Horton, *In Hope of Liberty*, 168; Malone, *Between Freedom and Bondage*, 5; Melish, *Disowning Slavery*, 189; Sweet, *Bodies Politic*, 363.

11. Kantrowitz, *More Than Freedom*, 44–45; Belknap, "Answer to Queries Respecting the Slavery and Emancipation of Negroes in Massachusetts," 208–209; de Tocqueville, *Democracy in America*, 373–374; Curry, *The Free Black in Urban America*, 132; *The Liberator*, January 15, December, 1831; Hooker, *Some Reminiscences of a Long Life*, 21–23.

12. Berlin, *Slaves without Masters*, 60; Piersen, *Black Yankees*, 46; Litwack, *North of Slavery*, 155; Daniels, *In Freedom's Birthplace*, 18–19; Horton and Horton, *Black Bostonians*, 8; Mayer, *All on Fire*, 108; "The Colored Population of the United States," *The Liberator*, January 22, 1831; Brown, *Life of William J. Brown*, 102–103; Quarles, *Frederick Douglass*, 11.

13. Cromwell, "The Black Presence in the West End of Boston," in Jacobs, *Courage and Conscience*, 156–157; Daniels, *In Freedom's Birthplace*, 17, 143; Horton and Horton, *Black Bostonians*, 2–3; Levesque, "Black Boston," 27; Nasta, "'Their Own Guardians and Protectors,'" 4; Warner, *New Haven Negroes*, 28; Karttunen, *Other Islanders*, 65; Horton and Horton, *In Hope of Liberty*, 77–79; White, "Salem's Antebellum Black Community," 99; Cottrol, *Afro-Yankees*, 53; LiBrizzi, *Lost Atusville*, 8. Thanks to Phil O'Brien and Ann Topjon not only for discovering *Lost Atusville* but also for giving me a copy.

14. Archer, *Fissures in the Rock*, 59–63.

15. Nell, *The Colored Patriots of the American Revolution*, 33–34; Price and Stewart, "Introduction," *To Heal the Scourge*, 6; Abdy, *Journal of a Residence and Tour*, 133–136.

16. Dempsey, "Benjamin Wheaton," *Brattleboro Reformer*, February 7, 1994. Thanks to John Carnahan of the Brattleboro Historical Society for alerting me to the Wheaton article and sending me a copy. Guyette, *Discovering Black Vermont*, 39–41.

17. Brown, *Life of William J. Brown*, 46; Finkenbine "Boston's Black Churches," 170–171, 174; Hinks, *To Awaken My Afflicted Brethren*, 95–96; Horton and Horton, *Black Bostonians*, 39, 52; Levesque, "Inherent Reformers," 492–493; Nasta, "African American Community in Middletown," 4; Warner, *New Haven Negroes*, 46–47.

18. Horton and Horton, *In Hope of Liberty*, 21; Moss, *Schooling Citizens*, 13, 161; Schultz, *Culture Factory*, 69; Zilversmit, *First Emancipation*, 26.

19. Horton and Horton, *In Hope of Liberty*, 21; Woodson, *Education of the Negro Prior to 1861*, 325–326; Hoar, *Autobiography of Seventy Years*, I, 16–17.

20. Cottrol, *Afro-Yankees*, 61; Hancock, "Elusive Boundaries of Blackness," 123; Kendrick and Kendrick, *Sarah's Long Walk*, 70–71; Moss, *Schooling Citizens*, 27; Schultz, *Culture Factory*, 159–160; Warner, *New Haven Negroes*, 71–72; White, "Salem's Antebellum Black Community," 107; Woodson, *Education of the Negro*, 95–96, 315–317, 317–319, 320.

21. Schultz, *Culture Factory*, 160–162; Kendrick and Kendrick, *Sarah's Long Walk*, 71; Shepard, "Public Schools of Boston," in Homans, *Sketches of Boston*, 215.

22. Schultz, *Culture Factory*, 168; White, "Black Leadership Class," 504–515; Woodson, *Education of the Negro*, 320–321.

23. "An Act for the Better Preventing of a Spurious and Mixt Isue," December 5, 1705, in *Acts and Resolves, Public and Private, of the Province of the Massachusetts Bay*, I, 578–579; "An Act for the orderly Solemnization of Marriages," June 22, 1786, in *Laws of the Commonwealth of Massachusetts*, I, 323–324; "An Act for Regulating Marriage," in Smith, *Laws of the State of Maine*, 420, 420n.; Martyn, "Racism in the United States," 223–224.

24. The Spanish word "mulatto" (little mule) literally means that such an offspring came from parents of different species (horse and donkey). The term first came to Virginia in the mid-seventeenth century. To what extent New Englanders understood its derogatory meaning or simply thought it meant a child of black and white parents is unclear. The Alabama physician, J. C. Nott, was proclaiming its negative meaning as late as 1843 in the *American Journal of the Medical Sciences*; so it must still have had some American currency. This certainly is a topic that needs a full investigation. In this book I will use "mixed" rather than "mulatto" unless the word is being quoted.

25. *Inhabitants of Medway v. Inhabitants of Natick*, 7 Mass. 88, October 1810, in Catterall, *Judicial Cases Concerning American Slavery and the Negro*, IV, 490; see also *Inhabitants of Medway v. Inhabitants of Needham*, 16 Mass. 157, October 1819, in Catterall, *Judicial Cases*, IV, 497; Weierman, *One Nation, One Blood*, 201n.

26. *1830 United States Federal Census*. I built a database with a record for each of the 21,214 New England African American residents as of 1830 from which these numbers come. There are minor discrepancies with the US Census Historical Statistics, some certainly their miscount and some most likely mine.

27. Horton and Horton, *In Hope of Liberty*, 164; Curry, *Free Black in Urban America*, 100–101; Savage, *A Chronological History of the Boston Watch and Police*, 66; Werner, *Reaping the Bloody Harvest*, 234; Grover, *Fugitive's Gibraltar*, 115.

28. Brown, *Life of William J. Brown*, 89–90; Cottrol, *Afro-Yankees*, 53–55; Sweet, *Bodies Politic*, 353; Werner, *Reaping the Bloody Harvest*, 230–231; Gilkeson, *Middleclass Providence*, 19–20.

CHAPTER 2

1. Archer, *Fissures in the Rock*, 88, 125–126, 155.

2. Vickers, *Farmers & Fishermen*, passim.

3. Archer, *Fissures in the Rock*, 127; John Winthrop to William Bradford, July 28, 1637, *Winthrop Papers*, III, 457; Israel Stoughton to John Winthrop, June 28, 1637, *Winthrop Papers*, III, 435; Hugh Peter to John Winthrop, July 15, 1637, *Winthrop Papers*, II, 450; Roger Williams to John Winthrop, November 10, 1637, *Winthrop Papers*, III, 509.

4. Most historians have agreed that the Peirce cargo marked the earliest presence of Africans in New England, but there have been dissenters. Lorenzo Greene argued that Samuel Maverick first owned slaves sometime between 1624 and the arrival of the Winthrop Fleet in 1630, *Negro in Colonial New England*, 16–17; and Twombly and Moore are convinced that "at least one Negro had arrived as early as 1633," "Black Puritan," 224–225. Winthrop, *Winthrop's Journal*, I, 260; Josselyn, *An Account of Two Voyages to New-England*, 24.

5. Emmanuel Downing to John Winthrop, c. August 1645, *Winthrop Papers*, V, 39–40.

6. Article ninety-one of the *Body of Libertyes*, in Moore, *Notes on the History of Slavery in Massachusetts*, 12–13; Greene, *Negro in Colonial New England*, 63, 126; Zilversmit, *First Emancipation*, 19; McManus, *Black Bondage in the North*, 59; Wood, *Origins of American Slavery*, 105.

7. Jordan, *White over Black*, 69–70.

8. McManus, *Black Bondage*, 59; Bartlett, ed., *Records of the Colony of Rhode Island*, I, 243; Jordan, *White over Black*, 70, 70n; Blackburn, *The Making of New World Slavery*, 239–240; Johnston, *Slavery in Rhode Island*, 10.

9. Berlin, *Many Thousands Gone*, 8; Morgan, "British Encounters with Africans and African-Americans," in Bailyn and Morgan, eds., *Strangers within the Realm*, 163; Vickers, *Farmers & Fishermen*, 59; Simon Bradstreet quoted in, Moore, *Slavery in Massachusetts*, 49; Winthrop, *Journal*, II, 227

10. Piersen, *Black Yankees*, 3, 13, 32, 59; Fowler, *Historical Status of the Negro in Connecticut*, 4; Morgan, "British Encounters," 167–169; Carvalho, *Black Families in Hampden County*, 12; Twombly and Moore, "Black Puritan," 237.

11. Breen, "Covenanted Militia of Massachusetts Bay," in Breen, *Puritans and Adventurers*, 37, 41; Jordan, *White over Black*, 125; Greene, *Negro in Colonial New England*, 187.

12. *Second Report of the Record Commissioners of the City of Boston, Boston Town Records, 1634–1660*, 141–142; *A Report of the Record Commissioners of the City of Boston, Containing the Boston Records from 1660 to 1701*, 5; Jordan, *White over Black*, 104.

13. Greene, *Negro in Colonial New England*, 177, 179, 187, 193, 236–237, 262; Fredrickson, *White Supremacy*, 72–73; Fowler, *Negro in Connecticut*, 21; Higginbotham, *In the Matter of Color*, 72; Horton and Horton, *In Hope of Liberty*, 26; Jordan, *White over Black*, 125; Zilversmit, *First Emancipation*, 19; Twombly and Moore, "Black Puritan," 226–227; Wood, *Origins of American Slavery*, 106–107.

14. Fowler, *Negro in Connecticut*, 21; Piersen, *Black Yankees*, 49, 51; Carvalho, *Black Families in Hampden County*, 12.

15. Winthrop, "A Modell of Christian Charity," in *Winthrop Papers*, II, 282; Archer, *Fissures in the Rock*, chap. 4; Fredrickson, *White Supremacy*, 70, 73. For definitions of ethnocentrism and racism, see Fredrickson, *A Short History of Racism*, 5–6; Painter, *History of White People*, xii; Hannaford, *Race*, 4–6; Dain, *A Hideous*

Monster of the Mind, 7; Feagin, Vera, and Batur, *White Racism*, 3; Smedley, *Race in North America*, 15.

16. Berlin, *Many Thousands Gone*, 369; Greene, *Negro in Colonial New England*, 23; Horton and Horton, *In Hope of Liberty*, 10; McManus, *Black Bondage in the North*, 14, 199–206; Moore, *Slavery in Massachusetts*, 48; Piersen, *Black Yankees*, 18; *A Report of the Record Commissioners of the City of Boston, Containing the Records of Boston Selectmen, 1701 to 1715*, 73–74, 232–233; *A Report of the Record Commissioners of the City of Boston, Containing the Records of Boston Selectmen, 1716–1736*, 82–83, 105–106.

17. Fryer, *Staying Power*, 20–21; Greene, *Negro in Colonial New England*, 24; McManus, *Black Bondage in the North*, 10; Zilversmit, *First Emancipation*, 3.

18. Berlin, *Many Thousands Gone*, 58; Peterson, "Selling of Joseph," 4 (2002), 2; Moore, *Slavery in Massachusetts*, 50–51; Piersen, *Black Yankees*, 14.

19. Jones, "Plantation Slavery in the Narragansett Country of Rhode Island," 157, 160–161; Woodward, *Plantation in Yankeeland*, 59, 72; Fowler, *Negro in Connecticut*, 14; McManus, *Black Bondage in the North*, 6–7, 39; Piersen, *Black Yankees*, 58; Berlin, *Many Thousands Gone*, 178; Bartlett, *From Slave to Citizen*, 9; Zilversmit, *First Emancipation*, 4.

20. Sewall, "Selling of Joseph," in *Diary*, II, 1117; also see Towner, "Sewall-Saffin Dialogue on Slavery," 40–52; and Peterson, "Selling of Joseph," 1–22.

21. Sewall, "Selling of Joseph," 1117–1121; Towner, "Sewall-Saffin Dialogue," 40–52; Peterson, "Selling of Joseph," 1–22; Jordan, *White over Black*, 196.

22. Saffin, "A Brief and Candid Answer to a late Printed Sheet, *Entitled*, The Selling of Joseph," in More, *Slavery in Massachusetts*, 251–256 (quotes on 252, 253, and 256); Towner, "Sewall-Saffin Dialogue," 48–49.

23. Zilversmit, *First Emancipation*, 51; *Records of Boston Selectmen*, May 26, 1701, 5; "An Act for the Better Preventing of a Spurious and Mixt Issue," in *Acts and Resolves*, I, 578–579; Sewall, *Diary*, I, 532.

24. "An Act for the Better Preventing of a Spurious and Mixt Issue," in *Acts and Resolves*, I, 578–579; Archer, *Fissures in the Rock*, 87; Fowler, "Northern Attitudes Towards Interracial Marriage," 49–51; Sewall, *Diary*, I, 532.

25. Horton and Horton, *In Hope of Liberty*, 43; Greene, *Negro in Colonial New England*, 50, 312–313; Zilversmit, *First Emancipation*, 13; Fowler, *Negro in Connecticut*, 46–50; Warner, *New Haven Negroes*, 7; Catterall, *Judicial Cases*, 413–414; Jordan, *White over Black*, 104–105.

26. Greene, *Negro in Colonial New England*, 140; *A Report of the Record Commissioners of the City of Boston, Containing the Boston Records from 1700 to 1728*, 173–175; *Journals of the House of Representatives of Massachusetts*, V, June 7, 17, 20, 21, 1723; August 13, 15, 22, 27, 1723; December 4, 5, 7, 10, 14, 17, 1723, 5:18–19, 36, 43, 48, 114, 121, 138, 145, 258, 259, 264, 274, 286, 292.

27. *Boston Town Records*, May 4, 1723, June 24, 1728, 176–177, 22; *A Report of the Record Commissioners of the City of Boston, Containing the Boston Records from 1729*

to 1742, 139; *A Report of the Record Commissioners of the City of Boston, Containing the Boston Records from 1742 to 1757*, 315; *A Report of the Record Commissioners of the City of Boston, Containing the Boston Records from 1758 to 1769*, 20.

28. Fredrickson, *White Supremacy*, 72–73.

29. For arguments that racism preceded slavery or that Europeans were so predisposed, see Vaughan, *Roots of American Racism*; Vaughan, and Vaughan, "Before *Othello*," 19–44; Davis, *Problem of Slavery in Western Culture*, 281–282, 447, 468; Jordan, *White over Black*; Bartels, "*Othello* and Africa," 61; Fryer, *Staying Power*, 144–145; Fredrickson, *Arrogance of Race*, 192.

30. Harris, *Patterns of Race in the Americas*, 70; Fredrickson, *Arrogance of Race*, 159.

CHAPTER 3

1. Breen, "Making History," in Hoffman, Sobel, and Teute, eds., *Through a Glass Darkly*, 70–71; Felt, *History of Ipswich, Essex, and Hamilton*, 120.

2. Harvey Amani Whitfield, *The Problem of Slavery in Early Vermont, 1777–1810*; Berlin, *Many Thousands Gone*, 229; Davis, *Inhuman Bondage*, 152; Higginbotham, *In the Matter of Color*, 90; Massachusetts Supreme Judicial Court, "The Massachusetts Constitution, Judicial Review and Slavery," www.mass.gov/courts/sjc/constitution-and-slavery.html; Charles Lowell to the Editor, May 17, 1847, *Boston Courier*, in *The Liberator*, June 4, 1847; Zilversmit, *First Emancipation*, 112–113, 116, 117, 121, 123–124, 202; Belknap, "Answer to Queries Respecting Slavery," 203; Steiner, *History of Slavery in Connecticut*, 400–401; Catterall, *Judicial Cases*, IV, 413–414.

3. Berlin, *Many Thousands Gone*, 369; US Bureau of the Census, *Negro Population, 1790–1915*, 57; McManus, *Black Bondage*, 199; *1830 United States Federal Census*.

4. US Bureau of the Census, *Negro Population, 1790–1915*, 57.

5. Sweet, *Bodies Politic*, 315–316, 344, 381; Melish, *Disowning Slavery*, 126; White, "'It Was a Proud Day,'" 35, 38; Belknap, "Answer to Queries Respecting Slavery," 198, 203; Kantrowitz, *More Than Freedom*, 44–45; Lott, *Love and Theft*, passim, but particularly 4–15; Roediger, *The Wages of Whiteness*, 97, 118.

6. The tabulations here and throughout this section come from a database I created that is based on the *1830 United States Federal Census*. That census only gives names for heads of household and does not identify relationships between those in the household, but it provides data for everyone for gender; range of age; state, county, and town place of residence; whether a person was slave or free; and whether a person according to the census taker was black or white (the only choices). My data sometimes depart from the Census Bureau's compilation, *Negro Population, 1790–1915*. For example, my database totals 21,224 African Americans while the Census Bureau uses the figure 21,331 (p. 57). Mistakes were made. I'll leave it to the reader to determine the subject of that passive sentence.

7. Database from the *1830 United States Federal Census*; Nash, "Forging Freedom," In Berlin and Hoffman, eds., *Slavery and Freedom in the Age of the American Revolution*, 10–11.
8. Database from the *1830 United States Federal Census*; Guyette, *Discovering Black Vermont, passim.*
9. Database from the *1830 United States Federal Census.*
10. Database from the *1830 United States Federal Census*; Malone, *Between Freedom and Bondage*, 14.
11. Database from the *1830 United States Federal Census*; Nash, "Forging Freedom," 27, and *Forging Freedom*, 78.
12. Database from the *1830 United States Federal Census*; Brown, *Life of William J. Brown*, 33.

CHAPTER 4

1. Brown, "'Not Only Extreme Poverty,'" 505–517 (the Haynes quote is on page 516); Saillant, *Black Puritan, Black Republican*, 63, 118–119.
2. Miller, *Search for a Black Nationality*, 20–21. For a full biography of Cuffe, see Thomas, *Rise to Be a People*.
3. Miller, *Search for a Black Nationality*, 4, 6; Horton and Horton, *Black Bostonians*, 91.
4. Easton, *A Treatise on the Intellectual Character*, in Price and Stewart, *To Heal the Scourge of Prejudice*, 105; "A Colored American" to Samuel E. Cornish, *Colored American*, August 2, 1837, in Ripley, ed., *Black Abolitionist Papers*, III, 236–237; Rael, *Black Identity and Black Protest in the Antebellum North*, 80, 91, 92, 94; Horton and Horton, *Black Bostonians*, 91.
5. A Subscriber to the Editor, *The Liberator*, July 16, 1831 (Garrison's response is in the same issue); Rael, *Black Identity and Black Protest*, 83, 102, 105; Horton and Horton, *In Hope of Liberty*, 201; Hancock, "Elusive Boundaries of Blackness," 119.
6. White, "'It Was a Proud Day,'" 15–16; Greene, *Negro in Colonial New England*, 255; Roediger, *Wages of Whiteness*, 103; Sweet, *Bodies Politic*, 346; Curry, *Free Black in Urban America*, 232; Rael, *Black Identity and Black Protest*, 55–57, 64, 65, 69.
7. *The Liberator*, January 29, March 4, 1831; Pease and Pease, *They Who Would Be Free*, 173.
8. *The Liberator*, March 12, 1831; Pease and Pease, *They Who Would Be Free*, 215.
9. Hinks, *To Awaken My Afflicted Brethren*, 110; Moss, *Schooling Citizens*, 31; Stewart, "Lecture at Franklin Hall," September 21, 1832, in *The Liberator*, November 17, 1832; Stewart, "An Address, Delivered at the African Masonic Hall," February 27, 1833, in *The Liberator*, May 4, 1833.
10. Horton and Horton, *Black Bostonians*, 31; Howard, *Conscience and Slavery*, 22, 25; Jacobs, "William Lloyd Garrison's *Liberator* and Boston's Blacks," 262; *The Liberator*, May 21, 1831, August 25, 1832, July 20, 1833; Bethel, *Roots of*

African-American Identity, 176–178; Wesley, "Integration versus Separatism," in Jacobs, *Courage and Conscience*, 214; Horton, "Generations of Protest," 50–252.

11. Fredrickson, *Black Image in the White Mind*, 9–10, 12, 16–17; Staudenraus, *African Colonization Movement*, vi, 210; Ignatiev, *How the Irish Became White*, 97; McKivigan, *The War against Proslavery Religion*, 35; Egerton, "'Its Origin Is Not a Little Curious,'" 470; Chambers, *Things as They Are in America*, 362–363.

12. Bay, *White Image in the Black Mind*, 23, 41, 44.

13. Goodman, *Of One Blood*, 42; Mayer, *All on Fire*, 79, 352; Kraditor, *Means and Ends in American Abolitionism*, 103–104; Garrison, *The Genius of Universal Emancipation*, February 12, 1830, in Garrison and Garrison, *William Lloyd Garrison*, I, 148.

14. Mayer, *All on Fire*, 107, 116; Horton and Horton, *Black Bostonians*, 84; Quarles, *Black Abolitionists*, 20; Ripley, "Introduction," *Black Abolitionist Papers*, III, 9.

15. *The Liberator*, January 1, 1831; Kendrick and Kendrick, *Sarah's Long Walk*, 45–46; Mayer, *All on Fire*, 115; Jacobs, "David Walker and William Lloyd Garrison," in Jacobs, *Courage and Conscience*, 2, 12, 15.

16. Mayer, *All on Fire*, 349–350; Chace, "My Anti-Slavery Reminiscences," in *Two Quaker Sisters*, 114.

17. Horton and Horton, *Black Bostonians*, 83; Mayer, *All on Fire*, 131; "New-England Anti-Slavery Society," *The Liberator*, February 18, 1832; *Fifth Annual Report of the American Anti-Slavery Society*.

18. Maria Weston Warren quoted in Quarles, *Black Abolitionists*, 36–37; Bowditch, "The Thirty Years' War of Anti-Slavery," quoted in Bowditch, *Life and Correspondence of Henry Ingersoll Bowditch*, I, 99–101.

19. Hansen, *Strained Sisterhood*, 6, 10–11, 19, 64, 74; Horton and Horton, *Black Bostonians*, 100; Jeffrey, *Great Silent Army of Abolitionism*, 84; Peace and Peace, *They Who Would Be Free*: 70–71, 86; Quarles, *Black Abolitionists*, 25, 49; Yee, *Black Women Abolitionists*, 89.

20. Gienapp, "Abolitionism and the Nature of Antebellum Reform," in Jacobs, *Courage and Conscience*, 41; Walters, *Antislavery Appeal*, xiii; Stewart, *Holy Warriors*, 127; Friedman, *Gregarious Saints*, 176; Mayer, *All on Fire*, 349–350; "New-England Anti-Slavery Convention," May 30, 1837, in *The Liberator*, June 2, 1837; Horton and Horton, *Black Bostonians*, 95; Yee, *Black Women Abolitionists*, 6; Chace, "My Anti-Slavery Reminiscences," in *Two Quaker Sisters*, 119–120.

21. Pease and Pease, "Antislavery Ambivalence," 695; Hartford, *Money Morals, and Politics*, 105; Abdy, *Journal of a Residence and Tour*, III, 218; Litwack, "Abolitionist Dilemma," 52; Adams, "Misconceptions of Shakespeare upon the Stage," in Hackett, *Notes and Comments upon Certain Plays and Actors of Shakespeare*, 224; Commager, *Theodore Parker*, 115–116, 199–202; Horsman, *Race and Manifest Destiny*, 179; Fredrickson, *Black Image in White Mind*, 157; Parker, "The Present Crisis in American Affairs," delivered on May 7, 1856 in *The Collected Works of Theodore Parker*, II, 244, 249.

Notes to pages 55–64

253

22. Stanton, *Leopard's Spots*, passim; Parker, "Present Crisis in American Affairs," II, 244, 249, and "The Present Aspect of Slavery in America, and the Immediate Duty of the North," in *Collected Works*, II, 289.

23. Garrison, *Thoughts on African Colonization*, 120; William Lloyd Garrison to Gerrit Smith, March 7, 1835, in *Letters of William Lloyd Garrison*, I, 458–459.

24. Mayer, *All on Fire*, 430–433 (Garrison quote on p. 430); Pease and Pease, "Antislavery Ambivalence," 687.

CHAPTER 5

1. Friedman, *Gregarious Saints*, 165; Stewart, "Emergence of Racial Modernity and the Rise of the White North," 200; S. T. U., "What Can the Free Colored People Do for Themselves?," *The Liberator*, February 11, 1832; Hansen, *Strained Sisterhood*, 79; *The Liberator*, July 16, September 24, October 31, 1831, May 19, 1832, August 17, October 12, November 23, 1833, February 1, March 15, May 24, August 2, September 13, 1834.

2. Warner, *New Haven Negroes*, 53.

3. Jocelyn, "College for Colored Youth," *New-Haven Advertiser*, in *The Liberator*, November 12, 1831; Warner, *New Haven Negroes*, 54.

4. Jocelyn, "College for Colored Youth"; William Lloyd Garrison, Philadelphia, June 10, 1831, in *The Liberator*, June 18, 1831; Minutes from the Convention, in *The Liberator*, October 22, 1831; Warner, *New Haven Negroes*, 54.

5. Jocelyn, "College for Colored Youth"; Minutes from the Convention.

6. Moss, *Schooling Citizens*, 49–50; Richards, *"Gentlemen of Property and Standing,"* 30–31; Staudenraus, *African Colonization Movement*, 126–127.

7. Jocelyn, "College for Colored Youth"; Warner, *New Haven Negroes*, 54–55; Stewart, "Emergence of Racial Modernity," 203.

8. *The Liberator*, September 17, 1831; Simeon S. Jocelyn, *New-Haven Herald* in *The Liberator*, September 24, 1831; Warner, *New Haven Negroes*, 55–56.

9. Samuel E. Cornish, Philadelphia, September 17, 1831, in *The Liberator*, September 24, 1831; Jocelyn, "College for Colored Youth."

10. "Riots at New Haven," *The Liberator*, October 22, 1831; *The Liberator*, October 29, 1831; Stewart, "Emergence of Racial Modernity," 203–204; Warner, *New Haven Negroes*, 58.

11. *The Liberator*, March 2, 1833, for both the advertisement and for Garrison's comments, "High School for Young Colored Ladies and Misses."

12. May, *Some Recollections of Our Anti-Slavery Conflict*, 40; Fuller, *Prudence Crandall*, 12–13.

13. *1830 United States Federal Census*; Strane, *A Whole-Souled Woman*, 22.

14. Strane, *Whole-Souled Woman*, 10–11; Fuller, *Prudence Crandall*, 13; May, *Some Recollections*, 40.

15. May, *Some Recollections*, 40–41; Prudence Crandall to Mr. Holbrook, May 7, 1833, *Brooklyn Advertiser*, in *The Liberator*, May 25, 1833; Abdy, *Journal of a Residence*

and Tour, I, 196; Fuller, *Prudence Crandall*, 17; Strane, *Whole-Souled Woman*, 22; Yacavone, *Samuel Joseph May*, 44; most accounts place Sarah Harris as a resident of Canterbury, but the 1830 *Federal Census* lists her father and the entire family at Norwich City and William Harris is named as *The Liberator*'s agent for Norwich in issues of the time; see also the State of Connecticut website for the Prudence Crandall Museum, www.cultureandtourism.org.

16. Prudence Crandall to Mr. Holbrook, *The Liberator*, May 25, 1833; Prudence Crandall to S. S. Jocelyn, April 17, 1833, in "Abolition Letters Collected by Captain Arthur B. Spingarn," 83; Prudence Crandall to William Lloyd Garrison, January 18, 1833, in Fuller, *Prudence Crandall*, 18; Strane, *Whole-Souled Woman*, 28.

17. Larned, *History of Windham County*, II, 492; Strane, *Whole-Souled Woman*, 34–35.

18. *The Liberator*, March 2, 1833.

19. May, *Some Recollections*, 42–43; George W. Benson to William Lloyd Garrison, March 5, 1833, in *The Liberator*, March 9, 1833; Strane, *Whole-Souled Woman*, 42, 47, 50.

20. This description and analysis of the town meeting in this and following paragraphs are based on these sources: May, *Some Recollections*, 43–50; Henry E. Benson to William Lloyd Garrison, March 12, 1833, in *The Liberator*, March 16, 1833; A Friend of the Colonization Cause to the Editor, *Norwich Republican*, in the *Liberator*, April 6, 1833; Select Men and Others to the American Colonization Society, March 22, 1833, in *The Liberator*, April 6, 1833.

21. Select Men and Others to the American Colonization Society, in *The Liberator*, April 6, 1833.

22. The quotations come from A Friend of the Colonization Cause to the Editor, in *The Liberator*, April 6, 1833.

23. Strane, *Whole-Souled Woman*, 61; *The Liberator*, May 18, 1833.

24. *The Liberator*, May 18, June 22, 1833; Archer, *Fissures in the Rock*, 149; Abdy, *Journal of a Residence and Tour*, I, 198.

25. Johnson, *Development of State Legislation Concerning the Free Negro*, 77; May, *Some Recollections*, 52; *The Liberator*, June 22, 1833; Strane, *Whole-Souled Woman*, 73.

26. May, *Some Recollections*, 52–56; *The Liberator*, July 6, July 20, 1833; Yacovone, *Samuel Joseph May*, 49.

27. May, *Some Recollections*, 57–59; Abdy, *Journal of a Residence and Tour*, I, 199–200, 205–207; *The Liberator*, July 6, August 17, August 24, 1833.

28. May, *Some Recollections*, 66–69; *Connecticut Courant*, August 26, 1833 in *The Liberator*, August 31, 1833; Strane, *Whole-Souled Woman*, 94–95, 103.

29. May, *Some Recollections*, 69; Daggett's Charge and other commentary, in *The Liberator*, October 26, 1833.

30. May, *Some Recollections*, 69–70; *The Liberator*, November 2, 1833, February 8, June 14, 1834; Abdy, *Journal of a Residence and Tour*, III, 210.

31. May, *Some Recollections*, 70; *The Liberator*, August 2, 9, September 27, October 11, 1834; Strane, *Whole-Souled Woman*, 148.

32. May, *Some Recollections*, 70–71; Abdy, *Journal of a Residence and Tour*, III, 303–305; *The Liberator*, September 13, 20, 1834.

33. *The Liberator*, September 29, 1832.

34. *The Liberator*, July 5, 19, 1834.

35. *The Liberator*, October 25, 1834; John Harris on behalf of the Trustees of Noyes Academy, *Herald of Freedom*, in *The Liberator*, October 3, 1835.

36. Database from the *1830 United States Federal Census*.

37. John Harris, *The Liberator*, October 3, 1835; the names of the students come from the Noyes Academy Study Group of the Canaan Historical Society, www.rootsweb.ancestry.com/~nhchs/Preservation/People/People.html.

38. John Harris, *The Liberator*, October 3, 1835; *Vermont Chronicle*, quoted in *The Liberator*, August 8, 1835.

39. John Harris, *The Liberator*, October 3, 1835; *Concord* (N. H.) *Patriot*, in *The Liberator* September 5, 1835.

CHAPTER 6

1. There is a long and substantial historiography on the New England mobs and race riots of the 1830s. I found the following most useful: Abbott, *Cotton and Capital*, 19–20; Lader, *Bold Brahmins*, 15; O'Connor, *Lords of the Loom*, 46; Strother, *The Underground Railroad in Connecticut*, 86; Hammett, "Two Mobs of Jacksonian Boston," 861, 863; Grimsted, *American Mobbing*, 18, 38; Ratner, *Powder Keg*, 4, 29, 64; Richards, *"Gentlemen of Property and Standing,"* 30–31, 36, 69; Hartford, *Money, Morals, and Politics*, 93–94; Fredrickson, *Black Image in White Mind*, 41; Curry, *Free Blacks in Urban America*, 110.

2. Grimsted, *American Mobbing*, 38; Arnold Buffum to Samuel E. Sewall, March 21, 1833, extract in *The Liberator*, April 6, 1833; Orson S. Murray, *Emancipator*, in *The Liberator*, March 8, 1834; *The Liberator*, June 13, 1834; Morse, *A Neglected Period of Connecticut's History*, 196.

3. Grimsted, *American Mobbing*, 36; Mayer, *All on Fire*, 200; Richards, *"Gentlemen of Property and Standing,"* 63–64; George Thompson to William Lloyd Garrison, October 28, 1834, in *The Liberator*, November 1, 1834; *Haverhill Gazette*, in *The Liberator*, December 13, 1834; *The Liberator*, October 10, 1835.

4. Mayer, *All on Fire*, 199–200; O'Connor, *Lords of the Loom*, 52; Chapman, *Right and Wrong in Boston*, 9–18; William Lloyd Garrison, *The Liberator*, November 7, 1835.

5. Chapman, *Right and Wrong in Boston*, 17–18, 27, 28; Garrison, *The Liberator*, November 7, 1835; Mayer, *All on Fire*, 200–201.

6. Charles C. Burleigh, *The Liberator*, October 24, 1835; Chapman, *Right and Wrong in Boston*, 29, 30; Garrison, *The Liberator*, November 7, 1835.

7. Chapman, *Right and Wrong in Boston*, 30–34, 37; Burleigh, *The Liberator*, October 24, 1835; Garrison, *The Liberator*, November 7, 1835; Samuel E. Sewall to Louisa

M. Winslow, October 22, 1835, in Tiffany, *Samuel E. Sewall*, 45–46; Mayer, *All on Fire*, 202–203.

8. Garrison, *The Liberator*, November 7, 1835; Sewall to Winslow, in Tiffany, *Samuel E. Sewall*, 48–49; Burleigh, *The Liberator*, October 24, 1835.

9. Garrison, *The Liberator*, November 7, 1835; Sewall to Winslow, in Tiffany, *Samuel E. Sewall*, 46–48; Burleigh, *The Liberator*, October 24, 1835; Mayer, *All on Fire*, 204.

10. Garrison, *The Liberator*, November 7, 1835; Sewall to Winslow, in Tiffany, *Samuel E. Sewall*, 49–50; Burleigh, *The Liberator*, October 24, 1835; Mayer, *All on Fire*, 204–207.

11. Chapman, *Right and Wrong in Boston*, 34; Garrison, *The Liberator*, November 7, 1835; Sewall to Winslow, in Tiffany, *Samuel E. Sewall*, 52.

12. Brown, *Life of William J. Brown*, 90; Providence Committee on Riots, *History of the Providence Riots*, 8; Werner, *Reaping the Bloody Harvest*, 235.

13. Brown, *Life of William J. Brown*, 95; Providence Committee, *Providence Riots*, 8–10; see Bolster, *Black Jacks* for a thorough examination of African American sailors.

14. Providence Committee, *Providence Riots*, 10–11.

15. Providence Committee, *Providence Riots*, 12–13.

16. Providence Committee, *Providence Riots*, 13–17.

17. Brown, *Life of William J. Brown*, 95; Providence Committee, *Providence Riots*, 8, 18; *1830 United States Federal Census*. Rosanna Jones was the one owner who may have been African American or of mixed ancestry.

18. Abdy, *Journal of a Residence and Tour*, III, 206–207.

19. *The Liberator*, April 30, 1831; *Hartford Intelligencer*, in *The Liberator*, May 7, 1831; J. K. to the editor, May 30, 1831, in *The Liberator*, June 4, 1831; Werner, *Reaping the Bloody Harvest*, 234.

20. *Hartford Review*, in *The Liberator*, June 20, 1835; Morse, *Neglected Period of Connecticut's History*, 196–197; Price and Stewart, *To Heal the Scourge of Prejudice*, 22; Price and Stewart make a strong case that the church's minister was Easton, 45, n. 27.

21. Grimsted, *American Mobbing*, 36–37; O'Connor, *Lords of the Loom*, 54; "Great Change in Connecticut," *The Liberator*, June 8, 1838.

CHAPTER 7

1. Laurie, *Beyond Garrison*, 41; Litwack, *North of Slavery*, 104–105; Pease and Pease, *They Who Would Be Free*, 12; Mayer, *All on Fire*, 351; Ripley, "Introduction," *Black Abolitionist Papers*, III, 20.

2. *The Liberator*, March 29, 1834; Susan Paul to the editor, April 1, 1834, in *The Liberator*, April 5, 1834; William Lloyd Garrison to Helen Garrison, April 16, 1836, in *Letters*, II, 77.

3. *The Liberator*, January 15, December 10, 1831; Bradlee, *Eastern Railroad*, 3, 8.

4. Bradlee, *Eastern Railroad*, 9, 19, 20; Marchione, "1835: The Year of the Railroads," www.bahistory.org/HistoryRailroads.html.

5. Bradlee, *Eastern Railroad*, 9–12, 14, 16–18.

6. Bradlee, *Eastern Railroad*, 27–28; Ruchames, "Jim Crow Railroads in Massachusetts," 62; Liberte Toute Entiere to the editor, April 9, 1842, in *The Liberator*, April 29, 1842. The earliest I've seen the use of the term "Jim Crow" is "The Color-Phobia as It Is," *Lynn Record*, in *The Liberator*, October 11, 1839. For a nuanced analysis of blackface minstrelsy, see Lott, *Love and Theft*.

7. "The Color-Phobia as It Is," *Lynn Record*, in *The Liberator*, October 11, 1839.

8. *The Liberator*, March 19, 1841; Ruchames, "Jim Crow Railroads," 67.

9. David Ruggles to the editor, July 24, 1841, in *The Liberator*, August 6, 1841; Ripley, "Introduction," *Black Abolitionist Papers*, III, 47.

10. Hodges, "David Ruggles," *American National Biography Online*, www.anb.org; David Ruggles to the editor of the *New Bedford Daily Register*, June 23, 1841, in *The Liberator*, July 9, 1841.

11. David Ruggles to the editor of the *New Bedford Daily Register*, June 23, 1841, in *The Liberator*, July 9, 1841; Meeting, June 30, 1841, *The Liberator*, July 9, 1841.

12. David Ruggles to the editor, July 24, 1841, *The Liberator*, August 6, 1841; Pease and Pease, *They Who Would Be Free*, 164–165.

13. "Treatment of Mr. Ruggles," *New-Bedford Morning Register*, in *The Liberator*, July 23, 1841.

14. David Ruggles to the editor, July 24, 1841, *The Liberator*, August 6, 1841; *Boston Times* in *The Liberator*, August 6, 1841; Pease and Pease, *They Who Would Be Free*, 165.

15. Douglass, *My Bondage and My Freedom*, 244; John A. Collins to William Lloyd Garrison, October 4, 1841, in *The Liberator*, October 15, 1841; William S. McFeely, *Frederick Douglass*, 92; Bradlee, *Eastern Railroad*, 16.

16. John A. Collins to William Lloyd Garrison, October 4, 1841, in *The Liberator*, October 15, 1841; Douglass, *My Bondage and My Freedom*, 244; McFeely, *Frederick Douglass*, 92–93; Johnson, *Sketches of Lynn*, 231–232.

17. John A. Collins to William Lloyd Garrison, October 4, 1841, in *The Liberator*, October 15, 1841; "Middlesex A. S. Society," *The Liberator*, October 22, 1841; "Resolutions from Worcester County North Division Anti-Slavery Society," *The Liberator*, November 26, 1841; Proceedings of the Plymouth County Anti-Slavery Society reported by the editor of the *Hingham Patriot*, in *The Liberator*, December 10, 1841; James N. Buffum, *Anti-Slavery Standard* in *The Liberator*, November 12, 1841.

18. John A. Collins to William Lloyd Garrison, October 4, 1841, in *The Liberator*, October 15, 1841; *The Liberator*, November 5, 1841; Jeffrey, *Great Silent Army of Abolitionism*, 127–128.

19. "The Disturbance on the Eastern Rail-Road," *Boston Daily Mail,* in *The Liberator,* November 5, 1841; John A. Collins to William Lloyd Garrison, October 4, 1841, in *The Liberator,* October 15, 1841.

20. H. Cummings to Brother Lee, October 25, 1841, *New-England Christian Advocate,* in *The Liberator,* November 12, 1841.

21. Committee Report for the town of New Bedford by John Bailey, J. B. Sanderson, William C. Coffin, Nathan Johnson, and George M. Bunker, in *The Liberator,* February 18, 1842; "Equal Rights," *Nantucket Islander* in *The Liberator,* March 25, 1842; Henry Hurd to William Lloyd Garrison, September 26, 1842, in *The Liberator,* October 7, 1842.

22. *The Liberator,* June 28, December 13, 1839; Maria W. Chapman, Hannah Robie, Mary G. Chapman, October 8, 1841, in *The Liberator,* October 15, 1841; *Concord Freeman,* January 17, 1842, in *The Liberator,* January 28, 1842; "Equal Rights of all Citizens in the Cars," *Bay State Democrat,* in *The Liberator,* February 25, 1842.

23. Bartlett, *Wendell Phillips,* 54, 58, and *passim*; Stewart, "Wendell Phillips," *American National Biography Online,* www.anb.org; Sewall, "Charles Lenox Remond," *American National Biography Online,* www.anb.org.

24. *The Liberator,* February 18, 1842.

25. *The Liberator,* February 25, 1842; Remond's remarks also are available in Testimony by Charles Lenox Remond Delivered at the Massachusetts State House, Boston, Massachusetts, February 10, 1842, *Black Abolitionist Papers,* III, 368–372.

26. *The Liberator,* March 4, 1842; Laurie, *Beyond Garrison,* 115–116.

27. *The Liberator,* April 8, 1842–February 10, 1843 and sporadically thereafter; Liberte Toute Entiere to the editor, April 9, 1842, in *The Liberator,* April 29, 1842; *Dover Star,* in *The Liberator,* May 13, 1842; Nathaniel Barney to the Proprietors of the New-Bedford and Taunton Rail-Road, April 14, 1842, in *The Liberator,* May 13, 1842; Bradlee, *Eastern Railroad,* 27; Mayer, *All on Fire,* 307.

28. *The Liberator,* February 17, 1843; Ruchames, "Jim Crow Railroads," 74–75; Laurie, *Beyond Garrison,* 115–116.

CHAPTER 8

1. Brown, *Life of William J. Brown,* 85–86; Cottrol, *Afro-Yankees,* 69.

2. Cottrol, *Afro-Yankees,* 70–71; Lemons and McKenna, "Re-enfranchisement of Rhode Island Negroes," 7.

3. Cottrol, *Afro-Yankees,* 73.

4. Cottrol, *Afro-Yankees,* 73–74; Lemons and McKenna, "Re-enfranchisement of Rhode Island Negroes," 8–9.

5. Cottrol, *Afro-Yankees,* 74–75; Lemons and McKenna, "Re-enfranchisement of Rhode Island Negroes," 9–10.

6. Brown, *Life of William J. Brown*, 173–174; Cottrol, *Afro-Yankees*, 75–77; Lemons and McKenna, "Re-enfranchisement of Rhode Island Negroes," 10–12.

7. "Latimer Meeting," *Salem Observer*, in *The Liberator*, December 9, 1842; "Case of George Latimer," as written in the *Boston Atlas*, in *The Liberator*, October 28, 1842; E. G. Austin to the Public, November 21, 1842, in *The Liberator*, November 25, 1842.

8. "Case of George Latimer," as written in the *Boston Atlas*, in *The Liberator*, October 28, 1842; E. G. Austin to the Public, November 21, 1842, in *The Liberator*, November 25, 1842.

9. "Case of George Latimer," as written in the *Boston Atlas*, in *The Liberator*, October 28, 1842; E. G. Austin to the Public, November 21, 1842, in *The Liberator*, November 25, 1842.

10. Rosenberg, "Personal Liberty Laws and Sectional Crisis," 27; Pease and Pease, *They Who Would Be Free*, 216; "Great Mass Meeting of Colored Citizens of Boston," *The Liberator*, December 23, 1842; "Case of George Latimer," as written in the *Boston Atlas*, in *The Liberator*, October 28, 1842; E. G. Austin to the Public, November 21, 1842, in *The Liberator*, November 25, 1842.

11. "Case of George Latimer," as written in the *Boston Atlas*, in *The Liberator*, October 28, 1842; E. G. Austin to the Public, November 21, 1842, in *The Liberator*, November 25, 1842.

12. E. G. Austin to the Public, November 21, 1842, in *The Liberator*, November 25, 1842.

13. "Case of George Latimer," as written in the *Boston Atlas*, in *The Liberator*, October 28, 1842; E. G. Austin to the Public, November 21, 1842, in *The Liberator*, November 25, 1842; *An Article on the Latimer Case*, 3–4; "Legal Injustice," *The Liberator*, November 4, 1842.

14. "Great Public Meeting," *The Liberator*, October 28, 1842; George Latimer note, *The Liberator*, November 4, 1842; "Latimer's Petition to the Boston Clergy," *The Liberator*, November 11, 1842; *An Article on the Latimer Case*, 4–8; the Faneuil Hall meeting as reported in a variety of newspapers, the speeches, and the resolutions are in *The Liberator*, November 4, 11, 1842.

15. E. G. Austin to the Public, November 21, 1842, in *The Liberator*, November 25, 1842.

16. Bowditch, *Life of Henry Ingersoll Bowditch*, I, 133–134; *An Article on the Latimer Case*, 8–12; *The Liberator*, November 11, 18, 1842; Campbell, *Slave Catchers*, 14.

17. E. G. Austin to the Public, November 21, 1842, in *The Liberator*, November 25, 1842; Maria Weston Chapman, "Sheriff Eveleth," *The Liberator*, November 25, 1842; James B. Gray's Account, *Boston Herald*, in *The Liberator*, December 9, 1842.

18. *The Liberator*, November 25, December 23, 30, 1842, January 6, 13, 20, February 3, 17, March 3, 1843; "The Latimer Petitions," *Boston Courier*, in *The Liberator*, March 17, 1843; Bowditch, *Life of Henry Ingersoll Bowditch*, I, 134; US Department

of State, *Aggregate Amount of Each Description of Persons . . . According to the Census of 1840*, 9.

19. "Great Mass Meeting of Colored Citizens of Boston," *The Liberator*, December 23, 1842; "Correspondence between the Authorities of Virginia and the Executive of Massachusetts, relative to the Latimer Case," *The Liberator*, February 3, 1843; Pease and Pease, *They Who Would Be Free*, 216.

20. "Legislative Report on the *Petition of George Latimer and Others*," in *The Liberator*, March 3, 1843; Rosenberg, *"Personal Liberty Laws,"* 27–28; *The Liberator*, April 7, 1843; Campbell, *Slave Catchers*, 14; Lader, *Bold Brahmins*, 117.

21. Kendrick and Kendrick, *Sarah's Long Walk*, 75–76; Moss, *Schooling Citizens*, 11; Curry, *Free Black in Urban America*, 162–163; Woodson, *Education of the Negro*, 320.

22. White, "Integration of Nantucket Public Schools," 59–60; Karttunen, *Other Islanders*, 82–83; *1830 United States Federal Census*; Polos, "Cyrus Peirce," *American National Biography Online*, www.anb.org.

23. White, "Integration of Nantucket Public Schools," 60; Karttunen, *Other Islanders*, 84.

24. White, "Integration of Nantucket Public Schools," 60; Nathaniel Barney to George Bradburn, quoted in *The Liberator*, March 11, 1842.

25. White, "Integration of Nantucket Public Schools," 60–61; Karttunen, *Other Islanders*, 85; Meeting and Address from the *Nantucket Islander*, in *The Liberator*, March 18, 1842.

26. White, "Integration of Nantucket Public Schools," 61; "Complexional Distinctions in Town Schools, *Nantucket Islander*, in *The Liberator*, March 31, 1845.

27. White, "Integration of Nantucket Public Schools," 61; Karttunen, *Other Islanders*, 85; "Public Meeting," *Nantucket Telegraph*, in *The Liberator*, March 15, 1844.

28. White, "Integration of Nantucket Public Schools," 61; Karttunen, *Other Islanders*, 85; Kendrick and Kendrick, *Sarah's Long Walk*, 86–87; "Speech on Hon. Mr. Wilson," *The Liberator*, March 7, 1845; "No Caste in the Public Schools," *Boston Courier*, in *The Liberator*, March 7, 1845.

29. White, "Integration of Nantucket Public Schools," 62; Karttunen, *Other Islanders*, 85; "Interesting Suit," *The Liberator*, September 26, 1845; R. to Garrison, February 11, 1846, in *The Liberator*, February 20, 1846.

30. White, "Salem's Antebellum Black Community," 108–110; "Costly Prejudice," *The Liberator*, August 23, 1834; *1830 United States Federal Census*.

31. White, "Salem's Antebellum Black Community," 110–114; "Resolutions of Salem School Committee," *Nantucket Telegraph*, and Richard Fletcher's Opinion, in *The Liberator*, July 12, 1844.

32. Curry, *Free Black in Urban America*, 166; Kendrick and Kendrick, *Sarah's Long Walk*, 79–80; Mabee, "A Negro Boycott to Integrate Boston Schools," 341–343.

33. Kendrick and Kendrick, *Sarah's Long Walk*, 81–82, 84; Mabee, "Negro Boycott," 343; "The Smith School," *The Liberator*, June 28, 1844.

34. "The Smith School" and "The Report . . . relative to the official conduct of Mr. Abner Forbes," *Boston Atlas*, in *The Liberator*, August 2, 1844; Kendrick and Kendrick, *Sarah's Long Walk*, 84; Mabee, "Negro Boycott," 344.

35. "Meeting of the Primary School Committee," and Henry I. Bowditch to William Lloyd Garrison, in *The Liberator*, June 27, 1845; Wightman, compiler, *Annals of the Boston Primary School Committee*, 208–209.

36. "Meeting of the Primary School Committee," and Henry I. Bowditch to William Lloyd Garrison, in *The Liberator*, June 27, 1845; "Boston Olive Branch," in *The Liberator*, August 8, 1845.

37. Henry I. Bowditch to William Lloyd Garrison, in *The Liberator*, July 10, 1846; Wightman, *Annals of the Boston Primary School Committee*, 212.

38. Extracts from the Majority Report, in *The Liberator*, August 21, 1846; Mabee, "Negro Boycott," 344–345.

39. Minority Report, in *The Liberator*, August 21, 1846; Mabee, "Negro Boycott," 345; Henry I. Bowditch to William Lloyd Garrison, in *The Liberator*, July 10, 1846.

40. Bowditch, "The Thirty Years' War of Anti-slavery," quoted in Bowditch, *Life and Correspondence*, I, 99–100.

41. These population figures come from my database of the *1830 United States Federal Census*.

42. Ralph Waldo Emerson's Journals, November, 1837, quoted in Gougeon, *Virtue's Hero*, 34.

43. Gougeon, *Virtue's Hero*, 82–83; Petrulionis, *To Set the World Right*, 54, 67; Emerson, *English Traits*, quoted in Philip Nicoloff, *Emerson on Race and History*, 145; R. to William Lloyd Garrison, October 27, 1845, in *The Liberator*, October 31, 1845; "New Bedford Lyceum," *New Bedford Register*, in *The Liberator*, November 28, 1845.

44. R. W. Emerson to W. J. Rotch, November 17, 1845, in *The Liberator*, January 16, 1846; Gougeon, *Virtue's Hero*, 103, 105, 133, 179, 185; Petrulionis, *To Set the World Right*, 54–55, 67. The current value of Emerson's $20.00 fee comes from Measuring Worth, www.measuringworth.com/ppowerus/.

CHAPTER 9

1. "An Act for the Better Preventing of a Spurious and Mixt Issue," in *Acts and Resolves*, I, 578–579.

2. "An Act for the orderly Solemnization of Marriages," June 22 1786, in *Laws of the Commonwealth of Massachusetts*, I, 323–324; Fowler, "Northern Attitudes Towards Interracial Marriage," 108; Levesque, "Black Boston," 131–132.

3. Fowler, "Northern Attitudes Towards Interracial Marriage," 108; Martyn, "Racism in the United States," 223–224; Weierman, *One Nation, One Blood*, 51–52; "An Act for Regulating Marriage," in Smith, *Laws of Maine*, 420, 420n.

4. Fowler, "Northern Attitudes Towards Interracial Marriage," 147; Kendrick and Kendrick, *Sarah's Long Walk*, 58–59; Pease and Pease, *They Who Would Be Free*, 163.

5. *The Liberator*, January 8, May 7, 1831; William Lloyd Garrison, "The Marriage Question," an extract from an address, in *The Liberator*, November 17, 1842; "A Wife Wanted," *The Liberator*, June 28, 1834; William Lloyd Garrison to Samuel J. May, July 23, 1834, in *Letters*, I, 381–382.

6. *The Liberator*, March 12, 19, 1831; John P. Bigelow to the editor of the *Boston Courier*, in *The Liberator*, April 30, 1831; database from *1830 United States Federal Census*.

7. *The Liberator*, March 19, 1831; J. G. W., *Amesbury Morning Courier*, February 11, 1839, in *The Liberator*, February 22, 1839; "Debate on Minot Thayer's Report Concerning the Dorchester Petition," Massachusetts House of Representatives, April 8, 1839, in *The Liberator*, April 19, 1839.

8. John P. Bigelow to the editor of the *Boston Courier*, in *The Liberator*, April 30, 1831; *The Liberator*, May 21, 1839.

9. *The Liberator*, January 28, February 4, February, 1832, February 9, March 9, 1838; Cosmopolite, March 5, 1838, in *The Liberator*, April 6, 1838; Kull, *Color-Blind Constitution*, 236, n. 17; Levesque, "Black Boston," 134; Moulton, *Fight for Interracial Marriage Rights*, 86–90; Ruchames, "Race, Marriage, and Abolitionism in Massachusetts," 255–256.

10. "Report Respecting Distinctions of Color," Massachusetts House of Representatives, February 25, 1839, in *The Liberator*, March 15, 1839; J. G. W., *Amesbury Morning Courier*, February 11, 1839, in *The Liberator*, February 22, 1839; One Who Knows to the Editor, *The Liberator*, February 8, 1839; *Dedham Patriot*, in *The Liberator*, April 12, 1839; Weierman, *One Nation, One* Blood, 149; Kendrick and Kendrick, *Sarah's Long Walk*, 58.

11. "Report Respecting Distinctions of Color," Massachusetts House of Representatives, February 25, 1839, in *The Liberator*, March 15, 1839; "Scurrilous Petition from Lynn," *Lynn Record*, in *The Liberator*, February 22, 1839; Ruchames, "Race, Marriage, and Abolitionism," 257.

12. "The Marriage Law," *The Liberator*, February 15, 1839; Correspondence on George Bradburn in the *Boston Atlas* and the *Hampshire Gazette*, in *The Liberator*, March 5, 1841.

13. "The Marriage Law," *The Liberator*, February 15, 1839; *The Liberator*, March 15, 1839.

14. "Report Respecting Distinctions of Color," Massachusetts House of Representatives, February 25, 1839, in *The Liberator*, March 15, 1839.

15. "Report Respecting Distinctions of Color," Massachusetts House of Representatives, February 25, 1839, in *The Liberator*, March 15, 1839.

16. "Debate on Minot Thayer's Report Concerning the Dorchester Petition," Massachusetts House of Representatives, April 8, 1839, in *The Liberator*, April 19, 1839; Sarah Baker to William Lloyd Garrison, April 15, 1839, in *The Liberator*, April 26, 1839; Petition of Lydia Maria Child to the Legislature of Massachusetts, March 20, 1839, in *The Liberator*, April 26, 1839; *The Liberator*, March 22, 29, July 5, 26, 1839.

17. *The Liberator*, February 7, March 20, 27, April 3, 17, 1840; Kull, *Color-Blind Constitution*, 24; A Member of the House to William Lloyd Garrison, in *The Liberator*, May 8, 1840.

18. *The Liberator*, January 29, February 5, 12, March 12, 19, 1841.

19. *The Liberator*, February 11, 29, March 4, 25, 1842.

20. *Lynn Record*, in *The Liberator*, February 12, 1841.

21. Fowler, "Northern Attitudes," 151; Laurie, *Beyond Garrison*, 111n.; Moulton, *Fight for Interracial Marriage Rights*, 70; Pease and Pease, *They Who Would Be Free*, 163–164; "Meeting of the Colored Citizens of Boston," *The Liberator*, February 10, 1843.

22. "Debate on the Marriage Bill," *The Liberator*, February 24, 1843 (also includes the petition and *The Liberator*'s comments on it).

23. "Debate on the Marriage Bill," *The Liberator*, February 24, 1843.

24. "Vote on the Intermarriage Law," *The Liberator*, March 10, 1843.

25. William Lloyd Garrison to Henry C. Wright, March 1, 1843, William Lloyd Garrison to Hannah Webb, March 1, 1843, in *Letters*, III, 134–135, 130–131.

CHAPTER 10

1. For Amos G. Beman: 1850, 1860, 1870 *United States Federal Census; Connecticut Deaths and Burials Index, 1650–1934*, online database, www.ancestry.com, FHL Film Number 3087; Beman Family Tree (www.ancestry.com); Warner, "Amos Gerry Beman," 218fn., 220–221. For Fred and Jane Little: 1850, 1860, 1870 *United States Federal Census*.

2. For Fred and Marian Clark: 1850, 1860, 1870 *United States Federal Census*. For Sylvester and Elizabeth R. Winslow Cazneau: 1850, 1860, and 1880 *United States Federal Census*; correspondence from Betty Miessner of the Scituate Historical Society. For Edward H. and Mary Jakes: 1850, 1860, 1870, 1880, 1900 *United States Federal Census*; US, *Civil War Draft Registrations Records, 1863–1865*, database online, www.ancestry.com.

3. Anderson, *American Census*, 35–40 and *passim*; Wright with Hunt, *History and Growth of the United States Census*, 42, 149, 152, 156, 157, 168, 171; US Bureau of the Census, *Negro Population*, 207; Spickard, *Mixed Blood*, 433, n27; Brown and Rose, *Black Roots*, xv.

4. Parentheses indicate maiden name.

5. Congdon, *Reminiscences of a Journalist*, 39.

6. Cifaldi, "Hammet Achmet, Middletown's Not-So-Famous Drum Maker," http://historyoftheancients.wordpress.com/?s=achmet; correspondence with Sue Cifaldi; *1840 United States Federal Census; Connecticut Deaths and Burials*, FHL Film Number 3076.

7. 1850, 1860, 1870 *United States Federal Census; Connecticut Deaths and Burials Index, 1650–1934*, online database, www.ancestry.com, FHL Film Number 3087;

Beman Family Tree, www.ancestry.com; Warner, "Amos Gerry Beman," passim; Beman, Amos G. Beman, Scrapbooks, online at the Beinecke Library, Yale
University, particularly for his letter of resignation (III, 132–133) and his busy
itinerary following his daughter's death (III, 154–156). Although it seems likely
that he was forced from his ministry in New Haven, there is no marriage record
of when he was united with his white wife, and his letter of resignation is vague
and ambiguous about his reasons for leaving. Warner offers conflicting testimony from thirty years after the event, 218n.

8. *Boston Traveller*, in *The Liberator*, August 7, 1846.

9. Guyette, *Discovering Black Vermont*, passim.

10. LiBrizzi, *Lost Atusville*, 15–29; 1820–1850 *United States Federal Census*; Quimby/
Edwards Family Tree, www.ancestry.com.

11. 1830, 1840, 1850, 1860, 1870, 1880 *United States Federal Census*; Quimby/
Edwards Family Tree, www.ancestry.com; LiBrizzi, *Lost Atusville*, 37, 39.

12. Wheeler and Wheeler, *History of Brunswick, Topsham, and Harpswell*, 75, 77,
98, 618, 624; 1830, 1840, 1850, 1860, 1870, 1880 *United States Federal Census*;
Maine Death Records, 1617–1922, roll 33, online database, www.ancestry.com;
Sukeforth Family Tree, www.ancestry.com.

13. 1830, 1840, 1850, 1860, 1870 *United States Federal Census*; *Massachusetts Vital
Records, 1841–1910*, online database, www.ancestry.com, v. 5, 248, and v. 76,
139; *Massachusetts, Town Vital Collections, 1620–1988*, online database, www.
ancestry.com; Karttunen, *Other Islanders*, 76, 106; correspondence with Frances
Karttunen.

14. *1860 United States Federal Census*; *Massachusetts, Marriage Records, 1840–1915*,
online database, www.ancestry.com; *Massachusetts, State Census, 1865*, online
database, www.ancestry.com.

15. Dempsey, "Town's Early Barber Shops Operated by Blacks," *Brattleboro Reformer*,
February 9, 1994; thanks to John Carnahan for sending me a copy of Dempsey's
article and more; 1850, 1860, 1870, 1880, 1900 *United States Federal Census*.

16. Smith, *History of the Town of Mont Vernon*, iv, 41, 59, 64, 120; 1830, 1840, 1850,
1860, 1870, 1880, 1900 *United States Federal Census*; *US Civil War Records and
Profiles*, online database, www.ancestry.com; *New Hampshire, Marriage Records
Index, 1637–1947*, online database, www.ancestry.com.

17. 1860, 1870, 1880 *United States Federal Census*.

18. 1850, 1860 *United States Federal Census*; *Massachusetts Vital Records, 1841–1910*,
v. 175, 57.

19. 1860, 1870 *United States Federal Census*.

20. 1850, 1860, 1870 *United States Federal Census*; *Massachusetts Vital Records,
1841–1910*, v. 164, 28; *The Boston Athenæum BOSBLACK database*, app.bos-
tonathenaeum.org/BosBlack/; *New Hampshire, Death and Burial Records Index,
1654–1949*, online database, www.ancestry.com. Most studies of the Irish and
their attitudes and behavior toward African Americans during the antebellum

period focus on antagonisms: Handlin, *Boston's Immigrants,* 132–133; Ignatiev, *How the Irish Became White,* 98–99, 112, 120; O'Connor, *The Boston Irish,* 82–83; Roediger, *Wages of Whiteness,* 134, 136, 149.

21. I constructed two appendices for this section somewhat differently. Some of the men changed occupations from time to time. That posed a problem concerning which occupation to list. Appendix 6 consists of occupations that were of the longest duration during the marriage. Appendix 7 uses occupations that were identified at the time of greatest real estate holdings. Thus, there are a few discrepancies between tables in the occupation of a particular person.

22. 1860, 1870, 1880 *United States Federal Census.*

23. 1860, 1870, 1880, 1900 *United States Federal Census; Brewster Massachusetts Vital Records,* book 2, p. 85, online database, www.ancestry.com; *Massachusetts, Vital Records,* v. 108, p. 3; *People of Color in the Massachusetts State Census, 1855–1865,* 146, online database, www.ancestry.com; *US Civil War Draft Registration Records.*

24. 1850, 1860, 1870, 1880 *United States Federal Census; Massachusetts Vital Records to 1850,* 279, 286; *People of Color,* 14677.

25. 1850, 1860, 1870 *United States Federal Census; US Federal Census Mortality Schedules Index,* online database, www.ancestry.com; *Massachusetts, Town Birth Records, 1620–1850,* online database, www.ancestry.com; *Connecticut Town Marriage Records,* www.americanancestors.com; correspondence with Christina Vida of the Windsor Historical Society.

26. 1850, 1860, 1870, 1880, 1900 *United States Federal Census; US Civil War Records; Maine Death Records, 1617–1922;* correspondence from a descendant of the Parkers who wishes to remain unnamed.

27. 1850, 1860, 1870, 1880, 1900, 1910 *United States Federal Census; Massachusetts Vital Records,* v. 101, p. 146; *Boston Athenæum BOSBLACK database; US Civil War Draft Registrations Records; People of Color,* 8746.

28. 1850, 1860, 1870, 1880 *United States Federal Census.*

29. 1830, 1840, 1850, 1860, 1870, 1880 *United States Federal Census; Massachusetts Vital Records,* 237, 559; *Springfield Republican,* August 8, 1862; Carvalho, *Black Families in Hampden Country,* 156–157; thanks to Cliff McCarthy of the Springfield Museums for his help with John N. Mars.

CHAPTER 11

1. McPherson, *Battle Cry of Freedom,* 70–77; Morris, *Free Men All,* 146–147.
2. McPherson, *Battle Cry of Freedom,* 80; Laurie, *Beyond Garrison,* 233.
3. Collison, *Shadrach Minkins,* 77; Kendrick and Kendrick, *Sarah's Long Walk,* 188; Quarles, *Black Abolitionists,* 199–200.
4. Laurie, *Beyond Garrison,* 245; "Colored Convention," Portland, Maine, in *The Liberator,* September 20, 1850; "Meeting of Colored Citizens of Springfield, Massachusetts," September 17, 1850, in *The Liberator,* October 4, 1850; "Meeting

of Colored Citizens of Boston," September 30, 1850, in *The Liberator*, October 4, 1850, "Declaration of Sentiments of the Colored Citizens of Boston on the Fugitive Slave Bill," October 4, 1850, in *The Liberator*, October 11, 1850.

5. Dalzell, *Enterprising Elite*, 211; O'Connor, *Lords of the Loom*, 97; Lader, *Bold Brahmins*, 155–156; *The Liberator*, October 11, 1850.

6. Collison, *Shadrach Minkins*, 80; *The Liberator*, October 25, 1850.

7. Faneuil Hall Meeting, October 14, 1850, *The Liberator*, October 18, 1850.

8. Faneuil Hall Meeting, October 14, 1850, *The Liberator*, October 18, 1850.

9. Faneuil Hall Meeting, October 14, 1850, *The Liberator*, October 18, 1850.

10. Faneuil Hall Meeting, October 14, 1850, *The Liberator*, October 18, 1850.

11. Craft, *Running a Thousand Miles for Freedom*, 1, 2, 10, 15, 31; Bowditch, *Life of Bowditch*, I, 205.

12. Craft, *Running a Thousand Miles*, 29–35.

13. Craft, *Running a Thousand Miles*, 42–68.

14. Craft, *Running a Thousand Miles*, 68–74.

15. 1850 *United States Federal Census*; Samuel May to John Bishop Estlin, November 6, 1850, in Craft, *Running a Thousand Miles*, 89; Bowditch, *Life of Bowditch*, I, 205–206; *The Liberator*, November 1, 1850.

16. Samuel May to John Bishop Estlin, November 6, 1850, in Craft, *Running a Thousand Miles*, 89–92; Bowditch, *Life of Bowditch*, I, 206–209; *The Liberator*, November 1, 1850.

17. *Boston Daily Atlas*, November 26, 29, 1850.

18. *Boston Daily Atlas*, February 17, 1851; *Boston Investigator*, February 19, 1851; Elizur Wright's account and Patrick Riley's deposition appear in *The Liberator*, February 21, 1851; Collison, *Shadrach Minkins*, 65, 110.

19. *Boston Daily Atlas*, February 17, 1851; *Boston Investigator*, February 19, 1851; *The Liberator*, February 21, 1851.

20. *Boston Daily Atlas*, February 17, 1851; *Boston Investigator*, February 19, 1851; *The Liberator*, February 21, 1851; Collison, *Shadrach Minkins*, 117, 125.

21. *Boston Daily Atlas*, February 18, 19, 20, 21, 22, 24, 27, 28, March 3, 4, 5, 7, 31, May 28, June 7, 18, 1851; *Boston Investigator*, April 2, July 23, 1851; *The Liberator*, February 28, March 14, June 13, 20, 1851; Collison, *Shadrach Minkins*, 125, 136; Robboy and Robboy, "Lewis Hayden," 591–603; Bowditch, *Life of Bowditch*, I, 215.

22. *Boston Daily Atlas*, April 7, 1851; *The Liberator*, April 11, 1851; Levy, "Sims' Case," 43–44.

23. *Boston Daily Atlas*, April 7, 1851; *The Liberator*, April 11, 1851.

24. *Boston Daily Atlas*, April 7, 1851; *The Liberator*, April 11, 1851; Levy, "Sims' Case," 46–47.

25. *Boston Daily Atlas*, April 7, 1851; *The Liberator*, April 11, 1851; Levy, "Sims' Case," 51–52; Pease and Pease, *They Who Would Be Free*, 222–223.

26. *Boston Daily Atlas*, April 7, 8, 9, 10, 11, 12, 14, 15, 16, 1851; *The Liberator*, April 11, 18, 1851; Levy, "Sims' Case," 52–69.

27. Bowditch, *Life of Bowditch*, 216–222; *Boston Daily Atlas*, April 14, 1851; *The Liberator*, April 18, 1851.

28. McPherson, *Battle Cry of Freedom*, 120–125; Abbott, *Cotton and Capital*, 26; Campbell, *Slave Catchers*, 94; Dalzell, *Enterprising Elite*, 214–215; O'Connor, *Lords of the Loom*, 98–99.

29. Schwartz, "Fugitive Slave Days in Boston," 204, 206; Shapiro, "Rendition of Anthony Burns," 36; Maginnes, "Anthony Burns," *American National Biography Online*, www.anb.org; *Boston Slave Riot, and Trial of Anthony Burns*; *Boston Daily Atlas*, May 26, 1854; *The Liberator*, June 2, 1854.

30. Shapiro, "Rendition of Anthony Burns," 36–37, 44; *Boston Slave Riot*, 83; *Boston Daily Atlas*, May 26, 1854; *The Liberator*, June 2, 1854; Bowditch, *Life of Bowditch*, 264.

31. Bowditch, *Life of Bowditch*, 264–265; Higginson, *Cheerful Yesterdays*, 147–151.

32. Higginson, *Cheerful Yesterdays*, 152–158; *Boston Slave Riot*, 10; *Boston Daily Atlas*, May 27, 1854; Maginnes, "The Case of the Court House," 31–33.

33. *Boston Slave Riot*, 10, 12, 19, 28–29; *Boston Daily Atlas*, May 29, 1854; Dana, *The Journal of Richard Henry Dana, Jr.*, II, 628; Shapiro, "Rendition of Anthony Burns," 40–41.

34. Shapiro, "Rendition of Anthony Burns," 41–44; *Boston Slave Riot*, 62–67, 80–83; *Boston Daily Atlas*, June 3, 1854; *The Liberator*, June 9, 1854.

35. *Boston Slave Riot*, 77, 84–86; Shapiro, "Rendition of Anthony Burns," 44–45.

36. Schwartz, "Fugitive Slave Days," 211–212; Maginnes, "Case of the Court House Rioters," 33–40; Morris, *Free Men All*, 168–173; May, *Fugitive Slave Law and Its Victims*, 43, 64 67, 107–109, 113; Davis, *Slave Power Conspiracy*, 30–31, 64–65; Formisano, *Transformation of Political Culture*, 331; Laurie, *Beyond Garrison*, 102–104.

CHAPTER 12

1. Mabee, "A Negro Boycott," 347; Levesque, "Black Boston," 217; Moss, "Tarring and Feathering," 229–231; Price and Stewart, "Roberts Case, the Easton Family," 105–108 (the Roberts quote is on p. 108); *Boston Daily Atlas*, September 7, 1847.

2. *1850 United States Federal Census*; Kendrick and Kendrick, *Sarah's Long Walk*, 111, 115, 137; Moss, "Tarring and Feathering," 231–232.

3. Jacobs, "Garrison's *Liberator*," 269–273; "The Smith School,--Meeting of Colored Citizens," *The Liberator*, August 18, 1848. For an extensive analysis of the clash between the two groups, framed as a dispute over black identity, see Hancock, "Elusive Boundaries of Blackness."

4. Levesque, "Inherent Reformers," 499–508; Kendrick and Kendrick, *Sarah's Long Walk*, 119–120; Moss, "Tarring and Feathering," 227–228.

5. "Meeting of Colored Citizens," *The Liberator*, August 10, 1849; *Boston Daily Atlas*, August 13, 1849; Mabee, "Negro Boycott," 348–349; Moss, "Tarring and Feathering," 228–229; *Massachusetts, Marriage Records, 1840–1915*, online database, www.ancestry.com.

6. "Meetings of Colored Citizens of Boston," *The Liberator*, September 7, 1849.

7. *Boston Daily Atlas*, August 30, 1849; Kendrick and Kendrick, *Sarah's Long Walk*, 128.

8. "Meetings of Colored Citizens of Boston," *The Liberator*, September 7, 1849.

9. Mabee, "Negro Boycott," 349–350; *Boston Courier*, September 20, 1849; William C. Nell, "The Smith School," in *The Liberator*, September 21, 1849.

10. William C. Nell, "Equal School Rights, *The Liberator*, October 5, 1849; Kendrick and Kendrick, *Sarah's Long Walk*, 137.

11. Thomas Paul Smith, "Vindication," *The Liberator*, October 5, 1849; Thomas P. Smith to J. McCune Smith, August 2, 1849, from the *Boston Chronotype*, in *The Liberator*, January 4, 1850.

12. William C. Nell, "Meetings of the Friends of Equal School Rights," October 23, 1849, in *The Liberator*, November 9, 1849.

13. *The Liberator*, December 28, 1849, January 11, 18, 25, February 1, 1850; Levy and Phillips, "The *Roberts* Case," 512–514.

14. *Boston Courier*, December 5, 1849, in *The Liberator*, December 14, 1849.

15. Massachusetts Supreme Court Decision of *Sarah C. Roberts v. the City of Boston*, *Boston Daily Advertiser*, in *The Liberator*, April 26, 1850; Levy and Phillips, "Roberts Case," 515–518.

16. *The Liberator*, April 26, June 7, 14, August 2, 9, 1850, April 4, 1851; *Boston Daily Atlas*, February 15, March 10, 1851; 1850 *United States Federal Census*.

17. Shepard, "Public Schools of Boston," in Homan, *Sketches of Boston*, 244; "Equal School Privileges," and "Anti-Colonization Meeting," *The Liberator*, April 4, 1851; Moss, "Tarring and Feathering," 234.

18. *Boston Daily Atlas*, May 7, 9, 10, 23, June 9, 14, July 22, 1851; 1860 *United States Federal Census; Massachusetts, Marriage Records, 1840–1915*; Moss, "Tarring and Feathering," *passim*, particularly 218–221, 232–235, 238–239; Archer, *As If an Enemy's Country*, 162–163, 211–212.

19. *Vermont Freeman*, in *The Liberator*, October 7, 1853; *The Liberator*, November 10, 1854; Kendrick and Kendrick, *Sarah's Long Walk*, 217–222.

20. Report of the Committee on Public Instruction, in *The Liberator*, August 18, 1854; Mabee, "Negro Boycott," 355.

21. Mabee, "Negro Boycott," 355–356; Mulkern, *Know-Nothing Party in Massachusetts*, 5–6; Von Frank, *The Trials of Anthony Burns*, 238–239; Kantrowitz, *More Than Freedom*, 167–168.

22. Report of the Committee on Education, March 17, 1855, in *The Liberator*, March 30, 1855; Kendrick and Kendrick, *Sarah's Long Walk*, 231.

23. Mabee, "Negro Boycott," 358–360; Kendrick and Kendrick, *Sarah's Long Walk*, 234–237; William C. Nell, "Improvement of Colored People," in *The Liberator*, August 24, 1855; *Boston Evening Telegraph*, September 3, 1855, in *The Liberator*, September 7, 1855; *Boston Post*, in *The Liberator*, September 7, 1855; "Abolition of the Smith and All Other Separate Colored Schools," *The Liberator*, September 14, 1855; *Boston Daily Atlas*, September 4, 12, 1855.

24. Davis, *Slave Power Conspiracy*, 64–65; Laurie, *Beyond Garrison*, 102–104; Levesque, "Black Boston," 234–235; Gorham, *Five Years' Progress of the Slave Power*, 84.

25. Cottrol, *Afro-Yankees*, 92; Grossman, "George T. Downing and Desegregation of Rhode Island Public Schools," passim, particularly 99–101; Pease and Pease, *They Who Would Be Free*, 156; William Howe to George T. Downing, February 10, 1857, in *The Liberator*, February 27, 1857; *The Liberator*, April 17, December 25, 1857, January 29, 1858, February 24, 1860.

CHAPTER 13

1. "The Colored Convention," from the *Hartford Republican*, October 3, 1854, in *The Liberator*, October 27, 1854.

2. "The Colored Convention," from the *Hartford Republican*, October 3, 1854, in *The Liberator*, October 27, 1854.

3. *The Liberator*, August 24, 1855.

4. Beman, "Letter" for the *Voice of the Fugitive*, May 15, 1851, in Scrapbooks, II, 19; Robert Morris, Speech at the Convention of the Colored Citizens of Massachusetts, August 2, 1858, in *The Liberator*, August 13, 1858; James Freeman Clarke, "Condition of the Free Colored People of the United States," from the *Christian Examiner*, March, 1859, in *The Liberator*, March 18, 1859; William Wells Brown et al., Committee to Fellow Citizens, *The Liberator*, June 3, 1859; *National Anti-Slavery Standard*, in *The Liberator*, December, 1860; Horton and Horton, *Black Bostonians*, 92; Kantrowitz, *More Than Freedom*, 171.

5. Gerrit Smith to Amos G. Beman, July 9, 1854, in Beman, Scrapbooks, III, 126; "Equal Suffrage in Connecticut," *The Liberator*, June 22, 1855; *The Liberator*, June 18, 1858; Strother, *Underground Railroad in Connecticut*, 92, 184.

6. *New Haven Journal and Courier*, June 9, 1855, in Beman, Scrapbooks, III, 93; *The Liberator*, June 22, 1855; Strother, *Underground Railroad in Connecticut*, 92, 184.

7. *The Liberator*, August 5, 1853; William J. Watkins to Editor, *Boston Herald*, April 22, 1853, in Ripley, *Black Abolitionist Papers*, IV, 154.

8. Kendrick and Kendrick, *Sarah's Long Walk*, 212–213; Pease and Pease, *They Who Would Be Free*, 159–160; *The Liberator*, August 5, 1853.

9. *Boston Evening Telegraph*, in *The Liberator*, August 17, 1855; both Clifford's letter to Governor Gardiner and Morris's letter come from the *Boston Evening Telegraph*, in *The Liberator*, September 14, 1855.

10. Kendrick and Kendrick, *Sarah's Long Walk*, 213; Pease and Pease, *They Who Would Be Free*, 160; *The Liberator*, September 10, 1858, October 7, 1859, March 2, 23, 1860.

11. "Progress of Equal Rights," *The Liberator*, July 17, 1857.

12. E. H. H. to William Lloyd Garrison, March 22, 1858, *The Liberator*, April 2, 1858; *The Liberator*, August 20, 1858; Charles K. Whipple to William Lloyd Garrison, *The Liberator*, January 6, 1860; Collison, "Antislavery, Blacks, and the Boston Elite," 426–428; *Hartford Republican*, "Colorphobia," in *The Liberator*, September 6, 1853.

13. "The Opera Ejection Case," *The Liberator*, June 10, 1853; Horton and Horton, *Black Bostonians*, 68; Wesley, "Integration versus Separatism," in Jacobs, *Courage and Conscience*, 216–218.

14. John Stephenson to the editor of the *Boston Evening Telegraph*, in *The Liberator*, October 3, 1856; *Boston Daily Atlas*, January 5, February 9, April 10, November 3, 1854, May 2, 28, June 2, 1855; "Franklin Celebration," *Boston Daily Advertiser*, September 19, 1856.

15. John Stephenson to the Editor of the *Boston Evening Telegraph*, in *The Liberator*, October 3, 1856.

16. *Boston Evening Telegraph*, in *The Liberator*, October 17, 1856.

17. Cottrol, "Robert Morris," *American National Biography Online*, www.anb.org; 1850, 1860 *United States Federal Census*.

18. Robert Morris to the editor, *Chelsea Telegraph & Pioneer*, September 6, 1858, in *The Liberator*, September 24, 1858.

19. Robert Morris to the editor, *Chelsea Telegraph & Pioneer*, September 6, 1858, in *The Liberator*, September 24, 1858; *1860 United States Federal Census*.

20. For an excellent account of Charlotte Forten's life and journals, see Stevenson, "Introduction," *Journals of Charlotte Forten Grimké*. Particular references in the paragraph are from *Journals*, I, 67, 87, 93, 94, 98, 100, 111, 133–134, 139–140, 147, 150, 153, 160–161; II, 182, 183, 274; III, 299.

21. Levesque, "Boston's Black Brahmin," 339; Chickering, *A Statistical View of the Population of Massachusetts, from 1765–1840*, 156; "Defending the Abused," *Portland Pleasure Boat*, in *The Liberator*, March 19, 1852; Moss, *Schooling Citizens*, 59–60; Bolster, *Black Jacks*, 158–159, 178; Laurie, *Beyond Garrison*, 271; Levesque, "Black Boston," 93; Pleck, *Black Migration and Poverty*, 198–199. For contrasting views on the extent of African American economic opportunity in the 1850s, see B. to the editor, *The Liberator*, March 28, 1856, and Speech by John Rock, delivered at the Meionaon, March 5, 1860, in Ripley, *Black Abolitionist Papers*, V, 63.

22. Amos Beman, "Letter," *Voice of the Fugitive*, May 15, 1851, in Beman, Scrapbooks, II, 19; W. P., "Encourage Colored Mechanics," *The Liberator*, October 10, 1851; "Give Him Your Patronage," *The Liberator*, October 10, 1851; William C. Nell,

The Liberator, January 27, 1854, August 24, 1855, April 25, 1856, June 17, 1859, August 3, 1860; Bethel, *Roots of African-American Identity*, 169.

23. "The Boston Massacre, March 5, 1770," *The Liberator*, March 12, 1858; Bethel, *Roots of African-American Identity*, 4; Levesque, "Boston's Black Brahmin," passim.

24. "The Boston Massacre, March 5, 1770," *The Liberator*, March 12, 1858; Levesque, "Boston's Black Brahmin," 340; Horton and Horton, *Black Bostonians*, 119–120; Pease and Pease, *They Who Would Be Free*, 102–103; Quarles, *Black Abolitionists*, 234.

25. "The Boston Massacre, March 5, 1770," *The Liberator*, March 12, 1858; Kantrowitz, *More Than Freedom*, 124.

CHAPTER 14

1. *The Liberator*, January 1, 1831, March 24, 1865.

2. *The Liberator*, May 26, June 2, 1865.

3. Johnson, *Development of State Legislation*, 77–80, 118, 124–126, 174–175; Grossman, "George T. Downing," 104.

APPENDIX 4

1. Brown and Brown, *Hanging of Ephraim Wheeler*; Hodes, *Sea Captain's Wife*; Guyette, *Discovering Black Vermont*; Cottrol, *Afro-Yankees*, 131–132; Catterall, *Judicial Cases*, IV, 490, 497; Horton and Horton, *Black Bostonians*, 21–23, 48; Brown, and Rose, *Black Roots in Southeastern Connecticut*, xv; Fowler, "Northern Attitudes," 52, 107; Belknap, "Answer to Queries Respecting Slavery," 209.

2. Every *United States Federal Census* from 1790 to 1920 used in compiling the database for New England mixed marriages may be found at www.ancestry.com.

Works Cited

1790–1920 United States Federal Census. Online database, www.ancestry.com.

Abbott, Richard H. *Cotton and Capital: Boston Businessmen and Antislavery Reform, 1854–1868.* Amherst, Mass., 1991.

Abdy, Edward Strutt. *Journal of a Residence and Tour in the United States of North America, from April, 1834, to October, 1834.* London, 1835.

"Abolition Letters Collected by Captain Arthur B. Spingarn." *Journal of Negro History* 18 (January 1933): 78–84.

Acts and Resolves, Public and Private, of the Province of the Massachusetts Bay: to which are prefixed the Charters of the Province, with Historical and Explanatory Notes, and an Appendix. Boston, 1869. I.

Adams, James T. "Disfranchisement of Negroes in New England." *American Historical Review* 30 (April 1925): 543–547.

Adams, John Quincy. "Misconceptions of Shakespeare upon the Stage." *New England Magazine* 9 (December 1835), in James Henry Hackett. *Notes and Comments upon Certain Plays and Actors of Shakespeare, with Criticisms and Correspondence.* New York, 1863, 217–228.

An Article on the Latimer Case from the March Number of the Law Reporter. Boston, 1843.

Archer, Richard. *As If an Enemy's Country: The British Occupation of Boston and the Origins of Revolution.* New York, 2010.

———. *Fissures in the Rock: New England in the Seventeenth Century.* Hanover, N.H., 2001.

Bailyn, Bernard, and Philip D. Morgan, eds. *Strangers within the Realm: Cultural Margins of the First British Empire.* Chapel Hill, N.C., 1991.

Bartels, Emily C. "*Othello* and Africa: Postcolonialism Reconsidered." *William and Mary Quarterly*, 3rd. ser., 54 (January 1997): 45–64.

Bartlett, John Russell, ed. *Records of the Colony of Rhode Island, and Providence Plantations in New England.* vol. 1, 1636–1663. Providence, R.I., 1856, I.

Bartlett, Irving H. *From Slave to Citizen: The Story of the Negro in Rhode Island.* Providence, R.I., 1954.

————. *Wendell Phillips: Brahmin Radical*. Boston, 1961.

Bay, Mia. *The White Image in the Black Mind: African-American Ideas about White People, 1830–1925*. New York, 2000.

Belknap, Jeremy. "Answer to Queries Respecting the Slavery and Emancipation of Negroes in Massachusetts." Massachusetts Historical Society. *Collections* 4 (1795): 191–211.

Beman, Amos G. Scrapbooks. I–IV. Beinecke Library, Yale University. Online at Beinecke Library, Yale University.

Berlin, Ira. *Many Thousands Gone: The First Two Centuries of Slavery in North America*. Cambridge, Mass., 1998.

————. *Slaves without Masters: The Free Negro in the Antebellum South*. New York, 1974.

Bethel, Elizabeth Rauh. *The Roots of African-American Identity: Memory and History in Antebellum Free Communities*. New York, 1997.

Blackburn, Robin. *The Making of New World Slavery: From the Baroque to the Modern, 1492–1800*. London, 1997.

Bolster, W. Jeffrey. *Black Jacks: African American Seamen in the Age of Sail*. Cambridge, Mass., 1997.

Boston Athenæum BOSBLACK database, The. app.bostonathenaeum.org/BosBlack/.

Boston Courier.

Boston Daily Atlas.

Boston Daily Advertiser.

Boston Investigator.

Boston Slave Riot, and Trial of Anthony Burns. Boston, 1854.

Bowditch, Vincent Y. *Life and Correspondence of Henry Ingersoll Bowditch*. 2 vols. Boston, 1902.

Bradlee, Francis B. C. *The Eastern Railroad: A Historical Account of Early Railroading in Eastern New England*. Salem, Mass., 1917.

Breen, T. H. "Making History: The Force of Public Opinion and the Last Years of Slavery in Revolutionary Massachusetts." In Ronald Hoffman, Mechal Sobel, and Fredrika J. Teute, eds., *Through a Glass Darkly: Reflections on Personal Identity in Early America*. Chapel Hill, N.C., 1997, 67–95.

————. *Puritans and Adventurers: Change and Persistence in Early America*. New York, 1982.

Brewster Massachusetts Vital Records, book 2, p. 85. Online database, www.ancestry.com.

Brown, Barbara W., and James M. Rose. *Black Roots in Southeastern Connecticut, 1650–1900*. Detroit, Mich., 1980.

Brown, Irene Quenzler, and Richard D. Brown. *The Hanging of Ephraim Wheeler: A Story of Rape, Incest, and Justice in Early America*. Cambridge, Mass., 2003.

Brown, Richard D. "'Not Only Extreme Poverty, but the Worst Kind of Orphanage': Lemuel Haynes and the Boundaries of Racial Tolerance on the Yankee Frontier, 1770–1820." *New England Quarterly* 61 (December 1988): 502–518.

Brown, William J. *The Life of William J. Brown, of Providence, R.I. With Personal Recollections of Incidents in Rhode Island.* Providence, R.I., 1883; reprint Freeport, N.Y., 1971.

Campbell, Stanley W. *The Slave Catchers: Enforcement of the Fugitive Slave Law, 1850–1860.* Chapel Hill, N.C., 1970.

Carvalho, Joseph, III. *Black Families in Hampden County, Massachusetts, 1650–1855.* Boston, 1984; revised edition 2011.

Catterall, Helen T. *Judicial Cases concerning American Slavery and the Negro: Cases from the Courts of New England, the Middle States, and the District of Columbia.* Washington, D.C., 1936, IV.

Chace, Elizabeth Buffum, and Lucy Buffum Lovell. *Two Quaker Sisters: From the Original Diaries of Elizabeth Buffum Chace and Lucy Buffum Lovell.* New York, 1937.

Chambers, William. *Things as They Are in America.* London, 1854.

Chapman, Maria Weston. *Right and Wrong in Boston: Annual Report of the Boston Female Anti-Slavery Society; With a Concise Statement of Events Previous and Subsequent to the Annual Meeting of 1835.* Boston, 1836.

Chickering, Jesse. *A Statistical View of the Population of Massachusetts, from 1765–1840.* Boston, 1846.

Cifaldi, Susan. "Hammet Achmet, Middletown's Not-So-Famous Drum Maker." http://historyoftheancients.wordpress.com/?s=achmet.

Collison, Gary L. "Antislavery, Blacks, and the Boston Elite: Notes on the Reverend Charles Lowell and the West Church." *New England Quarterly* 61 (September 1988): 419–429.

———. *Shadrach Minkins: From Fugitive Slave to Citizen.* Cambridge, Mass., 1997.

Connecticut Deaths and Burials Index, 1650–1934. Online database, www.ancestry.com.

Connecticut Town Marriage Records, pre-1870 (Barbour Collection), *Madison Vital Records,* 37. New England Historic Genealogical Society. www.americanancestors.com.

Commager, Henry Steele. *Theodore Parker, Yankee Crusader.* 1936; reprint Boston, 1960.

Congdon, Charles T. *Reminiscences of a Journalist.* Boston, 1880.

Cottrol, Robert J. *The Afro-Yankees: Providence's Black Community in the Antebellum Era.* Westport, Conn., 1982.

———. "Robert Morris." *American National Biography Online.* www.anb.org.

Craft, William. *Running a Thousand Miles for Freedom; or, The Escape of William and Ellen Craft.* London, 1860.

Curry, Leonard P. *The Free Black in Urban America, 1800–1850: The Shadow of the Dream.* Chicago, 1981.

Dana, Richard Henry Jr. *The Journal of Richard Henry Dana, Jr.* Ed. Robert F. Lucid. 3 vols. Cambridge, Mass., 1968.

Dain, Bruce. *A Hideous Monster of the Mind: American Race Theory in the Early Republic.* Cambridge, Mass., 2002.

Dalzell, Robert F. Jr. *Enterprising Elite: The Boston Associates and the World They Made.* Cambridge, Mass., 1987.

Daniels, John. *In Freedom's Birthplace: A Study of the Boston Negroes.* Boston, 1914; reprint New York, 1969.

Davis, David Brion. *Inhuman Bondage: The Rise and Fall of Slavery in the New World.* New York, 2006.

———. *The Problem of Slavery in Western Culture.* Ithaca, N.Y., 1966.

———. *The Slave Power Conspiracy and the Paranoid Style.* Baton Rouge, Louis., 1970.

Dempsey, Anne. "Benjamin Wheaton: Town's First Black Landowner." *Brattleboro Reformer,* February 7, 1994.

———. "Town's Early Barber Shops Operated by Blacks." *Brattleboro Reformer,* February 9, 1994.

Douglass, Frederick. *My Bondage and My Freedom.* Ed. William L. Andrews. Urbana, Ill., 1987.

Egerton, Douglas. "'Its Origin Is Not a Little Curious': A New Look at the American Colonization Society." *Journal of the Early Republic* 5 (Winter 1985): 463–480.

Feagin, Joe R., Hernán Vera, and Pinar Batur. *White Racism: The Basics.* 2d. ed. New York, 2001.

Felt, Joseph B. *History of Ipswich, Essex, and Hamilton.* Cambridge, Mass., 1834; reprint Ipswich, Mass., 1966.

Fifth Annual Report of the American Anti-Slavery Society. New York, 1838.

Formisano, Ronald P. *The Transformation of Political Culture: Massachusetts Parties, 1790s–1840s.* New York, 1983.

Forten, Charlotte. *The Journals of Charlotte Forten Grimké.* Ed. Brenda Stevenson. New York, 1983.

Fowler, David H. "Northern Attitudes towards Interracial Marriage: A Study of Legislation and Public Opinion in the Middle Atlantic States and the States of the Old Northwest." Ph.D. dissertation, Yale University, 1963.

Fowler, William C. *The Historical Status of the Negro in Connecticut: A Paper Read Before the New Haven Colony Historical Society.* New Haven, Conn., 1875; reprint Charleston, S.C., 1900.

Fredrickson, George M. *The Arrogance of Race: Historical Perspectives on Slavery, Racism, and Social Inequality.* Middletown, Conn., 1988.

———. *A Short History of Racism.* Princeton, N.J., 2002.

———. *The Black Image in the White Mind: The Debate on Afro-American Character and Destiny, 1817–1914.* New York, 1971.

———. *White Supremacy: A Comparative Study in American and South African History.* New York, 1981.

Friedman, Lawrence J. *Gregarious Saints: Self and Community in American Abolitionism, 1830–1870.* Cambridge, Mass., 1982.

Fryer, Peter. *Staying Power: The History of Black People in Britain.* London, 1984.

Fuller, Edmund. *Prudence Crandall: An Incident of Racism in Nineteenth-Century Connecticut.* Middletown, Conn., 1971.

Garrison, Francis, and Wendell P. Garrison. *William Lloyd Garrison, 1805–1879.* 4 vols. Boston, 1885–1889, I–III.

Garrison, William Lloyd. *The Letters of William Lloyd Garrison.* Ed. Walter M. Merrill and Louis Ruchames. 6 vols. Cambridge, Mass., 1971–1981, I–IV.

———. *Thoughts on African Colonization: or An Impartial Exhibition of the Doctrines, Principles and Purposes of the American Colonization Society, together with the Resolutions, Addresses and Remonstrances of the Free People of Color.* Boston, 1832.

Gilkeson, John. *Middleclass Providence, 1820–1940.* Princeton, N.J., 1986.

Goodman, Paul. *Of One Blood: Abolitionism and the Origins of Racial Equality.* Berkeley, Calif., 1998.

Gougeon, Len. *Virtue's Hero: Emerson, Antislavery, and Reform.* Athens, Ga., 1990.

Greene, Lorenzo. *The Negro in Colonial New England, 1620–1776.* New York, 1942.

Grimsted, David. *American Mobbing, 1828–1861: Toward Civil War.* New York, 1998.

Grossman, Lawrence. "George T. Downing and Desegregation of Rhode Island Public Schools, 1855–1866." *Rhode Island History* 36 (November 1977): 99–105.

Grover, Kathryn. *The Fugitive's Gibraltar: Escaping Slaves and Abolitionism in New Bedford, Massachusetts.* Amherst, Mass., 2001.

Guyette, Elise A. *Discovering Black Vermont: African American Farmers in Hinesburgh, 1790–1890.* Hanover, N.H., 2010.

Hammett, Theodore M. "Two Mobs of Jacksonian Boston: Ideology and Interest." *Journal of American History* 62 (March 1976): 845–868.

Hancock, Scott. "The Elusive Boundaries of Blackness: Identity Formation in Antebellum Boston." *Journal of Negro History* 84 (Spring 1999): 115–129.

Handlin, Oscar. *Boston's Immigrants.* Cambridge, Mass., 1959.

Hannaford, Ivan. *Race: The History of an Idea in the West.* Baltimore, Md., 1996.

Hansen, Debra Gold. *Strained Sisterhood: Gender and Class in the Boston Female Anti-Slavery Society.* Amherst, Mass., 1993.

Harris, Marvin. *Patterns of Race in the Americas.* New York, 1964.

Hartford, William F. *Money, Morals, and Politics: Massachusetts in the Age of the Boston Associates.* Boston, 2001.

Higginbotham, A. Leon Jr. *In the Matter of Color: Race and the American Legal Process, the Colonial Period.* New York, 1978.

Higginson, Thomas Wentworth. *Cheerful Yesterdays.* Boston, 1898.

Hinks, Peter. *To Awaken My Afflicted Brothers: David Walker and the Problem of Antebellum Slave Resistance.* University Park, Pa., 1997.

Hoar, George F. *Autobiography of Seventy Years.* 2 vols. New York, 1903, I.

Hodes, Martha. *The Sea Captain's Wife: A True Story of Love, Race, and War in the Nineteenth Century.* New York, 2006.

Hodges, Graham Russell. "David Ruggles." *American National Biography Online.* www.anb.org.

Homans, Isaac Smith. *Sketches of Boston, Past and Present, and of Some Few Places in Its Vicinity.* Boston, 1851.

Hooker, John. *Some Reminiscences of a Long Life, with a Few Articles on Moral and Social Subjects of Present Interest.* Hartford, Conn., 1899.

Horsman, Reginald. *Race and Manifest Destiny: The Origins of Racial Anglo-Saxonism.* Cambridge, Mass., 1981.

Horton, James Oliver. "Generations of Protest: Black Families and Social Reform in Ante-Bellum Boston." *New England Quarterly* 94 (June 1976): 242–256.

Horton, James Oliver, and Lois E. Horton. *Black Bostonians.* New York, 1979.

———. *In Hope of Liberty: Culture, Community and Protest among Northern Free Blacks, 1700–1860.* New York, 1997.

Howard, Victor B. *Conscience and Slavery: The Evangelistic Calvinist Domestic Missions, 1837–1861.* Kent, Ohio, 1990.

Ignatiev, Noel. *How the Irish Became White.* New York, 1995.

Jacobs, Donald M., ed. *Courage and Conscience: Black and White Abolitionists in Boston.* Bloomington, 1993.

———. "David Walker: Boston Race Leader, 1825–1830." *Essex Institute Collections* 107 (January 1971): 94–107.

———. "William Lloyd Garrison's *Liberator* and Boston's Blacks, 1830–1865." *New England Quarterly* 44 (June 1971): 259–277.

Jeffrey, Julie Roy. *The Great Silent Army of Abolitionism: Ordinary Women in the Antislavery Movement.* Chapel Hill, N.C., 1998.

Josselyn, John. *An Account of Two Voyages to New-England.* Ed. Paul J. Lindholdt. London, 1674; reprint Hanover, N.H., 1988.

Johnson, David N. *Sketches of Lynn; or, The Changes of Fifty Years.* Lynn, Mass., 1880.

Johnson, Franklin. *The Development of State Legislation Concerning the Free Negro.* New York, 1918.

Johnston, William. *Slavery in Rhode Island, 1755–1776.* Providence, 1894.

Jones, Rhett S. "Plantation Slavery in the Narragansett Country of Rhode Island, 1690–1790: A Preliminary Study." *Plantation Society* 2 (1986): 157–170.

Jordan, Winthrop D. *White over Black: American Attitudes toward the Negro, 1550–1812.* Baltimore, Md., 1968.

Journals of the House of Representatives of Massachusetts. Boston, 1723, V.

Kantrowitz, Stephen. *More Than Freedom: Fighting for Black Citizenship in a White Republic, 1829–1889.* New York, 2012.

Karttunen, Frances Ruley. *The Other Islanders: People Who Pulled Nantucket's Oars.* New Bedford, Mass., 2005.

Kendrick, Stephen, and Paul Kendrick. *Sarah's Long Walk: The Free Blacks of Boston and How Their Struggle for Equality Changed America.* Boston, 2004.

Kraditor, Aileen S. *Means and Ends in American Abolitionism: Garrison and His Critics on Strategy and Tactics, 1834–1850.* New York, 1969.

Kull, Andrew. *The Color-Blind Constitution.* Cambridge, Mass., 1992.

Lader, Lawrence. *The Bold Brahmins: New England's War against Slavery, 1831–1863.* New York, 1961.

Larned, Ellen D. *The History of Windham County, Connecticut.* 2 vols. Worcester, Mass., 1874, 1880, II.

Laurie, Bruce. *Beyond Garrison: Antislavery and Social Reform.* New York, 2005.

Laws of the Commonwealth of Massachusetts, from November 28, 1780 to February 28, 1807. 3 vols. Boston, 1807, I.

Lemons, J. Stanley, and Michael A. McKenna. "Re-enfranchisement of Rhode Island Negroes." *Rhode Island History* 30 (Winter 1971): 3–13.

Levesque, George A. "Black Boston: Negro Life in Garrison's Boston, 1800–860." Ph.D. dissertation, State University of New York, Binghamton, 1976.

———. "Boston's Black Brahmin: Dr. John S. Rock." *Civil War History* 26 (December 1980): 326–346.

———. "Inherent Reformers—Inherited Orthodoxy: Black Baptists in Boston, 1800–1873." *Journal of Negro History* 55 (October 1975): 491–525.

Levy, Leonard W. "Sims' Case: The Fugitive Slave Law in Boston in 1851." *Journal of Negro History* 35 (January 1950): 39–74.

Levy, Leonard W., and Harlan B. Phillips. "The *Roberts* Case: Source of the 'Separate but Equal' Doctrine." *American Historical Review* 56 (April 1951): 510–518.

The Liberator.

LiBrizzi, Marcus. *Lost Atusville: A Black Settlement from the American Revolution.* Orono, Me., 2009.

Litwack, Leon F. "The Abolitionist Dilemma: The Antislavery Movement and the Northern Negro." *New England Quarterly* 34 (March 1961): 50–73.

———. *North of Slavery: The Negro in the Free States, 1790–1860.* Chicago, 1961.

Lott, Eric. *Love and Theft: Blackface Minstrelsy and the American Working Class.* New York, 1993.

Mabee, Carleton. "A Negro Boycott to Integrate Boston Schools." *New England Quarterly* 41 (September 1968): 341–361.

Maginnes, David R. "Anthony Burns." *American National Biography Online*, www.anb.org.

———. "The Case of the Court House Rioters in the Rendition of the Fugitive Slave Anthony Burns, 1854." *Journal of Negro History* 56 (January 1971): 31–42.

Maine Death Records, 1617–1922. Roll 33. Online database, www.ancestry.com.

Malone, Christopher. *Between Freedom and Bondage: Race, Party and Voting Rights in the Antebellum North.* New York, 2008.

Marchione, William P. "1835: The Year of the Railroads." www.bahistory.org/HistoryRailroads.html.

Martyn, Byron Curti. "Racism in the United States: A History of the Anti-Miscegenation Legislation and Litigation." Ph.D. dissertation, University of Southern California, 1979.

Massachusetts Supreme Judicial Court. "The Massachusetts Constitution, Judicial Review and Slavery." www.mass.gov/courts/sjc/constitution-and-slavery.html.

Massachusetts, Marriage Records, 1840–1915. Online database, www.ancestry.com.

Massachusetts, State Census, 1865. Online database, www.ancestry.com.

Massachusetts, Town Vital Collections, 1620–1988. Online database, www.ancestry.com.

Massachusetts, Town Birth Records, 1620–1850. Online database, www.ancestry.com.

Massachusetts Vital Records, 1841–1910. Online database, www.ancestry.com.

May, Samuel J. *The Fugitive Slave Law and Its Victims.* Rev. ed. New York, 1861.

———. *Some Recollections of Our Anti-Slavery Conflict.* Boston, 1869.

Mayer, Henry. *All on Fire: William Lloyd Garrison and the Abolition of Slavery.* New York, 1998.

McFeely, William S. *Frederick Douglass.* New York, 1991.

McKivigan, John R. *The War against Proslavery Religion: Abolitionism and the Northern Churches, 1830–1865.* Ithaca, N.Y., 1984.

McManus, Edgar J. *Black Bondage in the North.* Syracuse, N.Y., 1973.

McPherson, James M. *Battle Cry of Freedom: The Civil War Era.* New York, 1988.

Melish, Joanne Pope. *Disowning Slavery: Gradual Emancipation and "Race" in New England, 1780–1860.* Ithaca, N.Y., 1998.

Miller, Floyd J. *The Search for a Black Nationality: Black Emigration and Colonization, 1787–1863.* Urbana, Ill., 1975.

Moore, George H. *Notes on the History of Slavery in Massachusetts.* New York, 1866; reprint New York, 1968.

Morris, Thomas. *Free Men All: The Personal Liberty Laws of the North, 1780–1861.* Baltimore, Md., 1974.

Morse, Jarvis Means. *A Neglected Period of Connecticut's History, 1818–1850.* New Haven, Conn., 1933.

Moss, Hilary J. *Schooling Citizens: The Struggle for African American Education in Antebellum America.* Chicago, 2009.

———. "The Tarring and Feathering of Thomas Paul Smith: Common Schools, Revolutionary Memory, and the Crisis of Black Citizenship in Antebellum Boston." *New England Quarterly* 80 (June 2007): 218–241.

Moulton, Amber D. *The Fight for Interracial Marriage Rights in Antebellum Massachusetts.* Cambridge, Mass., 2015.

Mulkern, John R. *The Know-Nothing Party in Massachusetts: The Rise and Fall of a People's Movement.* Boston, 1990.

Nash, Gary B. "Forging Freedom: The Emancipation Experience in the Northern Seaport Cities, 1775–1820." In Ira Berlin and Ronald Hoffman, eds., *Slavery and Freedom in the Age of the American Revolution.* Charlottesville, 1983, 3–48.

———. *Forging Freedom: The Formation of Philadelphia's Black Community, 1720–1840.* Cambridge, Mass., 1988.

Nasta, Jesse. "'Their Own Guardians and Protectors': African American Community in Middletown, Connecticut, 1822–1860." Bachelor's thesis, Wesleyan University, 2007.

Nell, William C. *The Colored Patriots of the American Revolution, With Sketches of Several Distinguished Colored Persons.* Boston, 1855.

New Hampshire, Death and Burial Records Index, 1654–1949. Online database, www.ancestry.com.

New Hampshire, Marriage Records Index, 1637–1947. Online database, www.ances-try.com.

Nicoloff, Philip. *Emerson on Race and History.* New York, 1961.

O'Connor, Thomas H. *The Boston Irish: A Political History.* Boston, 1995.

———. *Lords of the Loom: The Cotton Whigs and the Coming of the Civil War.* New York, 1968.

Painter, Nell Irvin. *The History of White People.* New York, 2010.

Palfrey, John Gorham. *Five Years' Progress of the Slave Power.* Boston, 1852.

Parker, Theodore. *The Collected Works of Theodore Parker: Discourses of Slavery.* Ed. Frances Power Cobbe. London, 1864, II.

Pease, Jane H., and William H. Pease. *They Who Would Be Free: Blacks' Search for Freedom, 1830–1861.* New York, 1974.

Pease, William H., and Jane H. Pease. "Antislavery Ambivalence: Immediatism, Expediencey, and Race." *American Quarterly* 17 (Winter 1965): 682–695.

People of Color in the Massachusetts State Census, 1855–1865. Online database, www. ancestry.com.

Peterson, Mark A. "The Selling of Joseph: Bostonians, Antislavery, and the Protestant International, 1689–1733." *Massachusetts Historical Review* 4 (2002): 1–22.

Petrulionis, Sandra Harbert. *To Set the World Right: The Antislavery Movement in Thoreau's Concord.* Ithaca, N.Y., 2006.

Piersen, William D. *Black Yankees: The Development of an Afro-American Sub-Culture in New England.* Amherst, Mass., 1988.

Pleck, Elizabeth Hafkin. *Black Migration and Poverty: Boston 1865–1900.* New York, 1979.

Polos, Nicholas "Cyrus Peirce." *American National Biography Online.* www.anb.org.

Price, George R., and James Brewer Stewart. "The Roberts Case, the Easton Family, and the Dynamics of the Abolitionist Movement in Massachusetts, 1776–1870." *Massachusetts Historical Review,* 4 (2002): 88–115.

———, eds. *To Heal the Scourge of Prejudice: The Life and Writings of Hosea Easton.* Amherst, Mass., 1999.

Providence Committee on Riots. *History of the Providence Riots, from Sept. 21 to Sept. 24, 1831.* Providence, R.I., 1831.

Quarles, Benjamin. *Black Abolitionists.* New York, 1969.

———. *Frederick Douglass.* New York, 1968.

Rael, Patrick. *Black Identity and Black Protest in the Antebellum North.* Chapel Hill, N.C., 2002.

Ratner, Lorman A. *Powder Keg: Northern Opposition to the Anti-Slavery Movement, 1831–1840.* New York, 1968.

A Report of the Record Commissioners of the City of Boston, Containing the Boston Records from 1660 to 1701, 1700 to 1728, 1729 to 1742, 1742 to 1757, 1758 to 1769. Boston, 1881, 1883, 1885, 1886.

A Report of the Record Commissioners of the City of Boston, Containing the Records of Boston Selectmen, 1701 to 1715, 1716–1736. Boston, 1884, 1885.

Richards, Leonard L. *"Gentlemen of Property and Standing": Anti-Abolition Mobs in Jacksonian America*. New York, 1970.

Ripley, C. Peter, ed. *The Black Abolitionist Papers*. 5 vols. Chapel Hill, N.C., 1985–1992, III–V.

Robboy, Stanley J., and Anita W. Robboy. "Lewis Hayden: From Fugitive Slave to Statesman." *New England Quarterly* 46 (December 1973): 591–613.

Roediger, David R. *The Wages of Whiteness: Race and the Making of the American Working Class*. New York, 1991.

Rosenberg, Norman L. "Personal Liberty Laws and Sectional Crisis: 1850–1861." *Civil War History* 17 (March 1971): 25–44.

Ruchames, Louis. "Jim Crow Railroads in Massachusetts." *American Quarterly* 8 (Spring 1956): 61–75.

———. "Race, Marriage, and Abolitionism in Massachusetts." *Journal of Negro History* 45 (July 1955): 250–273.

Saillant, John. *Black Puritan, Black Republican: The Life and Thought of Lemuel Haynes, 1753–1833*. New York, 2003.

Savage, Edward H. *A Chronological History of the Boston Watch and Police, from 1631 to 1865*. Boston, 1865.

Schultz, Stanley K. *The Culture Factory: Boston Public Schools, 1789–1860*. New York, 1973.

Schwartz, Harold. "Fugitive Slave Days in Boston." *New England Quarterly* 27 (June 1954): 191–212.

Second Report of the Record Commissioners of the City of Boston, Boston Town Records, 1634–1660. 3d ed. Boston, 1902.

Sewall, Samuel. *The Diary of Samuel Sewall, 1674–1729*. Ed. M. Halsey Thomas. 2 vols. New York, 1973.

Sewall, Stacy Kinlock. "Charles Lenox Remond." *American National Biography Online*. www.anb.org.

Shapiro, Samuel. "The Rendition of Anthony Burns." *Journal of Negro History* 44 (January 1959): 34–51.

Smedley, Audrey. *Race in North America: Origin and Evolution of a Worldview*. 3d. ed. Boulder, Colo., 2007.

Smith, Charles James. *History of the Town of Mont Vernon, New Hampshire*. Boston, Mass., 1907.

Smith, Francis O. J. *Laws of the State of Maine*. Portland, Me., 1834.

Stanton, William. *The Leopard's Spots: Scientific Attitudes toward Race in America, 1815–59*. Chicago, 1960.

Staudenraus, Philip. *The African Colonization Movement, 1816–1865*. New York, 1961.

Steiner, Bernard C. *History of Slavery in Connecticut*. Baltimore, Md., 1893.

Stewart, James Brewer. "The Emergence of Racial Modernity and the Rise of the White North, 1776–1840." *Journal of the Early Republic* 18 (Summer, 1998): 181–217.

———. *Holy Warriors: The Abolitionist and American Slavery*. New York, 1976.

————. "Wendell Phillips." *American National Biography Online*. www.anb.org.

Still, William. *The Underground Railroad: A Record . . .* Philadelphia, 1871.

Strane, Susan. *A Whole-Souled Woman: The Story of Prudence Crandall*. New York, 1990.

Strother, Horatio T. *The Underground Railroad in Connecticut*. Middletown, Conn., 1962.

Stuckey, Sterling. *Slave Culture: Nationalist Theory and the Foundations of Black America*. New York, 1987.

Sweet, John Wood. *Bodies Politic: Negotiating Race in the American North, 1730–1830*. Baltimore, Md., 2003.

Thomas, Lamont D. *Rise to Be a People: A Biography of Paul Cuffe*. Urbana, Ill., 1986.

Tiffany, Nina Moore. *Samuel E. Sewall: A Memoir*. Boston, 1898.

Tocqueville, Alexis de. *Democracy in America*. Ed. Henry Reeve, Francis Bowen, and Phillips Bradley. 2 vols. New York, 1945, I.

Towner, Lawrence W. "The Sewall-Saffin Dialogue on Slavery." *William and Mary Quarterly*, 3d Ser., 21 (January 1964): 40–52.

Twombly, Robert C., and Moore, Robert H. "Black Puritan: The Negro in Seventeenth-Century Massachusetts." *William and Mary Quarterly*, 3d Ser., 24 (1967): 224–242.

US Bureau of the Census. *Negro Population, 1790–1915*. Washington, D.C., 1918.

US *Civil War Draft Registrations Records, 1863–1865*. Online database, www.ancestry.com.

US *Civil War Records and Profiles*. Online database, www.ancestry.com.

US Department of State. *Aggregate Amount of Each Description of Persons . . . According to the Census of 1840*. Washington, D.C., 1841.

US *Federal Census Mortality Schedules Index*. Online database, www.ancestry.com.

Vaughan, Alden T. *Roots of American Racism: Essays on the Colonial Experience*. New York, 1995.

Vaughan, Alden T., and Virginia Mason Vaughan. "Before *Othello*: Elizabethan Representations of Sub-Saharan Africans." *William and Mary Quarterly*, 3rd. ser., 54 (January 1997): 19–44.

Von Frank, Albert J. *The Trials of Anthony Burns: Freedom and Slavery in Emerson's Boston*. Cambridge, Mass., 1998.

Walters, Ronald G. *The Antislavery Appeal: American Abolitionism after 1830*. Baltimore, Md., 1976.

Warner, Robert Austin. "Amos Gerry Beman—1812–1874: A Memoir on a Forgotten Leader." *Journal of Negro History* 22 (April 1937): 200–221.

————. *New Haven Negroes: A Social History*. New Haven, 1940; reprint New York, 1969.

Weierman, Karen Woods. *One Nation, One Blood: Interracial Marriage in American Fiction, Scandal, and Law, 1820–1870*. Amherst, Mass., 2005.

Werner, John M. *Reaping the Bloody Harvest: Race Riots in the United States during the Age of Jackson, 1824–1849*. New York, 1986.

Wheeler, George Augustus, and Henry Warren Wheeler. *History of Brunswick, Topsham, and Harpswell, Maine*. Boston, 1878.

White, Arthur O. "The Black Leadership Class and Education in Antebellum Boston."
    Journal of Negro Education 42 (Autumn 1973): 504–515.

———. "Salem's Antebellum Black Community: Seedbed of the School Integration
    Community." *Essex Institute Historical Collections* 108 (April 1972): 99–118.

White, Barbara. "The Integration of Nantucket Public Schools." *Historic Nantucket*
    40 (Fall 1992): 59–62.

White, Shane. "'It Was a Proud Day': African Americans, Festivals and Parades in the
    North, 1741–1834." *Journal of American History* 81 (June 1994): 13–50.

Whitfield, Harvey Amani. *The Problem of Slavery in Early Vermont, 1777–1810.* Barre,
    Vt., 2014.

Wightman, Joseph M, compiler. *Annals of the Boston Primary School Committee, from
    Its First Establishment in 1818, to Its Dissolution in 1855.* Boston, 1860.

Wilentz, Sean, ed. *David Walker's Appeal to the Coloured Citizens of the World.*
    New York, 1965; rev. ed. New York, 1995.

Winthrop, John. *Winthrop's Journal "History of New England," 1630–1649.* Ed. James
    Kendall Hosmer. 2 vols. New York, 1908.

Winthrop Papers. 5 vols. Boston, 1929–1947.

Wood, Betty. *The Origins of American Slavery: Freedom and Bondage in the English
    Colonies.* New York, 1997.

Woodson, Carter G. *The Education of the Negro Prior to 1861: A History of the Education
    of the Colored People of the United States from the Beginning of Slavery to the Civil
    War.* New York, 1915; 2d. ed., Washington, D.C., 1919.

Woodward, Carl R. *Plantation in Yankeeland: The Story of Cocumscussoc, Mirror of
    Colonial Rhode Island.* Chester, Conn., 1971.

Wright, Carroll D., with William C. Hunt. *The History and Growth of the United States
    Census, Prepared for the Senate Committee on the Census.* Washington, D.C., 1900.

Yacavone, Donald. *Samuel Joseph May and the Dilemma of the Liberal Persuasion,
    1797–1871.* Philadelphia, 1991.

Yee, Shirley. *Black Women Abolitionists: A Study in Activism, 1828–1860.* Knoxville,
    Tenn., 1992.

Zilversmit, Arthur. *The First Emancipation: The Abolition of Slavery in the North.*
    Chicago, 1967.

Index

Benson, George, 70
Besslow, Charlotte, 160
Besslow, P. J., 160
Bigelow, John P., 138–139
Bird, George W., 102
Birmingham, Samuel, 165
Bishop, Joel Prentiss, 101
blackface minstrelsy, 33
bobalition broadsides, 33, 34
Body of Libertyes, 19
Boston, 14
    and accomplishments of African
        Americans, 206
    Anthony Burns episode, 183–188
    Committee on Public Instruction,
        201–202
    creation of segregated schools, 12
    discriminatory laws, 21, 27–28
    division between blacks over
        integrating schools, 191–196
    efforts to integrate schools, 126–129,
        189–202
    exceptional characteristics, 189
    Frederick Minkins episode, 178–180
    fugitive slaves, 170
    geographical distribution of mixed
        marriages, 152
    housing and African Americans, 8–9
    number of free African
        Americans, 23
    number of mixed marriages, 152
    and opposition to abolitionists, 78–79
    percentage of African American
        population by ward, 37
    Pindall case, 201
    race riots, 14–16
    reaction to Fugitive Slave Law, 170,
        171, 172–174
    School Committee, 127–129, 190,
        192–194, 202
    segregated church seating, 209
    segregated theater seating, 210

    size of African American population
        in 1830, 14
    skilled work and African
        Americans, 8
    Thomas Sims episode, 180–183
    "Union" meeting, 178
    Vigilance Committee, 174, 177, 179,
        182, 185, 186
    violence against mixed couple,
        154–155
    William and Ellen Craft episode,
        174, 177
Boston, Absalom, 124
Boston Courier, 139
Boston Daily Atlas, 179–180
Boston Evening Telegraph, 203
Boston Female Anti-Slavery Society,
    78, 79–80
Boston, Phebe, 124
Boston Post, 140
Boston Traveller, 155
Bowditch, Henry Ingersoll
    on becoming an abolitionist, 130
    and the Crafts, 177
    difficulties being abolitionist, 53
    efforts to integrate Boston schools,
        127, 128, 129
    opposed Fugitive Slave Law, 172
    witnessed Sims' rendition, 182
Bowdoin College, 57
boycotts
    and dispute between integrationists
        and segregationists, 194–195
    effectiveness, 203
    feasibility, 102
    of Nantucket schools, 123
    of railroads, 99, 106
    of Smith School, 126–127, 129,
        189, 195
    of Salem schools, 125
Boynton, Nehemiah, 213–214
Bradburn, George, 95–96, 139, 141, 144

CPSIA information can be obtained
at www.ICGtesting.com
Printed in the USA
BVHW031312200720
584055BV00004B/24